To Nancy
*who provides the encouragement
for my Voyages*

and

Stephen A. Martin
*who continues to distill for me
the nuggets of wisdom
which inspire these meditations.*

Preface to the Third Edition

Let's deal with the problem right up front.

Ever since this volume was first published under its original title, *The Unauthorized Starfleet Daily Meditation Manual*, most bookstore browsers have assumed it was just another "Star Trek book."

It wasn't meant to be. And for the majority of people who ended up buying a copy, *it still isn't*.

Because the voyages of the starship *Enterprise* were never primarily about frontiers in space. They were about the frontiers within our *selves*.

Nor were all those fanciful aliens merely the inhabitants of distant planets. In reality they represented members of our own community whom we saw as "different," or who continue to challenge us in some way. Or they stood for aspects of our own personalities with which we are still struggling.

Even for the serious *Star Trek* fan, going boldly "where no one has gone before" was only a ruse, a gimmick to make our Inner Voyages seem more dramatic and compelling. "Space" made a convenient symbol not only for going within, but forging *ahead*—into the future.

As we journey into our Third Millennium, the words spoken by *Star Trek*'s diverse characters have a special ability to articulate our continuing efforts at self-discovery. But as profound as those words may be, there is nothing essentially new in them. They simply reconfigure the wisdom from centuries of human experience in the futuristic setting of starships and space stations, alien civilizations and "the undiscovered country."

As it turns out, Spock and Picard are only repeating lines spoken by earlier prophets and sages. Guinan and Kes merely echo the timeless voice of Mother Earth. Kirk and Dax, Worf and Chakotay, are simply reprising the venerable role of scriptural hero. And the clues to our own salvation—or "personal fulfillment," if you prefer—are only updated for us, not changed.

Of course, most of us who continue to enjoy an occasional TV episode, or the latest big-screen installment, don't tune in with all this symbolism in mind. In fact, as with any good film or book, moral and spiritual messages often have much greater impact if they reach us at a *sub*conscious level. And that's why, in order to get the most from this *Manual,* we're going to transport ourselves five centuries ahead, into *Star Trek*'s vision of the future.

In other words, we're going to pretend.

Using this Manual

This is how it works: We are no longer Americans or Europeans, Africans or Asians. We are Starfleet personnel whose homeworlds are scattered all across the galaxy. And now we're embarking on a year-long mission of exploration into even more distant regions of the universe.

To optimize our mental and spiritual health during this long and potentially dangerous Voyage, we're going to begin each new day with a thought-provoking meditation. And who better to provoke our thoughts than past Starfleet officers, crewmembers and other colorful characters whose words have been recorded in the chapters (also known as "episodes") of Federation logs?

The period after we wake up, but before we report for duty, is ideal for reading these meditations. So too is the hour or so before we end the day. If neither of these is convenient, we can always set aside some other regular time. And if we miss a few days, or prefer to read several meditations at one sitting, that's okay, too. However, as most spiritual disciplines confirm, developing a *daily* regimen will have the most lasting impact.

Starting our readings on the first day of the Solar Year might seem "most logical," as Spock would say—at least for humans (Terrans). But it's not required. Entering the cycle at *any* time should prove equally effective.

Since the numbering system at the top of each page corresponds to the traditional calendar, you may want to jump in on whatever today's date happens to be. Or you can simply let "1.01" represent the first day *you* start, whether it's June 29th or November 3rd. After all, somewhere in the galaxy, a brand new year is beginning *today*.

The quotations which precede each daily meditation were spoken in the context of "previous" voyages of exploration. For that reason alone they should have significance for us. But there are also deeper meanings hidden within them… meanings that transcend the boundaries between past, present and future… that blur the distinction between *Star Trek*'s warp-speed adventures through the galaxy and our own, more deliberate journeys within.

And it doesn't matter whether you're a seasoned Trekker, or you have only a passing familiarity with the series.

The stories of *The Enterprise, DS9* and *Voyager* are *our* stories. The challenges and obstacles their crewmembers faced are the same ones *we* face. And the inner resources they learned to call on, that gave them the strength to overcome those challenges and obstacles, are the same resources now available to *us*.

Hopefully, this book will help you become more aware of them. Equally important, the *Manual* encourages you to *apply* them in your daily life—to "learn by doing," as Captain Kirk put it.

Like other daily meditationals, the central theme for each reading has been condensed into a short affirmation or suggested action-for-the-day. If a different affirmation or action would be more appropriate to your circumstances, feel free to create another for yourself.

Either way, reading this closing thought out loud will increase its effect. Saying it more than once—with feeling—will help even more. *Applying* it at the first available opportunity will turn the daily lesson into genuine personal growth.

Inevitably, by the end of this year's Voyage, we'll be different people. By next year, chances are we won't simply be going along for the ride. We may find ourselves in the Captain's Chair.

And pretending will no longer be necessary.

Mark S. Haskett
Director, InnerFaith Resources
Terra: 1999/2000

SECTOR

CORRESPONDING TO THE TERRAN MONTH OF
January

1.01

A person's life—a future—hinges on each of a thousand choices. Living is making choices.

CAPTAIN PICARD: A MATTER OF TIME: 45349.1

Some decisions feel like they're "forced on us." Some events occur that seem beyond our control. And yet our lives are still basically in our own hands, if only because we can control our *reactions* to those "uncontrollable" events. We can choose to feel angry or helpless... or we can choose to learn from the experience and move on.

More importantly, we can also take the initiative. Because all around us are keys to our own future. These are the choices we make hundreds of times a day, that accumulate slowly, over time, to make us what we are. They're the opportunities to stop and listen to another person—or hurry off again because we're "late for an appointment." They're the frequent occasions we have to break old habits, to exert a little self-discipline; to say a kind word rather than an angry one; to forgive and release rather than hold on to the past.

We often fail to acknowledge how crucial these little choices can be. For they not only express Who We Are, they literally *re-create* us with each new moment. They take us along the same familiar path, or they point us in new, more promising directions—perhaps to where no one has gone before.

I am ready to go where I have never gone before, into the future I will create through my choices, by first accepting that I alone am responsible.

1.02

The greatest danger facing us is... our irrational fear of the unknown. But there is no such thing as the unknown. There are only things temporarily hidden, temporarily not understood.

CAPTAIN KIRK: CORBOMITE MANEUVER: 1512.2

A similar refrain is repeated not only in Terran history, but throughout most other planetary societies: *We have nothing to fear but fear itself.*

Biologically speaking, fear is a completely natural survival response. It tells us not to react hastily, not to get involved until we know what we're up against. We need to better understand the situation, to consider our options —assuming there's time. That's only logical. Fear is what "the need to know more" *feels like emotionally.*

But when we concentrate on the "fear itself" instead of the situation our fear is urging us to investigate, that emotion can paralyze us. And then it no longer serves its biological purpose.

Fear is the emotional trumpet blast that calls us to *advance,* not retreat. It's our sense of inner forces amassing themselves for The Mission, to go out in search of what is temporarily hidden and not yet understood.

Courage—*boldness*—is not the opposite of fear, not an "antidote." These qualities are its offspring.

I will acknowledge and embrace my fears, and look beyond them to the wonderful opportunities The Universe is now arranging for me.

1.03

Chance is irrelevant. We **will** succeed.

SEVEN OF NINE: NIGHT: 52081.2

It's a bold, even admirable sentiment. But the fact is, many people who make this statement *don't* succeed. Sometimes they fail… spectacularly.

What's admirable, then, is not so much the outcome, but the determination. Simply to make the attempt—to overcome inertia and decide to act—is already a kind of success. One that's equally spectacular.

In a parallel universe, a great sage taught his students, "Do, or do not. There is no try." His point was well taken. For if our aim is merely to "try," we often take our eyes off the goal. We focus on the effort alone. Or worse, we're *distracted* by it, worrying so much about the energy and the cost that we forget what we're trying to achieve. We soon forget the very relationship between trying and achieving until, at last, we see no reason to try at all.

But even this great sage would admit that, without trying, there is no doing. Doing is what trying *turns into,* if we keep working at it.

To say "Chance is irrelevant" isn't to deny the role of luck—or at least the unknown and unforeseen forces that luck represents. But, as Captain Sisko says elsewhere in the record, "Fortune favors the bold." And what fortune and luck often turn out to be, if only we had the determination to *try,* is The Universe itself rallying around us.

To try is to succeed. To make the effort is to give others, and The Universe, an opportunity to help.

1.04

I can't sacrifice the present waiting for a future that may never happen.

COMMANDER CHAKOTAY: RESOLUTIONS: 49690.1

As responsible Starfleet personnel we often think our goals should be about our next assignment, about career advancement, about future honors and achievements. Most of what we're striving for is "out there." We expect our efforts to be rewarded *someday*—when we've paid our dues, put in our time; when we've *earned* it.

If this attitude controls our thinking, we've made a fundamental mistake about what goals are *for*. Because planning for the future is not primarily about improving our conditions at some later time. The value of a goal is less in giving us something to "achieve" than something to guide our thoughts and actions *in the present*.

In short, we shouldn't select our goals based on the difference they may make in the future. We should choose a goal for the difference it makes in our lives *now*.

Is the discipline and effort of working toward our goals fulfilling in itself, whether or not "someday" ever arrives? Do our goals inspire us to look more closely at the world around us, and enable us to experience the present more fully? Can we feel ourselves being transformed by the pursuit of our goals into less isolated, more spiritually-connected, more joyfully *alive* individuals?

The right future for me is the one that helps me draw more growth and fulfillment—and more lasting joy—from each present moment.

1.05

The more difficult the task, the sweeter the victory.

COMMANDER RIKER:CAPTAIN'S HOLIDAY: 43745.2

It's a cliché in a thousand different languages, on a hundred different planets. But no less true.

It's also a good thing to remember—and to repeat as often as necessary—when frustrations pile up, when our best efforts fail, when defeat follows us like a plague.

We should be thankful there are no medals given for mediocrity. No one deserves cheers for doing "the minimum required," or for taking "the easiest route." Difficulty is necessary for excellence. And for a bigger payoff.

Then again, sometimes the payoff isn't what we think. Sometimes the real victory is one more hurdle away.

Which is why so many of the rewards of all our hard work turn out to be so unsatisfying. Our trophies and certificates of merit only end up gathering dust. Even the long-awaited benefits of "the good life" can turn sour.

Because the sweeter victories come from the difficult work we do *within.* Like overcoming our own anger and negativity. Like learning how to be a friend. Like knowing what you did was the right thing to do, even if it wasn't the most popular. Or like discovering that there's goodness and meaning in everything that happens to us.

Even in the events we once considered "defeat."

*I neither seek difficulty nor shrink from it. The choice is not whether the task is difficult, or how big the reward, but whether it is **right**.*

1.06

One can begin to reshape the landscape with a single flower.

SPOCK: UNIFICATION, PART II: 45245.8

As the ancient holy books say, Creation will always remain unfinished—if only because sentient beings like ourselves are essential to the "finishing" process.

But when we look around at what's yet to be done, we can easily lose heart: Poverty, ignorance and destruction still exist on a large scale, despite education and technological "progress." Physical and spiritual wastelands still occupy much of the galaxy, as well as the recesses of our own hearts. What difference can one person make?

(Which is exactly the excuse reeled out by those who prefer to avoid any responsibility.)

Fortunately, the ancient holy books also say that we're not required to *finish* our various tasks, only to contribute to their completion. Or sometimes, if The Universe so honors us, to begin a *new* task and thereby inspire *others* to contribute to its completion.

A single flower, symbolically speaking, can be enough. In fact, planting and nurturing that one tender shoot may be far more important in the scheme of things than the wholesale transformation of the landscape. Overcoming inertia, going ahead regardless of the odds—these are the hallmarks of redemption, not the final outcome.

I refuse to let the magnitude of the task prevent me from getting started. If I am sincere, and the goal worthy, The Universe will provide help.

1.07

Sometimes you have to go in blind. That's the exciting part.

CAPTAIN JANEWAY: INNOCENCE: Stardate Not Given

Naturally, we're more comfortable if we know what to expect. We feel more confident, more "in control." But sometimes we *can't* know what to expect; we don't have enough data. Or *any* data. Yet we're forced to act.

At times like this we must remember that we're never really "blind." We may use that term to describe how we *feel* at the moment. We may call ourselves "blind" because we're not conscious of the resources that might help us. But that doesn't mean we *have* no resources.

In fact the resources that often help us most are the very ones we are *not* conscious of, that work below the level of our awareness. For example, in critical situations where lightning-fast decisions must be made, it's often better to trust our instincts, and *not* try to think things through logically. If we're meditating regularly, if we've begun linking ourselves to others and to The Universe in our daily thoughts and actions—those "instincts" will come from our spiritual network, not just us.

And the "exciting part" is simply the anticipation of finding out that we *weren't* blind after all; that a higher Power was seeing *for* us; and that sometimes it's not a matter of knowing what to expect, but simply *expecting to know* when the time comes.

The Inner Voyage opens me to the inflowing of Universal Wisdom. Guidance comes as I ask for it.

1.08

The things I do for money!

QUARK: MERIDIAN: Stardate Not Given

Most of us have expressed the same surprise—or even horror—at what we sometimes give in trade for our standard of living.

Actually, our surprise is a healthy sign. It shows that we not only have a standard of living, but standards for *making* a living. And every now and then we find ourselves bumping up against them.

We shouldn't pass off these occasions too lightly. They are opportunities to further refine our standards, to ask ourselves what we would—and what we *wouldn't*—do for money. The answer can help us define Who We Are and what we believe.

Our beliefs, after all, are not mere theological "speculations." They're *what we do.* They're the priorities we establish, the values we demonstrate by our willingness to sacrifice our time and possessions on some things, less so for others.

What often surprises us is how easily we sacrifice what are presumably "higher" values—honesty, friendship, peace of mind—in pursuit of money. Which means we value money *more,* we "believe" in money *more.* We end up "serving" money in ways not unlike many ancient cultures served their idols.

But what happened to *them* need not happen to us.

My first priority is to learn and do what The Universe calls me to do. The money will follow.

1.09

Confidence is faith in oneself. It can't easily be given by another.

COUNSELOR TROI: LOUD AS A WHISPER: 42477.2

Most of us have less than we'd like. A few of us operate on very little. And *all* of us, sooner or later, will face that terrifying moment where our personal supply of it seems to have evaporated entirely.

We often talk about "confidence" in this way—as if it's some kind of commodity we can measure and use and sometimes "run out of" like the fuel in the combustion-powered vehicles of past centuries. And yet most of us also recognize that confidence is an *inner* quality. A *faith*.

The problem is, faith in oneself doesn't come out of the blue. We usually "earn" it by attempting new things and generally succeeding at them. And if, instead, we experience mostly failure in those attempts, then maybe it's just as well we're *not* confident since, that way, we're less likely to go out and fail *again*.

On the other hand, maybe the problem is our mistaken assumption that "faith in oneself" means relying solely on one's *own* resources. Or on needing to succeed.

Genuine confidence flows from our sense of being connected to resources *beyond* our own—or beyond anyone *else's*. It's the realization that the power which created the universe lies within us… that it nurtures us still, even when we "fail." And sometimes *because* we do.

My strength lies in being aware of my connectedness to The Universe—and through it, to others.

1.10

The real secret is, turn disadvantage into advantage.

RIVA: LOUD AS A WHISPER: 42477.2

It's nice to be handed things on a silver platter. To have our accomplishments come easily. To enjoy the benefits that are given by birth or position. Or plain, dumb luck.

But it's a far greater "gift" to have *earned* those benefits through planning and hard work; through successfully overcoming the interior and exterior obstacles that hold us back; through turning what seemed like a disadvantage into the very thing that leads to our salvation.

Of course, *how* to do that is one of life's enduring questions. Because the answer is different for everybody. But everyone who succeeds *does* begin in the same place.

The starting point is a *change in attitude*. It is our decision to stop calling the world "unfair" if it doesn't lay its riches at our feet as it seems to do for many other people. It's the recognition that the obstacles in our lives are really the urgings of a loving Universe to learn something essential to our spiritual progress, to win our fight against the flaws and weaknesses that impede us. It's our realization that the person we can become *after* we've fought that battle will be far wiser, far stronger, and far more fulfilled than we could ever be with*out* having fought it.

I accept my "disadvantages" as opportunities for growth. I recognize the obstacles in my Path as the secret gateways to a higher, stronger Self.

1.11

I prefer to confront mortality rather than hide from it.

DR. BASHIR : THE QUICKENING : Stardate Not Given

It's a psychological cliché to say that physicians like Dr. Bashir often seek out that profession as a way of confronting their own mortality. It's also no less true.

Because in their daily battles against pain and injury, physicians must come to grips with just how fragile our bodies are. *And* how resilient. In the inevitable circumstances where a patient's life is lost, they can't help but face their own inevitable death.

But these are events *we too* should face—if not daily (or as directly), then in such a way that we stop hiding from the issue. After all, to recognize our body's threshold for pain and injury is only prudent planning. To realize the possibility—and eventual *certainty*—of death is to begin deciding what we want from life.

Which often results in a radical reorganizing of priorities. Not that we should start living as if tomorrow we'll die. It simply means living as if we have specific goals to reach for, regardless of how much time we have left.

What goal would we like to achieve if we *did* have only one more day? What could we hope to achieve if all we had was a week? A month? A year? Fifty years? What can wait? And what can't we afford to put off any longer?

How precious is each remaining day in my life!
How grateful I am for each new opportunity to grow,
to love, to receive, and to give back even more.

1.12

We learn by doing.

ADMIRAL KIRK: THE WRATH OF KHAN : 8130.3

The opposite used to be called "book larnin'."

In most planetary cultures, learning from books—or computer files or video—has at times achieved a status far in excess of its true educational value. Amazing as it now seems, university degrees and special honors were once conferred on individuals not for demonstrated abilities or real life skills, but merely for absorbing the contents of certain prescribed repositories of information.

The fallacy of this approach was shown late in Terra's twenty-first century when methods were found for electronically transferring vast amounts of information and "book knowledge" directly into the human brain. What once took years of "study" could be accomplished in a few sessions of cortical data transmission (CDT).

Books, however, can still serve a purpose. *This* book has value—at least potentially. Because it's what we can learn *by applying it* that makes a difference. It's the information we absorb and refine by *living it* that empowers us. It's the knowledge that is eventually reflected in our behavior, that has seeped into our very muscles and nerves, that alone can transform our lives and our world.

Of course, in *doing* anything, we're bound to make mistakes. Fortunately, that's often how we learn best.

I welcome opportunities to turn mere "information" into genuine knowledge by applying it in my daily life and relationships. I do*, therefore I* know.

1.13

Curious how often you humans manage to obtain that which you do not want.

SPOCK: ERRAND OF MERCY: 3198.4

Insightful as ever, Spock has put his finger on it: It's almost as if we have some magnetic power to attract the very things we don't want. Or the things we fear most.

And it's not just humans. *Any* sentient being will attract what it thinks about often enough. Or with enough emotion. And since our psychic (or spiritual) energy can't be a negative force, *not* wanting something sends energy to that "something" just as much as if we wanted it!

Which simply means we'd better spend our time thinking about what we *do* want, not what we don't.

But even when we *get* what we want, it's "curious" how often we act as if we don't really want it. Many people with high-ranking positions, fancy shuttlecraft and luxurious domiciles are still as joyless and unfulfilled as ever. Why?

The answer is, what we truly "want" cannot be found in the world of objects and events. Though we *can* generate the energy to help bring these things about, genuine fulfillment comes from *inner* riches. Like developing an attitude of love and acceptance. Or learning to value relationships and experiences over material possessions.

Ironically, if we've been getting a lot of what we *don't* want lately, at least it shows that we *can* affect reality. And besides, maybe what we *do* want is a little clearer now.

*Starting today, I will devote less time to "wanting," and more time to thinking about what I really **need**.*

1.14

You gotta get in the spirit of things. Learn to be spontaneous... live in the moment.

DR. CRUSHER: GENERATIONS: 48650.1

There's something delightfully liberating about allowing oneself to embrace the moment, to "go with the flow."

But true spontaneity isn't blanket permission to do whatever "feels right." It's not about saying "yes" to every opportunity that pops up, to follow emotion over reason, to stop planning things and just let them "happen."

Spontaneity *requires* planning. Or at least preparation.

An ancient wisdom tradition talks about a process that underlies all existence, a Way, a *Tao* that seeks to express itself through nature as a whole, and through the actions of individual beings. Known as "Spirit" in other traditions, the Way works quietly, inevitably, toward wholeness and harmony. It blends the needs of each individual with every other, so that all things work for the greatest good.

In order to participate in this process, however, we must first acknowledge that we're part of it. We must also accept that our way is subservient to *its* Way—if only because its "consciousness" embraces the entire universe and ours doesn't. Finally, we must learn to tell the difference between its still, small voice, and the noisy shouting of our own limited perceptions.

To be prepared to listen, and act, is to be spontaneous.

I open myself to increasingly more opportunities for The Universe to act through me, by learning increasingly more about The Universe.

1.15

Only fools have no fear.

LIEUTENANT WORF: COMING OF AGE: 41416.2

The goal of spiritual growth is not to deny physical emotions, or somehow banish them from one's life—even if that were possible. Fear, for example, is one of the most universal emotions among physical beings. And one of the most *fortunate*.

In the evolution of autonomous life forms, those forms which could "feel" fear had a decisive advantage over those who could not. Fear, after all, heightens the senses; it pumps energy into the system. Surprisingly, it can also galvanize *community* because fear seeks safety in numbers, and a communal response is usually the most thoughtful and effective over the long haul.

To completely lose one's fear, therefore, means to cut oneself off from a valuable personal and communal resource. And if a "fool" is defined as an individual who acts without a genuine connection to self and community—what some people might call a "loose phaser"—then to act with no fear is indeed foolish.

Not that we should let our fears run rampant. Our Inner Voyage (or Spiritual Path) encourages us to acknowledge their existence, to honor them for the positive role they've played in bringing our species to this point. For only then can we enlist their energy in a higher service.

My fears are natural. But they do not control me. By facing them I will transform them. By accepting them, I can assign them a new role in my life.

1.16

To function in any human activity, you must learn to form relationships.

DATA: DEJA Q: 43539.1

All across the universe, the most successful species are those who balance personal independence with some form of "social contract." We live in groups of interacting individuals because we are thereby able to benefit from each others' strengths. We trade on what one person can produce for another. Our own knowledge and experience are multiplied by everyone else's in the community. Not to mention that the community provides protection.

In exchange for all these group benefits, we agree to interact according to certain rules and patterns. And in putting these rules and patterns into daily practice, we learn to "form relationships."

It seems less a question of "spirituality" than *what's practical.* Relationships help us live; sometimes our very survival depends on it. Still, in relating to one another we are doing more than exchanging goods and services. Our relationships provide the clearest mirror of what we think and feel, what we value, what we *believe.* In fact, we learn more about who we are by "relating" to others than by any other method of self-discovery.

And if we aren't satisfied by what we see, we can work to improve ourselves—by improving our relationships.

My relationships with others are extensions of Who I Am. I grow by nurturing those relationships, by learning from them, by celebrating them.

1.17

I seem to be the last to know just about everything around here!

THE DOCTOR: TIME AND AGAIN: Stardate Not Given

Voyager's holographic medical man often puts into words the frustrations we *all* feel. And one of the worst frustrations is living *re*actively rather than *pro*actively.

So much of our life is spent reacting to events instead of shaping them, in handling the latest crisis rather than carrying out a preconceived plan. That's why things can feel "out of control." Half the time we have no idea what's headed our way until it arrives. And by then it's too late.

The Doctor had an excuse: He was often "turned off" between medical emergencies. *We,* on the other hand, have the ability to remain *on* if we choose. And we do so not by trying to plan our lives down to the last detail, or by inventing some scheme that somehow eliminates all the surprises in our lives. (Not that we'd succeed, anyway. As one of Terra's most beloved troubadours wrote, "Life is what happens while you're busy making other plans.") Rather, we leave ourselves "on" by being more *present* to the world around us, by connecting with the world at deeper levels than the merely physical.

Meditation can help. Because by connecting with our selves we connect with The Universe. And The Universe already "knows" what's headed our way.

True "knowing" comes from within. I will look to my inner Source for help in guiding my actions, and my reactions will take care of themselves.

1.18

Give yourself some credit!

KES: PHAGE: 48532.4

Most recent converts to the practice of meditation probably know a lot about stress. Many are high achievers—both professionally and personally—and are usually more critical of themselves than any Starfleet officer.

Meditation is often begun as a necessary antidote to this kind of pressure-cooker lifestyle. But as Kes reminds us, there's another exercise that can also work wonders.

Everyone knows that emotionally healthy children are more often rewarded for good behavior than punished for the bad. Yet how often do we apply this simple strategy to our own development? How many times have we achieved some personal goal, or successfully overcome some inner flaw, and really *rewarded ourselves* for it?

Too often we think that, because we're adults, our achievements should be enough of a reward "in themselves." Or at least that doing the right thing will "eventually pay us back." Intellectually, we may know this to be true. The trouble is, our emotional lives thrive on immediate feedback. Our bodies need to *feel* it... *now*.

We can re-educate our bodies to enjoy learning and growing by giving ourselves the emotional equivalent of a warm hug or pat on the back. If this seems too childish, remember that new patterns and directions are *like* children. And we know how to produce healthy ones.

I deserve to celebrate my successes. I will reward myself as an incentive to continue growing.

Being an outsider isn't so bad. It gives one a unique perspective.

CONSTABLE ODO: THE SEARCH, PART II: Stardate Not Given

Most societies on M-type planets have a complementary expression. Each one talks about our tendency to become so embroiled in a given situation that we "can't see the forest for the trees."

In other words our personal, emotional involvement in some mission or relationship often causes us to lose our perspective—*and* our balance. Our focus on the details blurs The Bigger Picture. Our increasing investment of time and resources subtly shifts our needs and goals. We become disconnected from the reasons that motivated us to become involved in the first place.

This isn't necessarily wrong. Sometimes, in getting a closer look at the individual "trees," we're forced to re-evaluate our original view of the entire "forest." But even when this happens it's wise to get a second opinion. An objective opinion. An *outside* opinion.

By acting as one another's "outsiders" we can offer much-needed balance to our lives. What's more, we can learn to remove our*selves* from an emotional situation when necessary, to stand *outside* the turmoil, to remember Who We Are.

And hopefully, to remember who we can yet *become*.

I will watch for those times in life when I may be too close to a situation to remain objective. I am always open to the advice of others who care for me.

1.20

I'm not bothered by what people think of me!

LIEUTENANT TORRES: PARALLAX: 48439.7

It's an affirmation we would all do well to repeat.

Because what others think is no substitute for one's *own* internal guidance system. To let other people's view of us determine our thinking is dangerous not merely because they can't always be there every time we need guidance. What's worse is that we learn to distrust our *own* inner resources, our own innate ability to decide for ourselves, our own direct com-link with The Universe.

Which is not to say we should *ignore* what others think. Other people frequently have insights and experiences that can complement our own. Not to mention that seeing ourselves through others' eyes is a useful way to objectively assess our talents and flaws. Other people's opinions can also act as a check against "privatizing" reality, against our pretense that the world revolves solely around what *we* happen to think at any given moment.

In the end it's not a question of whether to ignore or to consider the views other people have of us. Or even whether we finally agree or disagree with those views.

It's simply a matter of *not being bothered* by them.

Other people may form opinions about me. But it's what I think about myself that determines my course of action... and my happiness.

1.21

Running away solves nothing.
CAPTAIN PICARD: COMING OF AGE: 41416.2

It's one of the hardest lessons to learn; and among the two or three most essential: Our relationships and our external conditions are primarily a reflection of our *internal* conditions. Our spiritual understanding and attitudes inevitably create the physical reality we live with. Our "world" mirrors our "self."

Running away therefore can't solve anything because we can never escape our *selves.* The same problems that plague us in our present surroundings or relationships will haunt us in the next, and the *next*—until we finally deal with the inner turmoil or spiritual defects that continue to generate those problems.

Not that "running away" is always useless. Sometimes the temporary respite we get from changing our physical environment gives us the mental distance we need to objectively face our problems. That's why there are spiritual retreat centers. That's why a regular "sabbath" is still practiced by many planetary cultures.

That's also why recreation is so important. Because to change our world, we must engage in *re-creation.* We must re-create our world from the inside *out.* And if we run anywhere, it must be to that sacred place within each of us where true transformation begins.

I'm through running. So that I may live fully with others, I will learn to live with myself. So that I can love others, I will learn to love myself. Starting now.

1.22

If we're going to do it, we're going to do it by the book.
CAPTAIN KIRK: THE FINAL FRONTIER: 8454.1

"Anything worth doing," an old proverb goes, "is worth doing *well*." And for everything worth doing, we might add, there's probably a dozen books telling you *how*.

Doing something "by the book" is simply another way of saying, "Let's do this task/project/assignment as well as we can—according to the most reliable, time-tested information we can find." This doesn't mean blindly following directions. It *does* mean admitting that many of the paths we walk were explored by others long before us. How foolish we would be to ignore the roadmaps they've left behind, or delete any Ships' Logs that might make our own voyages safer and more productive.

And yet that is often exactly what we do. Simply because other books—or traditions, or religions—were written in another cultural setting or a previous century, we assume they can't teach us anything useful. Which is like saying that anyone who speaks a foreign language doesn't have anything meaningful to tell us.

We might think of "The Book" as the accumulated wisdom of past generations—the collective resources which can tell us not only what works, but how to find answers for ourselves if the existing ones *don't* work. And that's when we become authors for the *next* generation.

I am grateful for the Book of Life others have left for me. I will strive to make my own contribution.

1.23

The stars are not just up in the sky. They're all around us.

COMMANDER SISKO: EXPLORERS: Stardate Not Given

Stars have played a symbolic role in almost every culture the Federation has encountered. Most often, stars represent other-worldly forces that somehow manage to affect—and even *control*—our lives. Or else they symbolize the hidden patterns in seemingly random events. Or the bright spots in our otherwise dark existence. Or the individuals who illumine our lives in some special way.

In the fables of several planets, stars are the "windows of heaven," portals in some celestial veil through which we glimpse the glories of a dimension beyond this one.

Each interpretation, in its own way, represents a truth. But what all of them seem to suggest is that these other powers and personalities are distant and distinct from us. They are inaccessible, above and beyond our ordinary experience or ability. We cannot understand or become like them, much less control them. Different rules apply.

Benjamin Sisko wisely reminds us that this view is flatly *wrong*. The forces that shape our lives *can* be known. The lights that brighten our lives and illumine our paths need not be limited to pinpoints in the night. If we open our spiritual eyes, they are everywhere, bathing us in their power. And we are made of the very same star-stuff!

The power of the Universe surrounds me, sustains me, energizes me. I can reach "up," or go within. I am a luminous body no less than the stars.

1.24

You can handle defeat in two ways: You can lose confidence, or you can learn from your mistakes.

COUNSELOR TROI: PEAK PERFORMANCE: 42923.4

Watching an infant learn to walk is an instructive, even inspirational, experience. The child gets up, stumbles, falls—cries, perhaps—then gets right back up and tries again. Confidence has nothing to do with it. Worrying about "how it looks" doesn't enter the child's mind. Nor do self-defeating thoughts about not being "allowed" or "able" or "deserving."

There is only an innate *knowing* that making an effort to walk *leads to walking*... along with the simple acceptance that falling down is part of the process.

We can look at our own failures or mistakes in life as "falling down." Unfortunately, as self-conscious adults we may become overly concerned about what others think, or whether our failures point to some deeper flaw in us. Or whether we'll ever, *ever* learn.

But learning is precisely the point. Our mistakes are among The Universe's best teaching tools. The most resounding victories often occur after the most abysmal defeats. Breakthroughs—revelations—are more likely to arise from failure than a steady string of successes.

The Spiritual Path knows this strange irony as Grace.

Failure will not stop me. Defeat is my opportunity to reassess and to learn. Success is sweeter, and more permanent, if it comes from raw experience.

1.25

The ride's going to get a little bumpy. Things are going to happen fast. Just keep alert, stay calm. Let's focus on what we're doing.

ENGINEER LA FORGE : ARSENAL OF FREEDOM : 41798.2

Sounds a lot like our lives, doesn't it?

The ride can be bumpy at times. Things happen fast. And the physical sensations can easily distract us from what we're doing—or what we're *supposed* to be doing. We get carried away with the thrills and turn the trip into a pointless joy ride. Or, more likely, all those bumps frighten and disturb us, and getting *rid* of them becomes more important than getting to where we're going.

The Inner Voyage helps us, first of all, by preparing us for the fact that the ride *is* bumpy. And if we expect all those bumps, maybe we'll be less likely to overreact.

More importantly, the Voyage reassures us that it's "we" who are going somewhere, not just "me." "Let's focus on what *we're* doing," La Forge says, as if to remind us that we're all on this ride together; that we depend on one another; that if we concentrate on our own assigned duties we may not even *notice* the bumps anymore.

And the mission—our *lives*—will be a success.

Today I will be alert, yet calm, focusing on my duties rather than my comfort, and thereby allow others to focus on theirs.

1.26

You want me to see past my programming. Then you must try to see past your doubts.

THE DOCTOR (as "The Warhead"): WARHEAD: Stardate Not Given

Speaking on behalf of the cybernetic entity inhabiting him at the time, The Doctor teaches us a lesson about changing our lives. And allowing others to change *theirs*.

The lesson begins by recognizing the flaws in the behavioral "programs" we've all inherited from our childhood and past experiences. That's hard enough. But what's *really* hard is giving each other permission to *re*program ourselves, to break through the current images we have of one another so we can feel free to act differently... to continue evolving.

It's hard because we so often put people in mental "boxes" based on past disappointments. We label others as untrustworthy or sloppy, lazy or rigid, careless, selfish.

And we assume they place similar labels on *us*.

Those expectations not only become constricting, but self-fulfilling. We may even reward others, unconsciously, for staying in the little boxes we've put them in. Which reduces the chances for change to just about zero.

Instead, let's agree to give each other permission to change... to see past our doubts. Even if we know it will take many more tries before a change is permanent.

After all, we could use a little slack ourselves.

I celebrate the ability of others to transform themselves. I will find a community of spirit where I, too, can feel free to become the person I intend to be.

1.27

...If we **can** help, we should.

CAPTAIN JANEWAY: STATE OF FLUX: 48658.2

As we grow into a relationship with The Universe, as we become more and more aware of our connection to everything around us, the idea of "luck" becomes less meaningful, less operative. We realize that events never truly happen "by chance."

We find new information and knowledge being given to us at the precise moment we're ready to absorb it. Events conspire to send us on new voyages of discovery soon after the urge to explore new vistas excites our imagination. And if we get into trouble along the way, help seems to come to us just when we need it.

The Universe, somehow, seems to be shepherding our lives, actively leading us along the paths of our becoming. And it's not just "events" that play a decisive role in our growth. It's *people*.

So it should not surprise us when we are asked to become the agents for growth or assistance in *other* people's lives. Whenever we find ourselves in a position to help someone who needs it, we ought to assume that this event, too, is no mere "coincidence."

In fact, whether or not we accept the opportunity to help becomes part of our *own* ongoing development. For as we help others grow, we help our*selves* grow.

I gratefully accept the help which The Universe continually arranges for me. And I open myself to the opportunities It provides for helping others.

1.28

Do not fear your negative thoughts. They are part of you. They are part of every living thing.

LIEUTENANT TUVOK: COLD FIRE: Stardate Not Given

Even Vulcans have been known to harbor low opinions of themselves or others. Or to be seized by the idea of doing something contrary to their own high standards.

Actually, negative thoughts are a natural by-product of a healthy imagination. The same mental process which makes us aware of our options does not also censor them for us. In response to the events in our lives, several possibilities for action will inevitably come to mind. It's not unusual when one or more of these are judged by our conscience as immoral. Or even repulsive.

The fact that we *have* these thoughts does not require us to act on them. In a sense, by giving us a wide range of choices, including negative ones, our subconscious is affirming its "trust" that we'll make the *right* one. In fact, the right choice is often all the more obvious and compelling precisely because we *can* imagine the negative possibilities. The mind is only doing its job.

Our job is to take the energy of our negative thoughts—the anger, the desire to lash out, the thrill of a secret fantasy—and transform it. Having had the negative thought, we are now empowered to be even more *positive*.

My negative thoughts arise from the same source as my positive ones. They are necessary building blocks that support my positive goals and actions.

1.29

Trust is earned, not given away.

LIEUTENANT WORF: THE WOUNDED: 44429.6

Relationships, we know, are particularly susceptible to the self-fulfilling prophecy. If we treat someone with kindness and respect, that individual is more likely to *become* kind and respectful. If we forgive others, they in turn become more forgiving.

Likewise, if we regard others with suspicion when we first meet, we may not only poison any future relationship, we can end up encouraging the very behavior that fuels our suspicion. In short, we literally create the attitudes and actions in others that we expect of them.

And yet it would be foolish to simply *assume* that other individuals possess certain qualities until we have sufficient reason to believe that they *do,* in fact, possess them. Trustworthiness is one such quality. Learning whether we can rely on someone else's abilities, or their levelheadedness during a crisis, or their loyalty to a cause, requires repeated demonstrations.

Neither can *we* expect to be fully trusted until we repeatedly prove our own trustworthiness. We shouldn't regard this as an affront to our integrity. Rather, we can look upon it as a "refresher course," as another opportunity to polish our skills—if not to reassure others, then to reaffirm Who We Are to our*selves*.

It is as important for me *to know I am trustworthy —and to learn to trust myself—as it is for* others. *I welcome opportunities to demonstrate it.*

1.30

You know what they say: Be careful what you wish for; you may get it!

COMMANDER UHURA: THE SEARCH FOR SPOCK: 8210.3

Long before it became a proverb on Terra, the truth behind Uhura's words was already well known. Centuries earlier, in fact, visitors' wishes were being routinely transformed into reality on the so-called "Amusement Park Planet." Frequently with less-than-desireable results.

Even under ordinary conditions, our consciousness has numerous mechanisms for bringing about the fulfillment of our dreams. Unfortunately, we often block these mechanisms with feelings of unworthiness or negativity. And because we therefore assume that our wishes will "never come true," we tend to let them run wild. We don't consider what consequences they might have if they ever *did* become real. Why *not* wish for unlimited power and pleasure if it'll never happen anyway?

And then suddenly it happens: A dream comes true. Perhaps it's because we finally throw off the shackles of self-doubt. Or because we finally accept the miraculous power of our own minds. The problem is, if our dream is a holdover from that earlier stage when we couldn't care less about "consequences," we may be in for a shock.

Which is simply to say that we must "be careful" even with our fantasies. Could we really live with them? Would they truly add meaning and purpose to our existence?

*Let my dreams be in harmony with the longings of my highest Self. I wish for no more... and no **less**.*

1.31

Change doesn't come easily. Change will come by itself if you're open to it.

ALIXUS: PARADISE: 47573.1

Such creatures of habit we are! Our bodies and nerves are literally imprinted with the patterns we've established over the years; and it becomes harder and harder to affect them, even when we're convinced change is needed.

The conflict often deteriorates into a battle between body and soul. All our "bad habits" or "primitive desires" are seen as products of an evil force which we personify as demons, The Devil, or our own "sinful natures." After all, something *else*—not us—must be holding us back.

Feeling this conflict is actually part of the growth process. It's the price we pay for being *conscious*—for realizing that we are more than our physical bodies, that we can transcend our previous limitations if we'd only work at it.

And fortunately, it's not as much work as we might think. We can see it as a battle if we insist. But we can also simply *envision the kind of person we want to be,* doing the things that type of person would be doing. As if by magic our transformation begins to unfold. And as long as we keep this "model" in our awareness, we inevitably become more and more like it. A new person emerges.

Not really "by itself," but because that's how transformation works. That's how The Universe works *in us.*

I will meditate daily on the stronger, more blissful, more spiritual person I have decided to be, thereby allowing The Universe to change me from within.

SECTOR 2

CORRESPONDING TO THE TERRAN MONTH OF
February

2.01

May cultural differences encourage us to build bridges of understanding to all that makes us unique.

SEVEN OF NINE: SOMEONE TO WATCH OVER ME: Stardate Not Given

To those aware of her background, the "toast" Seven offered on this occasion was the sign of a personal breakthrough. For her to acknowledge the value of diversity, to promote uniqueness as a quality to be preserved, was like a former slave announcing her freedom from bondage.

Many of us likewise need to set ourselves free: From the notion that cultural differences are roadblocks to unity. From the assumption that uniqueness and individuality are a hindrance to harmony. From the dogma that we need to be "the same" before we can be accepted.

Seven's words call us to celebrate and learn from our differences. But not merely for the purpose of adding new technology to our arsenals, to assimilate what others know so we can use that knowledge for our own benefit.

The fact is, building bridges between our differences creates new opportunities and new ideas neither could generate without the other. By respecting and preserving our "uniquenesses" we become resources for one another, models for looking at things differently, guides to lead us out of the ruts we're in, inspiration for our ongoing Voyages through the universe… and into ourselves.

Diversity is a gift The Universe has given me. Each month of this year, I will study another faith or culture, and reaffirm its relationship to my own.

2.02

A little less analysis and a little more action... that's what we need.

DR. McCOY: THE GALILEO SEVEN: 2821.5

Sometimes we must act before there's time to think. We can learn much about ourselves—our strengths and weaknesses—from watching our own behavior in these situations. "Gut reactions" reveal current programming.

But sometimes we have the luxury of analyzing the situation *before* we act. We can consider the variables, the possible outcomes, potential plans for action. And we can learn much about ourselves here, too.

Because in our need to "be right," we all-too-often *over*-analyze. We consider so many possibilities that we lose perspective. The law of diminishing returns kicks in.

Worse, we end up surrendering our responsibility. We let the Ship's Computer decide, or we seek the safety of decision-by-committee. We create a convenient excuse for failure, since we can always blame others for giving us faulty data or "insufficient information." Or we simply put off doing anything at all.

Except that we *can't* put it off. We grow not by "thinking about it," but by *acting*. And if we're mindful, the very action we undertake contains the clues to its own "rightness." The Way becomes clear *only as we begin to move*.

And mid-course corrections are always possible.

I acknowledge that I am Captain of the voyager that is my Self. I accept responsibility, and look for the lessons my own actions teach me.

2.03

We're not gods and prophets. We're **people**. We make mistakes.

COUNSELOR EZRI DAX: STRANGE BEDFELLOWS: Stardate Not Given

The description that we're only "people" bears repeating. Not to excuse our flaws, or our laziness. Not to free us to act out our worst impulses, but to act out our *best*.

In our quest for excellence and self-realization, we need to know that we'll often miss the mark. There will be long seasons of failure. Mistakes may haunt us for years.

...*Unless* we accept that we are imperfect, that life is about learning from our mistakes and then moving on.

But that's just half of it. Ezri's words aren't meant only to make *us* feel better. "We're not gods or prophets" is also the principle which should guide our relationships with *others*. For just as we must be free to fail (or else we can't grow), so must they. Forgiving others for their inevitable mistakes is inseparable from forgiving ourselves.

A Bajoran prophet echoed this universal sentiment when she said: "Be compassionate toward your neighbors, and to the strangers among you. Know that they are searching for self-understanding as you are. Do not think their struggles easier, nor their mistakes more grievous. In truth you are all on the same journey, and the comfort you offer them along the way becomes your own."

Sometimes comfort is all we need to keep moving.

I accept myself exactly as I am now, just as I accept others. Admitting my imperfections removes the obstacles between me and my ideal Self.

2.04

I'm just following the blueprint.

COMMANDER SISKO: EXPLORERS: Stardate Not Given

It's always good to have a blueprint. Whether you're working on a specific project or your life's goals, a plan sets guidelines, reinforces the need to proceed one step at a time (i.e. you can't build the penthouse before you've laid the foundation); and helps measure your progress.

Perhaps the biggest benefit is that you make your plan in a calm, objective state of mind. You line up resources in advance. You anticipate problems before they occur. You see things more clearly now than you will during the heat of construction. And later, when you're in the thick of it, when you're tired, distracted, maybe having second thoughts—you can still rely on the calm, clear vision you had earlier. You won't give in to pressure, or yield to temptation. You'll let your Blueprint think *for* you.

Of course, that strength is also its greatest weakness. Because reality is never so compliant as to follow your plans exactly. Problems will arise that no blueprint could foresee. Unexpected opportunities are just as likely. Both will have the potential to scuttle things entirely, or help them turn out better than you could ever have dreamed!

The best blueprints are therefore not *too* specific. They are *working* plans. Some of the details become clear only after we roll up our sleeves and start building.

My life is a construction zone. My blueprint gives me a specific direction, but enables me to develop and receive new guidelines as conditions change.

What the hell... nobody said life was safe!
COMMANDER RIKER: PEAK PERFORMANCE: 42923.4

There are two distinct components to the Commander's statement. The second contains the obvious truth.

Obvious, because experience has shown that our lives can't be both satisfying and totally safe. Growth can be dangerous. To fulfill our potential, we must often journey through the "badlands," or even uncharted space.

But the first part of Riker's statement is problematic. Too often we interpret *What the hell* to mean "It doesn't matter." It implies a tendency to do things carelessly or impulsively, without thinking about the consequences.

That's hardly the case here. Ryker *knows* what the consequences are. He's thought about it. He simply accepts the danger and prepares to go ahead anyway.

Which is exactly the attitude *we* need to succeed. Not that it doesn't matter, but that it *does*. To become the person The Universe calls us to be, we must accept risks. As one Terran holy book put it, we must be ready to "walk through the valley of the shadow of death."

A Twentieth Century "war movie" put it more bluntly. "Damn the torpedoes—full speed ahead!"

It's a line that might just as easily have come from the bridge of the *Enterprise*. Or, once we understand what's at stake, from our own personal lives.

I accept the risks and challenges of life as the price for becoming the person I want to be. Whatever happens on my journey, I am never alone.

2.06

You proceed from a false assumption. I have no ego to bruise.

SPOCK: THE WRATH OF KHAN: 8130.3

Unlike Spock, many of us still seem to organize our entire emotional lives around the protection of our egos: What will people think? How will I look? What if someone else is better? How can I save face?

It's as if we carry around a mental scorecard, giving ourselves points when we do something that impresses other people, and subtracting points when we *don't*—or worse, when someone else succeeds where we've failed and now everybody knows it. *Especially* our ego.

The problem is, our "ego" is an artificial identity given to us by others. To have an ego is to allow ourselves to be defined by *how others see us*. It means giving control of our very feelings to someone else: Now I can be proud; now I feel hurt. The ego is a marionette; pull my strings.

Not that the ego serves no purpose. In childhood, we must take on the standards of others—our parents, our peers, our culture—as a kind of "preliminary operating system". It's as necessary as baby food and diapers.

But adulthood is the process of taking responsibility, of discovering a core self that is beyond being proud or being "bruised," that's less concerned with how *others* see us than how *The Universe* "sees" us. Because, ultimately, its standards are the ones that truly count.

I will not seek so much to "protect" my ego as to dismantle it, and meet my true Self in the process.

2.07

It's hard to be philosophical when faced with suffering.

DR. CRUSHER: SYMBIOSIS: Stardate Not Given

The Inner Voyage does not demand that we suffer in order to grow spiritually. But some of our most important spiritual growth comes from *having suffered*.

Many ancient disciplines inflicted suffering on adherents for that very reason. Earth-centered traditions still require physical ordeals of some kind, from sweathouses to "walk-abouts" to self-flagellation. And while they are in a sense "artificial," they often teach valuable lessons.

But the ordeals of everyday life continue to be our most profound teachers: Facing the death of a loved one; recovering from a broken relationship; dealing with failure, (especially when others were counting on us). After the inevitable periods of suffering have passed—and they *do* pass—we can make sense of them, place them into the larger context of our lives. We can "be philosophical."

On the other hand, trying to be philosophical about a certain ordeal *while still undergoing it* is not just "hard." It's one of the worst things we can do. Because we need to *feel* the pain of our losses, not chat about them. We need to fully *experience* our experiences before we start analyzing them. For only then do we have the raw data—sometimes *very* raw—from which true wisdom comes.

I do not seek suffering, but I will not close my heart to it. Nor will I rush to "understand" my suffering, but allow any lessons to emerge in their own time.

2.08

No one is expendable.

DR. BASHIR: THE SEARCH, PART I: 47212.4

It's easier to see on a small scale: In an Away Team exploring a newly-discovered planet; on a Federation outpost in deep space, or a starship two generations from home. Here, every individual has a specific, *visible* function within the group. The unique talents of any one person can make a critical difference. And the loss of a single crewmember will create a vacuum that impacts everyone else... directly... *personally.*

How odd to think this kind of personal impact, this visible interconnectedness, no longer applies in larger groups. The sheer numbers fool us. We assume that people can be "replaced". Or at least that's the way most bureaucracies and economic entities treat us.

But we must not let *their* treatment of us determine *our* view of ourselves. Because that view is not only ultimately destructive, it's not even accurate. If we could only look more closely, we'd see that *every individual added or subtracted from a group changes it.* The energy may be spread over a broader area, like a single oboe in a vast concert hall. And when the whole orchestra is playing, we tend to hear the symphony rather than the individual instruments playing it. But take away the oboe, and the symphony isn't the same. People notice the difference.

Not the least of whom is the musician beside you.

My presence here makes a difference. Inevitably.
I will strive to make that difference a positive *one.*

2.09

The universe has been my playground.

Q: DEJA Q: 43539.1

It may seem odd to quote Q, that enigmatic being who is so contemptuous of human weakness. After all, in Q's eyes we are such pathetic creatures—for showing compassion, for forgiving one another, for all those attributes we celebrate as reflections of our deeper divinity.

Then again, Q himself could be compassionate and forgiving; and his contempt was more out of frustration for the high cost of those feelings than a conviction that we shouldn't *have* them. In fact, it is Q who teaches us that compassion requires the *most* strength.

And there are other things we can learn from Q. One of them is his attitude toward the physical world.

It's a kind of faith, really—a way of viewing one's life. According to Q, the world around us exists precisely to be used, experienced… *enjoyed*. We have far more to gain by treating life as an ongoing *game* than as some deadly-serious final exam. We'll learn the rules faster, with more lasting effect—and with more assurance—by running out there onto the playing field than by watching from the sidelines. Handbooks and holosuites are boring, anemic substitutes for a real playground.

And anyway, who do you think is out there supervising all the fun?

The Universe gives us our lives to **play** *with* **as well as** *to* **learn** *from. Playing by the rules is what makes the game* **more** *fun, not less.*

2.10

It's too easy to turn a blind eye to the suffering of a people you don't know.
CAPTAIN PICARD: INSURRECTION: Stardate Not Given

How far beyond our immediate circle—family, friends, community, nation, planet—must we go before we're no longer required to respond? Or, put another way, what are the limits of our responsibility to others in need?

Picard reminds us that we are often tempted to draw the line conveniently close. "We don't know those people" is an easy excuse. And there are plenty of others.

Like "The situation is more complicated than it looks." Or "Risking our own scarce resources is a cost we can't afford." Or simply, "We have no *right* to interfere."

Then again, what's "right" isn't only a matter of rights, of legalities. We are linked to others even before we may know them. Their sufferings—and their successes—can affect us both materially and spiritually, despite the fact that we're not even aware of their existence.

But when we *do* become aware of them, we can no longer avoid responsibility. Not just because we may discover something that compels us to come to their aid. It's because our failure to act would also harm our*selves*.

Karma extends equally to what we *don't* do as to what we *do*. And if we turn a blind eye to others, the universe will turn a blind eye to *us*.

Fortunately, the flip side is also true.

I earn help by giving it to others. I free myself from bondage as I work to release others from theirs.

2.11

> **You humanoids have a hard time giving up the things you love… no matter how much they might hurt you.**
>
> CONSTABLE ODO: HEART OF STONE: 48521.5

What Constable Odo means by "love," Bajoran and Terran gurus would call "attachment." It's not that we *love* certain objects or foods or activities. It's that we've become *attached* to them. They've become so intertwined in our lives that we simply can't imagine ourselves without them. They seem no less a part of us than our hands and feet and the face in the bathroom mirror.

Trouble is, some of these attachments aren't good for us. Like the Terulian brandy we enjoy (but which anesthetizes us to our problems). Or that secret, self-indulgent fantasy which may boost our ego (but prevents us from seeing the world as it really is). And even when we finally admit the damage they do, we still figure we're stuck with them, like a chronic limp or an untreatable disease.

The solution, ironically, is to lose one's attachments. Not just those that hurt us, but *all of them*. We must learn to see ourselves, our core identity, as separate from the habits and personal preferences that outwardly define us. Only then can we make a conscious choice about which ones to eliminate, and which to keep. Only then can we fully access the power we have to change our lives.

> *I am not what I eat, or what I like, or what I do. I am responsible for these things, but separate from them. Therefore I can change them as I see fit.*

2.12

Human intuition and instinct are not always right. But they do make life interesting.
GUINAN: THE LOSS: 44356.9

Though "intuition" and "instinct" are often used interchangeably, they are as different as thought and feeling.

Instinct refers to the physical drives and survival responses hard-wired into our bodies—almost as if our higher faculties didn't exist. (That's because our higher faculties *didn't* exist when our instincts evolved.) Intuition, on the other hand, *is* one of our higher faculties.

In fact, it may even be "higher" than rational thought. Because intuition not only draws on our mental abilities, it draws on our instincts, too. *And* on other subconscious processes we've only recently begun to understand.

When we "intuit," therefore, our minds are attempting to integrate information that may be intellectual, hormonal, sensory—and perhaps even *extra*-sensory. Some of these sources of information are not strictly logical, nor are they always compatible. So it should not surprise us that our intuition isn't always right.

But we diminish our capabilities if we simply label our intuition "wrong" and rely on logic alone, or only on what we can put into words. Instead, we must learn to listen even more carefully to our inner wisdom. We must learn to trust ourselves. *That's* what makes life interesting.

I will not discount my instincts and my inner guidance, even if they are sometimes wrong. I trust the diverse resources within me to help light my way.

2.13

> **There's a million things in this universe you can have and a million things you can't. It's no fun facing that, but that's the way things are.**
>
> CAPTAIN KIRK: CHARLIE X: 1533.6

The popular notion is that we can "be whatever we want"—and *have* whatever we want. After all, when we finally admit to ourselves that the universe is "good," and that its infinite resources supply everything we need, we can easily fall into the trap of thinking that the universe must therefore exist simply to satisfy all our desires.

We forget, in short, that getting everything we want is not always "good." And that, if we want a certain thing, we must often give up something *else*. We can't have both.

We can't drink the nectar of the gods for long and still keep our sobriety. We can't maintain committed, intimate relationships if we use others merely as tools to get what we want—or to satisfy our glandular needs. We can't reach the destination The Universe calls us toward if we refuse to learn any of the Paths required to get there.

To have the "million things" that truly enrich our lives, we must consciously choose to *not have* the other million that only *seem* enriching. The Ancient Ones called this process "repenting"—turning away from what *can't* give us life, so that we might turn back to what *can*.

In the end, the stakes are that high.

I accept the fact that Life has rules, and that "the way things are" is ultimately for my own good.

2.14

Until I saw you, there was nothing in my heart. It sustained my life, but nothing more. Now it sings!

NATIRA: FOR THE WORLD IS HOLLOW AND I HAVE TOUCHED THE SKY: 5476.3

On Terra there is still a minor holiday which celebrates the joys of love and physical attraction. Its origins are now obscure, as is the source of the figurine which is its mascot—an infant angel, or "cherub," who shoots heart-tipped arrows that turn "victims" into instant lovers.

The symbolism is not as obscure as the origins. The cherub, for example, signifies that genuine love exhibits a childlike innocence and playfulness. The arrows represent the fact that feelings of love often strike us as if from an outside source, unexpectedly, without our "permission" and without any logical justification. It's as if we have no control.

But in return for our seeming lack of control, there *are* compensations. The pleasure lovers take simply by being in each other's presence cannot be duplicated. Every sense, every emotion, is heightened. A touch, a smile, a mere glance from one's lover can communicate more information than a Ship's Computer. The heart *does* sing!

Of course there are complications. And as sentient beings, we can't always permit the heart to rule our minds. But there are days when we enjoy *pretending* that it can.

It is good to feel. I give myself permission to enjoy the presence of another person, to practice caring for someone else—as The Universe cares for me.

2.15

Communication is a matter of patience …imagination.

CAPTAIN PICARD: DARMOK: 45047.2

"Why don't you just *say* what you *mean*—?!"

How impatient we are with others, and with their words. Yet we're just as guilty: We beat around the bush, we hold the most important things back. We make others pry the truth out of us, instead of saying it flat out.

On the other hand, these are ways of "communicating," too. If we would only use a little imagination, if we would stop insisting that all meanings be boiled down into words—which they often can't, anyway—we might find that the messages others are sending us are as obvious as the headline on an old-fashioned newspaper.

Because what is *not* being said can convey far more than what *is*. What someone can't seem to express, or refuses to talk about, is usually the real message.

We need to stop setting boundaries around what we'll accept as the other half of a "conversation." If we've been meditating for long, chances are we've learned to recognize the volumes that are communicated in our silences. We need to practice receiving that same depth of information from others… in a feeling, a touch, a look.

Listening is far too important to rely on our ears alone.

What I need to know from others lies not only in, but between and around, their spoken words. When I open my mind to these other levels, I hear fully.

2.16

Sometimes people blindly make the same mistakes again and again.

ENSIGN D'SORA: IN THEORY: 44932.3

Nobody would dispute these words from Data's one-time paramour. Except perhaps to say that many of our mistakes aren't made all that "blindly." We often seem to commit the very same act that got us into trouble once before with our eyes wide open.

The question is, *why*—? Didn't we get hurt enough? Or do we simply enjoy the punishment?

First, let's give ourselves a little credit. Maybe we had reason to believe things would turn out differently the second time. Perhaps we thought we'd grown enough to know where things went wrong, and we could prevent the same disaster from happening again. Besides, an even bigger mistake would be to assume that, just because something didn't work before, we should give up trying.

But when the same failure occurs repeatedly, it means we probably *are* blind. We're not seeing something crucial. We missed the lesson. Or maybe we *do* feel some "need" to punish ourselves, and we aren't aware of it.

Whatever the case, it's not as if the universe is being cruel. It simply doesn't want us to "get things right" *by accident.* Or to go on ignoring something that requires our undivided attention. It wants us to *know* something.

Let's be grateful for another chance to learn.

I open my eyes to the messages hidden within my mistakes. If I repeat them, I will look deeper.

2.17

For everything there is a first time.

SPOCK: THE WRATH OF KHAN: 8130.3

"Are you serious? No one's *ever* done that before!"

"Me—? I could *never* do that!"

I could never... No one's ever... These litanies of negativity act as reverse affirmations. If we tell ourselves we can't, we usually *can't*. If we keep pointing out that a certain goal has never been achieved, we build more barriers against achieving it. Or at least *our* achieving it.

And yet, everything good that was ever done had once *never* been done. If we let that stop us, there would be no new achievements, no breakthroughs. Our barriers are often less a problem of difficulty than of attitude.

Then again, sometimes not. Many of the things we haven't yet accomplished—whether as a species, or in our personal lives—*are* genuinely difficult. Achieving them requires stretching our abilities, taking risks, making sacrifices... perhaps even changing certain aspects of ourselves. But that's why "firsts" get into record books. That's why firsts are such a major cause for celebration. They are hard won. And they deserve to be celebrated, if only to encourage us to achieve more of them.

A continuing succession of these firsts is another definition for "growth."

I will search my life for opportunities to do for the first time the things I know I must do eventually. I will act boldly and celebrate my successes.

2.18

We prefer permanence... the reward of relationships that endure and grow deeper with the passing of time.

CAPTAIN JANEWAY: PRIME FACTORS: 48642.5

As convenient as it may be, our brave new world of instant gratification also carries some unfortunate side effects. A tray of food appears at the push of a button. We access libraries of information with a single word to the Ship's Computer. Transporters and holodecks take us to other worlds—both real and imaginary—in moments.

It's no wonder we sometimes treat one another with little more regard than holographic images. We're so busy moving from one experience to another that we tend to forget that another *person* is involved—a *real* person not unlike us, with dreams... with *feelings*.

And while real people may not respond to our whims like some computer-generated fantasy figure, there *are* rewards: Knowing that the feelings you have are shared by another; imagining what the other person is doing when you're apart; anticipating the next time you meet.

It's because life *is* so full of activity and technology and impermanence that person-to-person relationships are so precious. Enduring friendships provide emotional grounding, constants in a universe of Relativity. They are worth all the effort we put into them. And more.

My relationships are an important gauge of my emotional health... and a tool for improving it. I grow as they grow, and endure as they endure.

2.19

We're big enough to take a few insults.

"SCOTTY": THE TROUBLE WITH TRIBBLES: 4523.3

How sensitive we are to criticism, or even to verbal abuse, is a good indicator of our self-confidence. For example, if someone's cutting remark elicits a strong emotional reaction, it's often because we're not sure of ourselves. Or else we suspect there's some truth to it.

Rather than simply feel hurt by the remark, we need to *process* it. Instead of lashing back, or immediately constructing arguments to prove how wrong it was, we need to stop and ask "why." *Why* did a certain comment cut so deep? *Why* did we feel a need to respond so defensively?

There may be several possibilities. The criticism may point to a real flaw we tried to keep secret, and now we've been exposed. Or maybe we're worried that someone important to us will be influenced by the remark—whether it's true or not. Perhaps the insult seems out of character for the person who made it, and now we don't know what to think of them. Or we simply decide the remark is unjustified, in which case we dismiss it and *get past it*.

Being "big enough," as Scotty puts it, means doing all of this processing before we respond—if a response is even necessary. More importantly, it means we're content with the truth. Because Who We Are—as revealed in our actions—always speaks louder than anybody's words.

Insults say most about the person giving them. Nevertheless, I will look for any kernels of truth they may contain, and learn from what I find.

2.20

We're lost... but we're making good time!

COMMANDER SULU: THE FINAL FRONTIER: 8454.1

How often we repeat Sulu's observation—and what we're really talking about is *our own lives!*

After all, we seem to be going *some*where in a hurry, don't we?—our engines at warp speed, our daily lives filled with all sorts of activities (and maybe even a taste of personal satisfaction). And all that activity is sometimes a good sign that we know what our lives are about.

Then again, it can also be a good sign that we *don't* know.

Because being busy often results from our *lack* of direction. We rush breathlessly through our lives, hardly stopping, often taking on new projects in a desperate search—though usually an unconscious one—for something that might give our lives meaning and focus. Or we simply keep ourselves so preoccupied and "rushed" that we don't have time to reflect on how lost we really are.

But we *must* stop; we must give ourselves time to breathe, to reflect, to ask the important questions: What does The Universe uniquely want to say *through me?* What is the Prime Directive in *my life?*

Without an answer—even a tentative, changing one—"making good time" is only the joke Sulu meant it to be.

I hereby commit myself to regular times for reflection. The busier I am, the more I will stop to review where I'm going, and whether I'm getting there.

2.21

Man stagnates if he has no ambition, no desire to be more than he is.

CAPTAIN KIRK: THIS SIDE OF PARADISE: 3417.3

It is one thing to enjoy the fruit of one's labors, to rest on one's laurels. Or, as the ancient ballad says, to stop and smell the roses.

But to call a halt to one's aspirations, to say that "I've achieved enough," is to commit spiritual suicide.

The Inner Voyage, after all, is a journey of continual self-improvement. The Voyage may have its way-stations, but it does not come to an end. Not in this life, anyway.

Someone's ambition to "be more than he is" begins with his first glimmerings that there are deeper dimensions to existence. We perceive, dimly at first, that we are not defined by our physical limitations, not confined to the conditions in which we originally find ourselves. We may translate that realization of "more" into a desire for *material* things—pleasure, possessions, power or honor. But what The Universe is trying to teach us, even in our mistaken pursuit of these trinkets, is that *we do deserve more;* that we are mirrors of what the Ancients called "the divine image"; that we can continually expand our limited notions of Who We Are until we reflect the goodness, creativity, and limitless bounty of The Universe itself.

Certainly more than we do now.

Even my materialistic ambitions hide spiritual truth: If I can have *more, I can also* be *more. I choose "being" over "having," character over possessions.*

2.22

You can't hide from your feelings.
COUNSELOR TROI: NEW GROUND: 45376.3

The old cliché about "getting in touch with your feelings" still contains some of life's best advice. Not just because feelings convey important (and usually-reliable) information. It's because knowing exactly *what* those feelings are trying to tell us is an art.

The same feeling might convey an intuitive message that someone we've just met can't be trusted, or that we're still unsure what to think about an earlier meeting with someone *else*. Either way, our subconscious is trying to tell us *something,* using physical cues which, if we were only in touch with our feelings, would be as clear a message as the flashing lights on the Ship's Panels.

One of the most common of these messages is that we still need to resolve some emotional issue from our past. When we suffer humiliation or loss, for example, we often "deal with it" by simply ignoring or supressing our memory. But our built-in Mental Management System knows better. Even a suppressed memory can affect our judgment and emotional stability. And our subconscious will send a "reminder"—continually—until we face it.

It's not just that "hiding" from these distress signals is futile. It's that we should *embrace* them. We should be following where they lead us. For our own good.

My emotional feelings are messages of love and concern from my deeper Self. I commit myself to learning how to decipher my own "secret code."

2.23

The way I see it, freedom is a whole lot better than slavery.

COMMANDER SISKO: THROUGH THE LOOKING GLASS: Stardate Not Given

Sisko's observation isn't all that controversial or profound, is it? Notwithstanding the Borg, everyone prefers freedom to the kind of political, racial or economic sanctions that once enslaved billions. *Don't* they...?

You'd think so. Yet the fact remains that many of us are living in slavery right now, without even realizing it.

We are restrained from further growth by our addictions. We are chained by our own unwillingness to break out of established patterns and comfortable lifestyles that limit our options or drain our creative energies. We continue to be ensnared by the notion that life itself is somehow against us; that we are essentially evil, sinful beings whose only hope for salvation lies in "external" answers.

Mental or spiritual slavery is a lot more powerful, and certainly more insidious, than the outward kind. Freeing ourselves from *those* chains ought to be our top priority.

Freedom implies having options and choosing between them. By acknowledging our own "slave mentality" we can choose to overcome it. By becoming aware of our own patterns of action and thought, we can decide if we wish to maintain them or transcend them.

Freedom *is* better. But only because we must earn it.

Today I will list all the ways I am free, and all the ways I am not. I will meditate on how I can secure freedom from my own spiritual bondage.

2.24

'Tis at the heart of our natures to feel pain and joy. It is an essential part of what makes us what we are.

CAPTAIN PICARD: THE BONDING: 43198.7

The most crucial component of this quotation is the word "and." Pain *and* joy… Sorrow *and* pleasure…

Because we can't have one without the other. It's a requirement of our emotional hardware. We can choose to turn off our agony, yes; but the ecstacy circuit will shut down at the same time. Without fail.

The Terran poet, Khalil Gibran, framed this relationship in a simple question: "Is not the lute that soothes your spirit the very wood that was hollowed out with knives?" His own answer makes it even clearer. "The deeper that sorrow carves into your being, the more joy you can contain."

Too often we assume that our emotions are independent of one another. We think we can—or *should*—feel happy all the time. (Or at least that we shouldn't feel any pain.) We forget that our capacity to feel one emotion is the direct result of having experienced its opposite.

Not that we should *pursue* pain. It will find us on its own. But, if only in retrospect, we can be grateful for our seasons of sorrow. Without them, we could not harvest such profound joy.

I will accept and embrace my pain so that I may deepen my capacity for happiness.

2.25

For any event, there is an infinite number of possible outcomes. Our choices will determine which outcomes will follow.

DATA: PARALLELS: 47391.2

Even Data could exaggerate to make a point.

Whether the possibilities really *are* infinite is debatable, if not downright mistaken. But the point is, *they may as well be infinite* if we truly accept the awesome power we have to choose our own future.

"I had no choice" is a line we often employ to excuse our actions, or our blindness to other alternatives. Our behavior may even be understandable—when we're unprepared or frightened, or when a certain choice is likely to bring us pain, or when the world seems to be against us. But "I had no choice" is never really *true.* Never.

As people who make thousands of choices in the course of a single day, it is to our advantage to continually expand our awareness of the possibilities. The Inner Voyage increases those possibilities if only because it offers alternatives that do not depend on outer circumstances. We can choose self-control even if we can't control "the world." We can choose *inner* peace even when those around us are in conflict.

And the irony is, inspired by our choice, the world is more likely to conform itself to *us,* than we to *it.*

My choices determine my future. I always have a choice; and in choosing, I choose the person I am.

2.26

Never judge a fruit by its skin.
NEELIX: CARETAKER: 48315.6

...Or, as Terrans used to say, "a book by its cover."

Some of the sweetest fruits have the thickest husks. And, alternatively, many of the least enriching works of literature have had the most attractive covers.

In fact, by the end of Terra's Second Millenium, the ability to make all sorts of products appear wholesome and enriching—despite the fact that they were *not*—had become a major art form. From petroleum to politicians, "image" became more important than substance. And the bottom line was, people fell for it left and right.

Things are not so different today. We are still easily deceived by appearances. That may explain why we often compensate—consciously or not—by learning to deceive others. Or at least by concentrating more on looks than character. Which amounts to deceiving our*selves*.

To "never judge a fruit by its skin" is certainly a way to guard against deception. But the statement also reminds us that opportunities and treasures sometimes lie hidden in the most unexpected places and relationships. If we expect the worst, if we react only to outward appearances or first impressions, we will probably get what we expect. But if we search deeper, we may discover more beauty—and sweeter fruit—than we ever thought possible.

I will not equate appearance with substance—not merely because I might be deceived, but because I might miss something truly wonderful!

2.27

> **Maybe we weren't meant for paradise. Maybe we were meant to fight our way through... struggle, claw our way up... scratch for every inch of the way.**
>
> CAPTAIN KIRK: THIS SIDE OF PARADISE: 3417.3

Life ain't easy. No one promised you a rose garden. Welcome to the School of Hard Knox.

There are thousands of ways to say it. And the underlying message is not merely that our lives can be tough and we'd better get used to it. The message is, *that's the way it's supposed to be.*

After all, our biggest triumphs never come from the victories handed us on a silver platter. We draw our greatest satisfaction from taking on a new challenge, perhaps risking something of value in the process, pushing ourselves beyond previous limits. And the prize has less to do with the outcome than the struggle itself.

It would be tempting to ascribe that "satisfaction in the struggle" to our roots in the Animal Kingdom—nature's emotional enticement to keep our survival skills in working order. But it's more than biological. It's *spiritual*. It's the realization that there's always more for us to learn; a reminder that "perfection" is an action verb, not an adjective; a lesson that heaven isn't so much a place where all our needs are fulfilled and provided for, but a lifestyle in which we're all fulfilled by providing for our needs.

I will face whatever Life sends my way, knowing that the rewards are in the effort, not the outcome.

2.28

You are making a statement about the sanctity of life, and it will be heard!

LWAXANA TROI: HALF A LIFE: 44805.3

Talk is cheap. Which is why a good argument or a well-polished speech might move us temporarily, but it will rarely transform our thinking in the long run.

It's the statement people make by *doing* something that has power to change the world. It's the *eloquence of action* that cuts through public apathy, that brings home an otherwise remote issue, that reaches into our hearts and minds with images that compel us to respond.

Think of the human rights movement of the late Twentieth Century—from Ghandi's March to the Sea to King's March on Washington. Consider the war protester who loses his legs on the railroad tracks at an ammo dump, trying to stop a train carrying bullets and bombs. Recall the courage of a single Chinese student blocking a tank in Tienamen Square as he demonstrates for democracy.

Such "statements" do more than raise our consciousness about an issue, or mobilize us to join hands—although that would be enough. They also teach us that life is sacred, that our lives must have meaning to be worth living, that some common chord connects us all at a level that runs much deeper than speech, beyond race, that outlasts time.

They teach us that our *lives* are our loudest voices.

I will meditate on what I truly believe in, and what actions would visibly demonstrate those beliefs.

2.29

> **It's so easy to become jaded... to treat the extraordinary like just another day at the office. But sometimes there are experiences that transcend all of that.**
>
> CAPTAIN JANEWAY: EMANATIONS: 48623.5

There are hidden layers, deeper dimensions, in everything that happens. Like exploring the miniature worlds that surround us—the thriving community in a single plant leaf, or the dance of DNA in our own cells, or the electromagnetic energies filling the space between and inside us... We have only to shift our point of view to discover how much *more* life offers.

For most of us, unfortunately, it's "business as usual." We draw lines around the experiences we'll permit ourselves, or the feelings we'll allow. We enforce our own "tunnel vision." After all, we have jobs to do. Sometimes it's critical to our very survival that we stay focused and not get distracted. And if we've developed an ability to concentrate on the work we're doing, we've learned an important life skill, haven't we?

Perhaps. But if we continually tune out the deeper dimensions that underlie our existence, we pay dearly for that "skill." We lose the capacity for awe, for surprise, for the ability to imagine that things can be different, better.

Without these, we lose the power to change.

It is only my own tunnel vision that hides the deeper layers of existence from me. I will open myself to new ways of seeing, and see my life anew.

SECTOR

CORRESPONDING TO THE TERRAN MONTH OF
March

3.01

Our function is to contribute in a positive way to the world in which we live.

DATA: THE OFFSPRING: 43657.0

You'd think it would be obvious. But even with the best intentions, short-term self-interest can cloud our vision. After all, we can *see* the results of selfish efforts. We try to do something to benefit ourselves—and either it works for us or it doesn't. Even if it fails, at least we *know*.

Long-term self-interest is harder to track. We often lose the connection between what we did, and the benefit we finally receive. We may not *feel* rewarded, even if we *are*.

Contributing "to the world" is even more obscure. We can rarely see the slow, cumulative effects of our altruistic efforts. The positive influence we've had on certain people, the difference we've made in the wider scheme of things—these are difficult to identify, much less take credit for. So we fall back on the behaviors that give us immediate reinforcement: Being selfish.

What we don't realize is that our contributions to the world *are* selfish. Computer scenarios have proven it: Members of a theoretical society who work toward the "greater good" actually produce more benefits to the *individual* than if each member worked only for himself.

But computers don't help us *feel* that fact. It comes down to having faith. And acting on it.

Each day for the next month, I will do at least one nice thing for someone else—a different person every day—without thought of my own benefit.

3.02

Logic is the beginning of wisdom, not the end...

SPOCK: THE UNDISCOVERED COUNTRY: 9522

...And knowing the *limits* of logic is the next step.

Clearly, there are places where even the most skilled application of logic cannot penetrate. One such place is referred to by Terran romantics as "the human heart."

One needn't be romantic to recognize that our minds are more than "intellect." Even Vulcan culture acknowledges that the biological system which supports all that rational firepower has its own needs, its own "language." And if many Vulcan rituals seem to be among the most *illogical* in the galaxy, it is because those rituals speak to an entirely different component of the Vulcan mind.

In fact, for most sentient beings the concept of "mind" includes *affective components*. Emotional "well-being," for example. A sense of meaning and purposefulness. A connectedness of one's self to others and to something that transcends space and time. In a word, *wholeness*.

To recognize these components is only logical. But logic alone can't satisfy them. "Wisdom" is the art of dealing with the *whole* person, the *whole* community, the *whole* universe... as if every part plays an essential role.

Because they *do*.

I will honor those dimensions in others, and in myself, which lie beyond the limited horizon of logic. I celebrate my whole self.

3.03

> **You explore the universe. We've discovered that a single moment in time can be a universe in itself... full of powerful forces.**
>
> ANIJ : INSURRECTION : Stardate Not Given

No matter how small or large the "world" we inhabit—from the space inside our skulls to an entire galaxy—there remain uncharted realms ripe for exploration. One of these still-mysterious realms is Time.

No less real than length, depth and height, time is the dimension that connects cause and effect... that links our actions to their consequences. And every moment of it, like the smallest particle of matter, contains great energy.

If we could dissect each moment like Anij's people have, we would see it reaching into every other dimension. We would also be amazed at how the energy from even the most trivial action is carried far into the future, and far beyond our immediate relationships.

But what if we didn't *like* what we saw? What if we wanted to take back the energy we already set in motion?

To a greater degree than we think, *we can.* Not by going back in time, or stopping it, but by using the powerful forces each new moment presents. Because every new action sends energy through time and space, too; and just the *right* one can counteract the mistakes of our past.

If we are mindful of our moments, we can create new worlds, and go boldly into a future of our own choosing.

I will close my eyes and feel the power of this moment. I accept its energy as fuel for my growth.

3.04

You need to run a self-diagnostic.

LIEUTENANT PARIS: TIME AND AGAIN: Stardate Not Given

Androids do it. So do Ships' Computers. Even the chips in ordinary household gadgets are designed to do it.

Whenever performance falls below prescribed levels, or if other warning signs appear, these "intelligent" machines automatically run a program to uncover possible malfunctions. The more sophisticated systems can take action based on their findings, essentially repairing themselves. Less sophisticated systems will flash lights and sound buzzers to summon outside help.

We could all take a lesson.

Trouble is, most of us aren't sensitive to the warning signs our own systems send us. Or else we're so busy rushing though our daily routines that we don't even realize we're malfunctioning until the lights and buzzers are going off all around us. And by that time the damage may be difficult or impossible to repair.

Our Inner Voyage provides regular opportunities for self-diagnosis—either in supportive groups and relationships, or in private meditation. Through its disciplines we are re-sensitized to our psyche's subtle messages, helping us re-connect with our own higher Self. *And* with the deeper Source from which solutions come.

In fact, proper diagnosis is already half the solution.

I cannot be whole if I lose touch with myself. I will make my spiritual discipline my top priority.

3.05

> **Like all humans, you depend on feelings and instincts to guide you, and they invariably let you down.**
>
> LIEUTENANT TUVOK: STATE OF FLUX: 48658.2

No one is suggesting that we ignore our feelings. The damage caused by dissociating ourselves from our emotions can't be overstated. An ability to repress feelings *without* damage would require genetically re-engineering our entire nervous systems. Or else transforming ourselves through thousands of years of evolutionary change.

As a matter of fact, our systems *have* been transformed by thousands of years of evolution. And the result is precisely that we now *have* feelings and instincts—because they serve a purpose. We feel, therefore we act.

But evolution has also provided us with *sentience.* And that too was purposeful. Because being aware of our feelings and instincts allows us to recognize when they are *in*appropriate guides for action, and to transcend them.

The Vulcan disdain for emotion isn't because feelings are *always* inappropriate. Or because they mislead us half the time, or a tenth of the time. It's because the situation will arise, sooner or later, when they simply aren't able to clearly point the way. Or they point the *wrong* way. And if we rely on feelings alone, if we don't back them up with Mind and Spirit, they can't help but let us down.

*I'm grateful for the counsel of my feelings, but I do not **depend** on them. I will balance my emotional life with reason and spiritual discipline.*

3.06

You won't last long bangin' into walls. I'll be there for you... believe me.

ENGINEER LA FORGE: Q WHO?: 42761.3

Even by ourselves we are powerful. Even *alone* we can stand up to the forces of negativity and destruction.

Because we're *not* alone if we're aligned with The Universe. As one tradition put it, "God plus one is a majority."

Unfortunately, the Divine Presence can be difficult to feel. In the thick of our daily struggles—and especially during the tough times—nothing is quite so reassuring as the physical presence of a sympathetic friend. Having another person around to "be there for us" can be a lifeline.

But not to rely on. Not to become dependent upon every time we face a crisis. The true friend is "there" not so much to save us, but to *help us save ourselves.*

In fact, we may still end up banging into a few walls. A friend isn't doing his job by protecting us from the harsh realities of life. "Being there" is about comforting us when we *do* get banged up, cheering us up when our spirits sag, reminding us we'll survive when we're not so sure.

Mostly, a friend is someone who reconnects us with our own resources. By seeing love and strength in our friend, we remember those same qualities in ourselves.

Find yourself a friend. More important, *be* one.

I am not alone. Whenever I need help, there is at least one special friend who can remind me of the deeper resources I already possess.

3.07

Fencing tones the muscle, sharpens the eye, improves the posture.

LIEUTENANT SULU: THE NAKED TIME: 1704.2

You're catching on. This isn't really about fencing.

It's about doing *something* to keep our physical machinery in good working condition, fencing or otherwise. It's about our realization that The Inner Voyage includes both mental and *physical* disciplines.

Among the gifts The Universe provides in this life, our material form is primary. Though we are in a sense "separate" from that form, our body is our most useful tool for knowing and refining our spiritual identity. It's not simply that our bodies are the vehicles by which we act in the world, thus revealing Who We Are—to our*selves* as well as others. The fact is, how we deal with our bodies is *the training ground for the way we treat others.*

Which means that a balanced exercise program does more than improve our posture. It becomes our stance toward life. By toning our muscles, we learn the discipline to keep our relationships healthy. By using our body wisely, we learn to use *all* our possessions wisely. (Of course, if our body monopolizes our time, chances are we've become self-centered in many other ways, too.)

Through our body, we affirm the goodness of physical existence, and our gratitude to The Universe.

My body is a tool, not an idol. I will be mindful of its needs, but also of its limits. Without comparing my body to others', I affirm and give thanks for it.

3.08

When you're under conditions of extreme stress, the mind manufactures all kinds of things.

DR. CRUSHER: FRAME OF MIND: 46778.1

The effects of extreme or chronic stress are well documented. The heightened energy levels designed to galvanize us for action can end up eating away at our own bodies. *And* our psyches.

Because without any clearly-defined problem to focus on, to analyze, to *solve,* our minds literally invent a substitute. We imagine problems that don't exist. We project our frustrations and fears onto others, and onto the world. Those projections sometimes manifest as hallucinations, but more often as a vague uneasiness, or even the feeling that everything and everybody is "out to get us."

The fact that we have such feelings much of the time should give us pause. More importantly, it should remind us that *we need to pause* more often in our daily routines —to close our eyes and mentally remove ourselves from the moment; to regain our objectivity; to seek guidance.

One of Terra's sacred traditions would have us stop for meditation and prayer five times each day. Another counsels us to "Pray unceasingly." Whatever our Path, finding *some* way to regularly reconnect with a Higher Reality is essential. Because when we *are* connected, the mind stops "manufacturing." It's too busy... *receiving.*

I will be sensitive to the signs of my own stress, and take a "time out" whenever my body/mind needs it.

3.09

In a crunch, I wouldn't like to be caught without a back-up system.

CHIEF O'BRIEN : DESTINY : 48543.2

DS9's plain-talking engineer reminds us of a question we must all answer—if only because our lives may depend on it: What is *our* back-up system?

What can *we* rely on in a crunch? What can *we* turn to when our usual coping mechanisms fail... when all our hopes and dreams seem to be crumbling around us?

From computers to Starships, our technologies have incorporated fail-safe features and back-up systems almost from their inceptions. How ironic that many of the people who designed these life-enhancing (and life-*saving*) systems haven't taken the lesson to heart.

But *we* still can. Before it's needed. Or needed *again*.

We can start by building a network of others who will care for us, and for whom we'll care, when crunchtime comes. People who have lived through their own personal crises, who can point to resources they've already used successfully, can be especially valuable.

Chances are those resources will involve the kinds of spiritual disciplines that help people transcend their pain; that allow them to take the longer view; that can connect them to the power which turns even loss into learning. That's the Back-Up System behind *all* back-up systems.

Knowing what my ultimate resources are gives me strength and confidence. Through my spiritual community, I will come to know those resources better.

3.10

You cannot take away what someone does not have.

LT. COMMANDER WORF: THE WAY OF THE WARRIOR: 49011.4

Through the centuries, dictators and preservers of the status quo have recited a similar statement almost as a portent of their doom: "The most dangerous people are those who have nothing to lose."

All over the Quadrant, governments have been toppled by ordinary people who no longer felt any "ownership" in The System—or sometimes ownership in *any*thing. Under such conditions people are quite willing to risk their lives, to work (or fight) for change; to wipe the proverbial slate clean and start over.

The political message here points to a spiritual truth. From Hindu, Sufi, and Native American to Klingon and Bajoran, various traditions have encouraged this same nothing-to-lose attitude through the practice of "non-attachment." By not becoming dependent on the objects they "own" and the materialistic lifestyle that goes with them, people become far more adaptable to change. They also recover from loss more easily, take risks more willingly, and try new paths more readily.

Which means *they grow more*.

What they've willingly given up already, no one can take away. More importantly, what they gain as a result, no one can take away either.

I hereby make my top priority those "personal possessions" which cannot be taken away.

3.11

> **The future contains wonders you can't even imagine. The universe could be your playground.**
>
> Q: TRUE Q: 46192.3

Though he wouldn't be called "religious" in any traditional sense, *Q* is nevertheless talking about faith.

Because he's talking about our world-view here. He's referring to the way we look at what's going on around us, the level of excitement and joy we bring to each new day, the way our vision of the future can affect our lives *now*.

He's reminding us, in so many words, that too many of us seem to wear blinders through life. We focus on our daily chores, hardly taking notice of other events or other people unless they bump into us. We lose sight of future possibilities. We lose touch with our imagination. It's almost as if, in trying to "fit" into this world, we end up *blending* into it. Like the Borg, we become "assimilated."

Q suggests a different approach: *Don't* be assimilated. Instead, we must look on this world as if we're tourists from another dimension, scientists on holiday, seeking answers to the riddles of this strange new existence by exploring everything, questioning everything. And the best way to do this is to take on the identity of one of its residents—even as we remember who we *really* are.

Maybe *Q*'s suggestion is more than it seems.

I've waited long, studied hard, and now I can go out and play! I must play fair, and take care of my playground, but I can do anything else I want!

3.12

Who's trying to break any records? I'm doing this because I enjoy it!

CAPTAIN KIRK: THE FINAL FRONTIER: 8454.1

It's not so much that we enjoy what we do well. It's that we do well what we enjoy.

One of life's lessons is that personal fulfillment is ultimately what matters. Money, power, "breaking records"—these are hollow rewards for our labors. That which gives us *joy* is what makes life worthwhile.

But make no mistake: True "enjoyment" is no simple pleasure. We're not talking about the passing satisfactions of a full body massage, or a well-played game of softball, or a stimulating afternoon in the holosuite. Joy is more like the "bliss" of Terra's Hindu or Sufi mystics. It's the abiding sense that something we are doing is connected to the very purpose of our lives—that *this* is what we were meant for. It's the biofeedback system designed by The Universe to guide us along our personal Path.

Too often we turn off that system because it conflicts with what society tells us. Yet if we follow society's advice, we are usually left unfulfilled, even enslaved.

The irony is that if we follow the guidance of our bliss instead—if we seek first what gives us true joy, *lasting* joy—we end up doing so well that what society values often comes to us as a by-product. And if we don't break any records, at least we've broken some of our chains.

Fulfillment is my first priority. I will look for the signs of true joy that illumine my path through life.

3.13

The game isn't big enough unless it scares you a little.

COMMANDER RIKER : PEN PALS : 42695.3

Here's one of those truths you can take to the Federation Credit Center: There is no learning without challenge. There is no growth without overcoming some obstacle, without pushing the limits of what you've done before.

If you *knew* you'd succeed every time out, if there was no doubt you'd return safely—if you weren't *scared*—the journey would be little more than round-trip transportation back to where you started. It's the voyage into the Unknown that opens up new possibilities.

And opens up our blood vessels.

Because there's an emotional, visceral *rush* that comes from the prospect of discovery, from knowing that you're about to learn something, but you're not sure *what*. Being a little bit afraid, as Riker points out, isn't your body's warning to cut your potential losses, to fold your hand without playing it out. It's a message from your own psyche that the potential gain is worth the risk, and now you're mobilizing your energies for the effort.

"Big enough" is about *growing room*—or more specifically, our need to make room in our lives for personal growth. In this case, if it's too comfortable, it doesn't fit!

I enjoy the "game" of improving myself. I accept the risks; I feel invigorated as my body rises to the challenge; I am fulfilled by having made the effort.

3.14

Live long and prosper.

SPOCK: AMOK TIME: 3372.7

The traditional Vulcan benediction is now repeated so often, and in so many parts of the galaxy, that it's become one of the most common slogans of our time. *So* common that we rarely pause to reflect on what it means anymore.

Certainly it means more than the parting words Terrans uttered for centuries—the lukewarm "Good day" or, later, "Have a nice day." Then again, compared with some of Terra's *other* benedictions—like "Peace be unto you" or "May the Lord shine his face upon you"—the Vulcan "Live long and prosper" sounds almost... *commercial*.

But the literal meaning is less important than what happens when one person speaks the words to another. Because it's *more* than the words. It's what the Ancients called "well-wishing" or, in spiritual terms, a "blessing."

When we bless someone, we are essentially affirming their connection to The Universe. We are reminding them that all the bounty and goodness the universe has to offer can be theirs—in fact is *already* theirs.

And that reminder is not lost on our *own* ears, either. Because if we can affirm the goodness of the universe for others—and even "bless them that curse you"—we not only claim it for ourselves, we unleash such a positive flow of energy that lives can be changed overnight.

I will wish others well in both word and thought— especially my so-called "enemies"—and watch as my relationships, and my world, are transformed.

3.15

> **Sometimes it's healthy to explore the darker side of the psyche. Jung called it "owning your own shadow."**
>
> COUNSELOR TROI: FRAME OF MIND: 46778.1

More often than not, Who We Are and who we *think* we are don't match up. It's so easy to fool ourselves—and not just in our tendency to regard ourselves too highly. Almost as often we don't regard ourselves highly *enough*. Ironically, the same self-denial accounts for both.

Like sentient beings throughout the galaxy, our species' consciousness emerged only after an evolutionary journey which imprinted our bodies with all the earmarks of the Animal Kingdom. Within our very cells is the legacy of that journey: A physical (and psychological) urge to reproduce; a tendency toward agressive behavior that once promoted our species' survival; and, in general, an emotional toolkit designed for a harsher, more primitive environment that no longer exists.

That ancestral "toolkit" frequently conflicts with social custom, which is why we label it our "darker side." And yet it's an irrepressible part of us. If we fail to acknowledge it, we may assume a moral "superiority" that we don't truly earn until we've faced and struggled with it. Or else we grow to distrust and dislike ourselves, not realizing that those darker tendencies are perfectly natural.

And, if only we would *own* them, a source of strength.

I accept the evolutionary legacy that lies within me. And in accepting it, I can now begin to transcend it.

3.16

It is possible to commit no mistakes and still lose. That is not a weakness. That is life.

CAPTAIN PICARD : PEAK PERFORMANCE : 42923.4

One of the most difficult lessons to learn is that even if we do our best, even if our phasers are charged and ready, success is not guaranteed. We can still be defeated.

There are limits to technology. Unknown factors inevitably come into play. An old Terran proverb suggests that anything that *can* go wrong, *will* go wrong.

But as another Ancient One said, we are responsible not for the outcome, but for *making the effort.*

Failure, in spite of our best efforts, is a great teacher. It keeps us humble. It reminds us that we're only a finite part of an infinite Whole.

More importantly, failure teaches us to live fully in the present, to do the very best we can *now,* and then trust that the future will take care of itself... if only we'd *let go.*

Of course, the expected outcome can motivate us to make the effort, just as a destination can energize us to begin a voyage. But life—and personal growth—lies in our voyaging, not in our arriving.

I derive satisfaction from making the effort. I will concentrate on doing my best now, and turn over responsibility for the outcome to The Universe.

3.17

Indulging in fantasy keeps the mind creative.

GARAK: OUR MAN BASHIR: Stardate Not Given

Fantasy is to the mind as sports are for the body.

A game like *Karo-Net* (Odo's favorite), or the recently-revived Terran pastime of "baseball," not only provides a physical workout but fine-tunes our concentration and channels our energies. While masquerading as "fun," these sports actually serve to enhance our physical fitness for the rigors of our jobs and our daily lives.

Our minds, too, can be enhanced by a similar kind of workout. While also masquerading as fun, fantasy provides an arena in which we can experience new situations, take on challenges and invent solutions—and thereby practice the same mental skills we need in our jobs and daily activities. Psychologists have long known that the richer our fantasy lives, the better our creative skills in our "real lives." The more we indulge our imaginations, the more likely we'll explore reality and extend the boundaries of factual knowledge. The more we dream, the more intently we pursue our goals.

Our fantasies are like prayers. "Universe, let my life be *this* way," our fantasies say. And more often than not, The Universe answers. We must remember the power of that.

And the responsibility.

My fantasies are "practice" for the life I want to lead, not a substitute for it. The person I imagine and continually meditate on, is person I will grow into.

3.18

We are far from the sacred places of our grandfathers, and from the bones of our people.

CAPTAIN JANEWAY: THE CLOUD: 48546.2

One of the risks of "going boldly where no one has gone before" is the possibility that we may lose touch with where we've *been*. Unfortunately, where we've been —our past—very much affects who we are *now*. And if we make a wrong turn, sometimes the only way to get back on course is to retrace our steps.

The "bones of our people" provides a powerful symbol for "where we've been" and "who we are." The ancient practice of setting aside sacred ground for the dead may seem primitive. But burial was never meant primarily to preserve bodies for an afterlife. Its major effect was to keep us connected to those who went before, to preserve their hard-won lessons—to keep their legacy alive *in us*.

It should not be surprising that physical separation from hometowns, much less home *planets,* will sometimes unsettle us. The evolution of a species in a certain environment can't help but produce psychic patterns which only that environment can satisfy. To remember "sacred places" and honor ancestors is to reaffirm our roots—not for the purpose of living in the past, but to keep our bearings as we venture into uncharted territory.

Where I came from remains part of me now. In learning to accept and celebrate those who went before me, I am better prepared to face the future.

3.19

Perhaps you would be happier... in another job...?

DATA: UNIFICATION, PART II: 45245.8

Data's question, though made in jest, is a serious one —serious enough to ask ourselves on a regular basis: Is our work making us happy? Is it personally fulfilling... or simply a task we must engage in to "earn a living"?

One of Terra's ancient languages preserves the notion that our careers are meant to be an expression of Who We Are on the deepest levels. Ideally our work is our *vocation*—literally our "calling"—from the Latin word *vocaré*, meaning "voice."

The Universe, if we listen, is *calling us* to do something: To prepare for a life's mission; to perform a special task as only *we* can. No employer, no corporation—not even The Federation—can call us to this job. The most they can do is provide an *avenue* for it. And if that avenue doesn't exist, then we must create it for ourselves.

Fortunately, if The Universe needs a job done, it will also supply the energy and the means to *do* it. Which is why we must concentrate first on what *kind* of work might make us happy, on what "mission" would best express the unique capabilities within us. Once we begin to follow that path—a spiritual path, really—The Universe assigns us more than a "living." It gives us our *life*.

My work is what I do... what I do... what I do.
I will strive continually to make my job part of my
life's work, and my life's work my job.

3.20

Perhaps you know of Russian epic of Cinderella...? If shoe fits, **wear** it!

COMMANDER CHEKOV: THE UNDISCOVERED COUNTRY: 9521.6

One of Chekov's more charming traits was his unabashed assumption that every useful invention, every scientific breakthrough, every classic of literature was a product of Russian culture. (Actually, Checkov was playing off his shipmates' assumptions *to the contrary*—an admission he makes in his memoirs.) But the Cinderella "epic" not only echoes a theme common to every human culture, it can be found all across the galaxy.

Equally charming is Chekov's assumption about what the Cinderella story *means.* (Or was he playing games here, too?) Surely he isn't suggesting that the message is merely about accepting the personal foibles others help us to see. Cinderella's glass slipper can't simply be a symbol for the personal qualities we must "own" before we can reach an accurate understanding of ourselves.

Or *can* it?

Because one of the qualities we sometimes have the most trouble accepting is *our own inherent goodness.* Unlike many of us, Cinderella was true to that "royalty" within her, despite being treated like a slave. And the message is, if only we would be true to *our* higher Self, our royal destiny will come looking for *us,* too.

The Universe has already outfitted me with the divine image. Today I will remember to put it on; to wear it, act it, **become** *it.*

3.21

The ways our differences combine to create meaning and beauty!

SPOCK: IS THERE IN TRUTH NO BEAUTY?: 5630.7

One clear sign of our spiritual progress is our capacity to appreciate differences. We may feel more at home in a certain culture. We may find one spiritual tradition more conducive to our growth and understanding of reality. But our recognition of the positive role other cultures and traditions play is an essential step along our Path.

Despite all the shared traits that make us essentially alike, each of us is different. Our childhoods shape us in ways that make us more or less sensitive to certain experiences, more or less receptive to various approaches to learning. So, what conveys meaning or beauty to one person may have little impact on someone else.

Which simply means that our spiritual unfolding may happen in very different ways. Ironically, only by using a wide *diversity* of symbols, disciplines and experiences can The Universe teach us the same identical Truth.

But what's amazing is, once we realize this, we begin to see that same Truth in all its variations. We enable ourselves to gain new insights from a broader spectrum of sources. We can leave the confines of our own racial, social or religious circles and feel no less "at home."

Besides, a garden with only red roses soon loses its appeal... unless there are yellow tulips nearby.

I celebrate the diversity of forms beauty and truth can take, and by which The Universe can teach me.

3.22

A lifetime of building emotional barriers... they're very difficult to break down.

CAPTAIN PICARD: UNIFICATION, PART I: 45236.4

Transformation is almost never quick, rarely easy. We mustn't lose heart in our struggle to change ourselves—and our world—simply because the results are so long in coming. Or less than we'd hoped for.

We forget that we've fashioned ourselves over years of practice. Just think of it: If we'd consciously set out to become the person we are now—with all our imperfections and emotional defenses—it would probably have taken exactly *this long* to achieve our goal! How unrealistic we are to expect any rapid reversals.

Not to mention that some of our problems may stem from childhood traumas we've repressed so completely that we're simply unaware of them. Memories of abuse, for example, often don't resurface until we're better prepared to deal with them. Or until we've given "permission."

The fact that we *want* to change is a good sign that we *are* prepared, and we've given ourselves permission.

And there *is* hope. If we can find others with whom we can openly reveal ourselves, emotional barriers can crumble in surprisingly short order. And if we can surrender to the Power that is far greater than the combined emotional energy we've spent in an entire lifetime—or a million lifetimes—no barrier can stand in our way.

I cannot expect immediate results. But I know they will come if I persevere. And I will *persevere.*

3.23

It's not a crime to believe in yourself.

LT. COMMANDER DAX: THE QUICKENING: Stardate Not Given

For many of us, the past is little more than a case study in self-disappointment. We can hardly count the number of times we've failed to accomplish what we set out to do, or we end up accomplishing exactly the opposite. It's no wonder we've stopped believing in ourselves!

Trouble is, our resulting lack of confidence only makes matters worse. We stop trying—or at least trying anything *new*—for fear of failing again. We defer too easily to what others think, or what others want, or what others say we should do. We give up responsibility for our lives.

And that's the real crime here: Giving up.

For one thing, we'll never regain our confidence if we won't even give ourselves the *opportunity* to succeed. More importantly, each of us has a mandate from The Universe to *keep trying*. No matter how many mistakes we've made in the past, no matter how many more times we may fail, every one of us is divinely authorized to continue believing in our selves.

And if it's admittedly difficult to believe in the person we've *been*, we can still believe in the person we *can be*.

That person exists within us even now, calling us out, challenging us to live up to our potential. If we sit quietly, we can hear that voice. And in hearing, we become.

I affirm the Self blossoming within me, the Self I will become, and therefore the Self I am already.

3.24

Personally?—I'd rather go down fighting!

LIEUTENANT TORRES: TWISTED: Stardate Not Given

Looking beyond the specific situation in which she spoke these lines, B'Elanna's comment reflects her entire attitude toward life. One we'd do well to imitate.

Because, like all warriors, we too must ask ourselves if there are some things more valuable than life itself; what it is we'd do everything in our power to get or keep, and without which our spirits might as well be dead. And then, symbolically at least, we must *fight* for those things.

In fact we must *go down fighting*. And if that language sounds rather extreme, it's simply to emphasize how high the stakes are. The truth is, our daily lives put us in just as much physical jeopardy as a warrior going into battle, since what we stand for and believe in can have immediate, tangible consequences on how we live. Or whether we *ever truly live* to begin with.

B'Elanna's words also remind us that fighting for our beliefs is a struggle to which we must commit the rest of our lives—whether we have five more years or fifty. It's not like our jobs; we do not "retire" after putting in a prescribed number. In fact, remaining committed until the very end, until the final moment of our "going down," may be what the struggle is ultimately *about*.

I value the life given me not by trying to preserve it, but by using it up. I will know my true purpose in life because it will keep me "fighting" to the end.

3.25

The Borg... party poopers of the galaxy.

THE DOCTOR: DRONE: Stardate Not Given

"The Borg" has always served as a useful metaphor for the forces that rob us of our individuality, that reduce us to interchangeable parts in an impersonal, mechanized whole. To be a Borg, symbolically speaking, is to let some exterior framework determine Who You Are, to allow it to substitute *its* thoughts for yours. The Borg can stand for the clique we belong to, or a culture or religion whose precepts and customs we unthinkingly follow.

In a more literal sense, The Borg represent the temptations of technology, whose "progress" and products we blindly embrace (whether we truly need them or not)—and which insidiously transform us over time until we're no longer aware how much of ourselves we've lost, and we no longer care anyway.

To call The Borg "party poopers" is simply to inject a little humor into an otherwise serious situation: The loss of our own identity and autonomy. Ironically, many spiritual traditions would also have us lose our identity, by finally merging with the universe... or, as The Borg might say, to assimilate with the Ultimate Collective.

But that kind of assimilation takes place only when each individual has been fully developed. And thankfully, the process of unfolding our individuality *never ends*.

I celebrate my quest for autonomy. I am grateful for the freedom to make choices that are considerate of others, without being determined by them.

3.26

That's the thing about faith. If you don't have it, you can't understand it. And if you do, no explanation is necessary.

MAJOR KIRA : ACCESSION : Stardate Not Given

We've all heard this argument used by people to justify actions they can't defend otherwise. "It was a matter of personal faith," they'll say. "You wouldn't understand because you're not..." And then they fill in the blank with whatever religion they happen to be, and you aren't.

But just because the argument is misused, doesn't mean it's not true. Faith *isn't* something you can readily understand without having it, without *living* it. And trying to explain an action motivated by faith is rarely satisfying, because there's so much more involved than logic.

For example, try to logically justify your love for someone else, and why that love motivates you to do all the things you do. Try to explain why we should have compassion for a total stranger, freely give them our food or clothing or hard-earned latinum even though we may never see them again. We can't explain it. We just *do* it.

The concepts and disciplines that give direction and meaning to our lives are, in a sense, indefensible. They justify themselves only *by their effect on us*—on how we feel about ourselves, how we treat others, and whether they inspire us to reach for our highest potential.

I need not justify my beliefs to others. But I can affirm their truth for me by the positive effects they are having on my life, and on my relationships.

3.27

We all have our assigned duties.

ADMIRAL KIRK: THE WRATH OF KHAN: 8130.3

It's as if The Universe is calling us to do something, to perform some important task for which our lives have uniquely prepared us. Some of us are lucky enough to discover our mission early in life, others only later. If at all.

Many of us *think* we know what it is. We may even get offended if anyone should question us about it. "Mind your own business," we might say, bluntly suggesting they focus on *their* assigned duties and leave us to *ours*.

Which is usually a clue that we *don't* know what our mission is, because few of us can work completely on our own, without input (and sometimes hard questioning) from others. In fact, others can often help us *discover* our mission and continually refine it as we go through life.

But once we *do* discover it, nothing can distract us. Our "assigned duty" takes precedence over everything else.

An ancient tradition tells the story of a man whose duty was to plant fruit trees for the next generation to enjoy. As he was planting one such tree, a neighbor rushed up to tell him that the long-awaited Messiah had finally come, and that they should immediately go to greet him. "Later," the man replied, "after I'm done planting my tree."

He was right to finish. That was his life's mission. And who's to say the man's dedication—and that of others like him—isn't precisely what *made* the Messiah come?

I have an essential role to play. If I meditate and open myself, The Universe will teach me what it is.

3.28

You may eliminate the symbols, but that does not mean death to the issue those symbols represent.

COMMANDER RIKER: ANGEL ONE: 41636.9

During Terra's Nineteenth and Twentieth Centuries, certain reactionary groups often held "book-burnings." Publications deemed heretical or unwholesome were thrown into a huge pile and torched. The bonfire would supposedly rid the community of their influence.

The practice is hardly isolated. Literally hundreds of planetary societies have sought to suppress unwelcome messages by destroying the vehicles which carried them. And not just the words and symbols. Writers and prophets have also been torched or otherwise put to death.

But trying to eliminate the "vehicle" without dealing directly with the message has always failed. In fact it's likely to draw even *more* attention to the message.

So it is with our personal lives. We can't heal our moral or spiritual illnesses by applying "band-aids." We can't finally rid ourselves of emotional pain by anesthetizing our minds with drugs or endless "entertainment." If anything, our problems will only become worse.

We must confront the deeper issues which our behavior and our feelings *represent.* Our lives are an open message to others, and to ourselves. Stop and listen.

I am learning to see through my life's experiences to the messages they hold for me. If I don't like what they tell me, I know that help is available.

3.29

Somewhere along this journey we'll find a way back.

CAPTAIN JANEWAY: CARETAKER: 48315.6

For many of us—and for many religions—this statement is a concise summary of the very Purpose of Life: To find our way back home. Whether conceived as "Heaven" or "Nirvana" or "walking with the Prophets," some final reunion with our Creator or Source is the ultimate goal.

The irony is that, according to these same traditions, we've never really *left* to begin with. We are, deep within us, in contact with our Source even now. But in the course of our lives we've built up layers of crust and corrosion; we've bound ourselves with chains of karma or sin. We've not so much lost our way as *lost our connection.*

"Finding our way back" makes a powerful symbol for *re*-connection and recovery. The "journey" reminds us that we can expect many wrong turns, many side trips, and many ongoing adventures which will teach us important lessons. For most of us, returning will take time.

In fact, we will finally come to realize that "getting back" is less important than *the journey itself.* The final destination is not so much a goal as an excuse to undertake the voyage. And our patient expectation of returning *someday,* regardless of how long it may take or what we must go through along the way, is the Faith that sustains us.

"Somewhere" is here. My "way back" is within. I welcome and celebrate this voyage of spiritual reunion as it expresses itself in my physical life.

3.30

Without the darkness, how would we recognize the light?

LIEUTENANT TUVOK: COLD FIRE: Stardate Not Given

The debate has raged on a thousand planets: Why is there good *and* evil? Why can't we have beauty without ugliness? Why must darkness co-exist with the light?

It's true one can't exist without the other. But that truth is less a description of the universe than about *how we think*. Opposites are simply a necessary part of our mental framework. We bring our values into focus by visualizing how things might be *without* those values, or by imagining a "force" which seems to actively work against them. Even if that force is, well, *imaginary*.

Like darkness.

Darkness is not a real "thing"—material or otherwise. It is simply the absence of light. It is a linguistic construct, a verbal convenience.

Having a word for it does not confer existence. What it *does* do, unfortunately, is give us the illusion that darkness is something we can "fight." So we end up boxing shadows and chasing phantoms when the real solution is to step over to the window, raise the blinds, and expose the corners of our lives that could use a little illumination.

"Darkness" is still a useful term for talking about our inability to see. But in developing strategies to improve our vision, let's remember what's real... and what *isn't*.

I can try to fight the darkness, or I can embrace the light and shine it on others. I choose the latter.

3.31

Thy will be done.

"SCOTTY": THE VOYAGE HOME: 8390

It's the most common meditation, the most common prayer, in the universe. It is also the most deeply *religious,* for it symbolizes what amounts to our own salvation.

The fact is, sooner or later we realize who—or what—is truly in command of this Voyage. After trying to live as if we were the center of the universe, something comes along to turn our world upside down. The "precipitating event" is as different as *we* are. But all of us learn, at last, that our lives are in the grasp of the same Power that fashioned the stars and the planets; and that, under its direction, we are like so much soft clay.

We also figure out that *other* lives are likewise being shaped and sustained by that Power. And we realize that our very survival—both together and individually—depends not on trying to carry out our own separate wills, but in *aligning ourselves with its Universal Will*.

Ironically, this life-changing realization can't come through meditation. Even as "Thy will be done" becomes our mantra, we can't learn its truth except through life experience. We must hit the streets, interact with other people, perhaps even live as if we *are* the center of the universe. Until, inevitably, reality catches up with us.

Or sometimes pounds us into pancakes. And the saving grace is, it's the best thing that could've happened.

By surrendering my will to The Universe, I do not lose it. I find it—transformed and empowered.

SECTOR

CORRESPONDING TO THE TERRAN MONTH OF
April

4.01

At least I'm consistent.

QUARK: VISIONARY: Stardate Not Given

By itself, consistency is no virtue. Reminding people that our bad behavior is simply "to be expected" doesn't make that behavior any more acceptable. Quark surely knew this even as he repeated these words.

Actually, the value of consistency lies in helping us to measure the *kind of people we are* now. What attitudes and thoughts do we consistently reflect? What behaviors and actions can we be expected to perform? (We're not talking about thinking or doing something continuously or *invariably*—just enough to know that there's an established pattern.) We may consider ourselves charitable, honest, and non-judgmental, for example. But if we don't actively reflect those characteristics far more often than not, we *aren't*.

On the other hand, we may think of ourselves as morally weak or self-serving. But if we would only count how often we resist temptation or act compassionately toward others, we'd see how strong and generous we really are.

"Counting" our thoughts and actions, in fact, allows us to begin taking responsibility for Who We Are. By documenting the regularity with which we have certain feelings or thoughts, or act in certain ways, we gain the insight we need to change ourselves. *And* change our destiny.

Transformation begins with understanding. Over the next month I will record the things I do and think consistently. Then I will know what to change.

4.02

A man does not own land. He doesn't own anything but the courage and loyalty in his heart.

COMMANDER CHAKOTAY: INITIATIONS: 49005.3

Most societies throughout the galaxy still retain some notion of "ownership." In a positive light, the concept embodies the notion of "personal responsibility." Because I *own* this, I'd better take care of it; I alone am responsible.

Of course, certain things *can't* be owned by anyone—at least, not as some societies see it. The indigenous peoples of Terra's North America were one such society. In their view, people could no more own land than they could possess the sunset or the seasons. They could take from the land what they needed to live—that's why the Great Spirit had provided it. But even those "necessities" were meant to be used and recycled, just as our bodies grow and age and revert to the elements.

As another society put it, "You can't take it with you."

But what *can* be taken, what you *do* own—and are therefore solely responsible for—is Who You Are. The "courage" Chakotay mentions really stands for all our personal qualities. "Loyalty" represents our sense of interconnectedness with others, with the network of Life, with The Universe. This is what truly matters. And as Chakotay went on to say, "That's where my power comes from."

My strength comes not from things, but from character. I do not seek possessions or honors—or even knowledge—so much as a brave heart.

4.03

The only person you are truly competing against is yourself.

CAPTAIN PICARD: COMING OF AGE: 41416.2

It's not that we shouldn't look to other people as role models—for examples of how to live our lives, or perhaps how *not* to. It's just that, in the end, those other people don't live *in our shoes.* They can't fully appreciate the challenges we're up against. Or the possibilities *this* life offers that theirs doesn't.

In short, there is no ideal role model, no concrete standard to measure yourself against, except...

Except for *you.*

Which doesn't mean there *are* no standards. The Universe, in its mysterious way, "knows" the person each of us is capable of becoming at any particular stage in our lives. Deep down, *we do too.* And we can allow previous habits and external circumstances to continue their hold on us, or we can work diligently toward our higher vision.

But first we must *get in touch* with that highest and best vision of ourselves—the person only *we* can be, despite the challenges we face, and *because of* the unique possibilities our life offers. We must measure ourselves by *that* standard and, in a sense, compete with it like an athlete striving to beat his own "personal best."

If we're lucky, the competition never ends.

I will measure my failures and successes not by what other people think, but by my own highest aspirations—mine, together with the Universe's.

4.04

Words are here, on top. What's **under** them—their meaning, is what's important.
RIVA: LOUD AS A WHISPER: 42477.2

There's no avoiding the fact that the right words can be crucial. The ground-breaking Treaty of Alliance between the Federation and the Klingon Empire would've been useless without wording that offered no chance for misinterpretation. Ordinary business contracts, too, require careful selection of words to define obligations and relationships, not only for the parties directly involved, but for those who may inherit their provisions.

Interpersonal relationships, however, often rely on meanings that can't be captured by words. In fact, what is *not* said can be more important that what *is.* Sometimes the real meaning may flatly contradict the words. Even strong criticism can communicate love if delivered with compassion, or with an arm gently encircling another's shoulders. The most bumbling, clumsily-worded apology—or compliment, or proposal of marriage—can sound like poetry if one's heart is in it.

Words, after all, are only tools. We must practice listening *through* the words we hear to what lies "under them." And we must measure our own words in the same way—not by the mere sounds our vocal chords make, but by what resonates *within us,* and by what we *do.*

Genuine meaning lies deeper than words. Without discounting what people say, *I will look into their eyes, I will listen to their hearts. And to my own.*

4.05

Logic dictates caution in the face of a superior enemy.

TUVOK: THROUGH THE LOOKING GLASS: Stardate Not Given

Storytellers have known this truth for thousands of years: No "hero" can exist without a worthy adversary. Tales about easy victories won by confident protagonists are undramatic, uninteresting, and uninstructive.

The best stories confront the leading character with a seemingly insurmountable obstacle or a clearly superior enemy. The first reaction to this challenge is usually fright or flight—or both. Because it's not just "the enemy" that our hero must overcome. It's the inner turmoil, the lack of confidence, the feeling of inability or unworthiness or isolation. In the end, victory is less about an external threat than the *internal* resources the hero discovers to meet it.

Such stories come in a million different forms. They're told from one end of the galaxy to the other because *they distill the essence of what our own lives are about.* And they all advise us to exercise caution, not so much as a battle tactic or because "logic dictates," but because that's the only way to fully integrate what is happening to us.

What's happening is nothing less than our own salvation. In the "enemies" we face, The Universe is forcing us to realize the redemptive power we have within us. And the final, heroic deed is to embrace one's true Self.

My life's challenges are invitations to connect with the heroic Self that overcomes all opposition.

4.06

They don't arrest people for having feelings.

DR. McCOY: THE UNDISCOVERED COUNTRY: 9521.6

Not now, maybe. But there have been times when the opposite was true. On some planets, it's *still* true.

Because feelings can be dangerous. After all, they're so "irrational." Not to mention *compelling:* they often make us do things we never intended.

What's worse, they're *communicable.* One person's public display of emotion will often infect another with the very same feelings. Group passions can be aroused. More than one rebellion has been sparked when a single person expressed deep feelings of discontent. The broken dam starts with a small crack.

Then again, it's the holding back of those emotions— the building up of churning waters behind the dam—that allows a single crack to have such a devastating effect. If only we could release our natural feelings as they arise, the damage would be reduced. If not eliminated.

Not that they would no longer be "communicable." The fact is, feelings have been *designed* by the universe for communication. They link us at the level where we all "live"—where all of us are equal despite differing I.Q.'s and languages and cultures. *To feel is to be connected.*

We are meant to share one another's joy and sadness. Because only through others are we made whole.

My feelings are not only natural, but empowering. I will neither hide my feelings from others, nor hide from the feelings of others.

4.07

Hollow is the sound of victory without someone to share it with. Honor gives little comfort to a man alone in his home and in his heart.

GENERAL MURTOK: YOU ARE CORDIALLY INVITED: 51247.5

The blessings of companionship and love are only one aspect to this reflection from Worf's friend and fellow warrior. At face value, the General is pointing out that our personal triumphs in life are magnified when those close to us can join in celebrating them. Equally important, sharing our victories yields psychic rewards that reinforce our gains and inspire us to face even greater challenges.

But there's a deeper level to Murtok's musings. Because sometimes our victory and honor is bought at the expense of those we love. Sometimes we struggle so hard to win, to always be "right," that we drive away the people around us. We prove our point but poison our relationships. We defend our ego and offend everyone else's.

In short, Murtok reminds us, *winning isn't everything.* Being "right" isn't always about having the facts on our side. Rather, it's about nurturing harmony in our lives, about empowering and encouraging those around us.

The true victor knows when letting others "have their way" is a small price for keeping the peace. The truly honorable are those who know that how things *look* on the surface is no substitute for how things *are*... in their homes, and in their hearts.

Today I will strive to get right in my relationships. Love and friendship are the honors that sustain me.

4.08

I hardly believe that insults are within your prerogative.

SPOCK: THE CITY ON THE EDGE OF FOREVER: 3134.0

One of Terra's great Spiritual Teachers tells the story of a man who is always quick to point out the specs of dirt in other people's eyes. Yet this same man can't see the logjam in his own eyes that makes him all but blind.

Psychologists tell a similar story. Just as most people who are genuinely insane don't recognize their insanity, the people who most need an ethical overhaul don't realize that they do. And the people who continually point fingers, who are most often critical of others, are usually the ones most in need of help.

The Magic Mirror strikes again. It works like this:

The negative traits our fragile egos won't permit us to see in ourselves, we project onto others. The character flaws, the moral failures, the "sins" we find in everyone else are really reflections of our *own* flaws, failures and sins. Our subconscious mind is trying to show us what we can't—or *won't*—see, using other people as mirrors.

So if we notice ourselves being critical of others, it's time to ask ourselves what it is about *us* we need to change. And if we've actually *insulted* somebody, it's a pretty good sign that things are getting desperate. We need to change our ways... *now.*

I will concentrate first on changing myself. *And I will be more understanding of others who face the same uphill battle in their own lives.*

4.09

> **The acquisition of wealth is no longer the driving force in our lives. We work to better ourselves and the rest of humanity.**
>
> CAPTAIN PICARD: FIRST CONTACT: 50893.5

Easy for Picard to say.

For when society has evolved to the point that the average citizen lives better than the kings and queens of centuries past, it's easy for people to turn their attentions to other things besides "making a living."

But bettering ourselves isn't something we should focus on only *after* we've "made it," only when we finally achieve some predetermined level of wealth.

Not that Picard meant to imply this. He understood that bettering ourselves *is* acquiring wealth. Serving our fellow beings *is* the way to grow richer.

In fact, spiritual traditions throughout the galaxy have always advised us not to "lay up" material possessions, but to concentrate on the kind of treasures no one can take away. Like an appreciation for the simple things. Or the satisfaction of having helped someone, just when help was needed. Or having a faith in the goodness of the universe so powerful, so radiant, that you literally *make it so*.

To develop personal—or rather *spiritual*—qualities like this should be our first priority. And the good news is, once this spiritual quest becomes the driving force in our lives, material wealth tends to take care of itself.

I seek the spiritual riches The Universe has placed within me, and in my relationships with others.

4.10

I don't have a life. I have a program!

THE DOCTOR : TATTOO : Stardate Not Given

For many of us, *our* lives have become programs, too. Our reluctance to try anything new; our fear of falling behind if we pause now and then to review where we're going; our willingness to let our jobs take priority over everything else—these are signs that we are no longer controlling our lives so much as *being controlled.*

Not that we can avoid responsibility. Things could've been different. But we made choices. And now we've accepted our routines as if they were installed by our manufacturer, and any tampering might crash our system!

Ironically, our personal programs are very much like the "software" of the early Computer Age. They are easily frozen by conflicting commands, highly sensitive to hidden viruses. And when we develop a program which seems to work for us, we are *very* reluctant to change.

Pre-computerized societies called it "habit." Or being "stuck in a rut." But life is about getting *un*stuck, about setting off on new paths. Because one of the programs our manufacturer *did* install is the ability to *rewrite* those programs. Beginning with the "Pause" command.

And if that doesn't work, software upgrades are available from several dependable sources. Not the least of which is the One we're already connected to.

I am my own programmer. I can diagnose the glitches—with others' help, if I want it. And I can install new "software" whenever I decide.

4.11

You can't be afraid of rejection.

COMMANDER SISKO: THE HOMECOMING: Stardate Not Given

The "traveling salesman" of Terran legend is the paradigm case. The Ferengi deep space businessman is a more contemporary example.

And the most successful ones rarely make more than one sale in ten. In other words, for every ten product presentations these entrepreneurs make, the proverbial door slams in their face *nine times!* That's a rejection ratio of ninety percent. Or, as Sisko might have put it, a batting average of .100. How can any player cope with that?

More than not being "afraid," it's a matter of redefining the game. It means recognizing beforehand that you'll "process" ten potential customers in order to filter out the one with whom you were meant to do business. It means identifying the nine who *don't* need your services, so you can better serve the one who *does*. It means practicing on the nine, so that the tenth will truly understand and appreciate what you have to offer.

And what you're practicing is not your "sales presentation." What you're offering is not a product. What you're really "processing" is not your customers but your *self.*

In facing rejection, we are all like the salesman. Overcoming it is a process of affirming one's self-worth despite the outcome. Selling that *to ourselves* is the real success.

*Rejection is a loving process for refining Who I Am. I acknowledge the Self within me that **can't** be rejected because The Universe already accepts it.*

4.12

When you lie or steal, you not only dishonor yourself, but your family.

LIEUTENANT WORF: NEW GROUND: 45376.3

It's not that the readers of this *Manual* need a lecture about lying and stealing. There is a deeper issue here.

At some point in our lives we finally come to accept responsibility for the choices we make. This is a healthy, necessary stage. The problem is, it often brings with it a tendency to think of ourselves as autonomous, self-made beings no longer bound to those who originally shaped us, whether through influence or genes... or both.

And the fact is, all of these people—parents, teachers, siblings, friends—*continue* to have a stake in us, if only because of the time, sweat, and emotional energy they've invested in our development. That doesn't give them the right to use their "investment" to make us feel unduly obligated, of course. Honor is also about *releasing attachments,* about having the freedom to leave the nest, to try our wings, to make our own mistakes.

But our actions link us to the people in our past nevertheless. When our actions demonstrate our own higher qualities, they reaffirm *theirs.* When our behavior falls painfully short, it recalls the anguish of times they too missed the mark. "Honor" is Worf's word—an ancient, venerable, *visceral* word—for recognizing these links.

I will live and act as if the people who cared for me and encouraged me... who believed the most in my potential... are present with me now.

4.13

> **It is the struggle itself that is most important. It does not matter that we will never reach our ultimate goal. The effort yields its own rewards.**
>
> DATA: THE OFFSPRING: 43657.0

Data's statement can stand quite nicely on its own, thank you. Nothing further is necessary...

Except, perhaps, for this footnote:

Religious traditions on many planets have envisioned a kind of personal salvation which claims to be a once-in-a-lifetime event. One's vow of submission to a certain diety's authority, or one's performance of a particularly heroic deed, was enough to secure the Eternal Reward.

Admittedly, there *are* turning points in our lives. Certain actions or realizations may stand out as life-transforming events. Religions are right to celebrate these decisive moments by giving them some kind of sacred status.

But this kind of recognition also gives the impression that the struggle is over. Or that the struggle is worthwhile only as a means toward an end. Data properly reminds us that our salvation lies in *doing*, not in *having done*.

We should be suspicious of life goals that are too close, too easily achieved. The voyage whose destination is always just beyond the horizon is the only one that can reward us eternally.

Perfection is a verb, *not an adjective. I reaffirm my commitment to the never-ending voyage of self-discovery and self-improvement.*

4.14

You cannot put a price on life!
CAPTAIN PICARD: BLOODLINES:47829.1

From a purely practical point of view, it's hard to disagree with Picard's statement. We know, for example, how impossible it is to predict the course of someone's life. A person born into poverty may end up giving more wealth to his community—in service if not money—than a dozen self-indulgent millionaires. Intelligence hasn't been a reliable gauge of someone's "worth" either. Nor have good looks, or racial qualities, or social standing.

Not to mention how wrong we can be in valuing our *own* lives. Even those of us who harbor doubts about our self-worth may go on to play decisive roles. Or at least go on to decide that our lives aren't really so bad after all.

But practical considerations are not, finally, what makes Picard's statement true. The fact is, we have no business trying to judge the worth of a person's life in the first place. The Universe has its own "reasons" for creating us all. How any individual fits into the wider Scheme of Things is not merely beyond the human (or Vulcan, or Betazoid) capacity to know. It is beyond *knowing*.

What lies deep within each of us—deeper than all the external descriptions of Who We Are—is not subject to evaluation. Let's remember to treat each other that way.

I will not judge others—or myself—by any standard of "value." We exist; The Universe has given us the right to be here. That is enough.

4.15

I have considerable leeway to bargain in these circumstances: Name your terms.

QUARK: THE SEARCH, PART I: 47212.4

In many ways, living is similar to running a business. And we, like Quark, are self-employed entrepreneurs.

Because it's ultimately *our* business. No one else is responsible. *We* are the managers and the custodians. We sit behind the big desk, and we sweep up the floors. Our choices make it a success, or lead to bankruptcy.

Much depends on wise bargaining. Everything is subject to negotiation. Even goods that are "free" often require that we change our attitude in order to receive them.

Most things, however, will cost us *some*thing out-of-pocket. Yet surprisingly, The Universe allows us to set the terms. We can agree in advance what we're going to give up in return for what we get. Or we end up paying later.

The safest terms, as countless other entrepreneurs will testify, are based on a by-the-book, pay-in-advance contract. By investing a certain amount of time and effort, we can usually predict what our return will be. Progress may be slow, but it's steady. We get exactly what we earn.

But there are also times for risk, for taking advantage of opportunities even when we can't predict the outcome. And just *taking* those risks, for the sake of our own spiritual progress, can yield the biggest payoff of all.

Life is a bargain. The Universe has given me power to set my own terms through the "considerable leeway" (options) my life continuously offers me.

4.16

If there are self-made purgatories and we all have to live in them, mine can be no worse than someone else's.

SPOCK: THIS SIDE OF PARADISE: 3417.3

According to one Terran tradition, "purgatory" was the place all human souls were sent after death—when they hadn't yet qualified for entrance to Heaven, but neither were they doomed to Hell.

A common spin on this tradition is that *our present lives are purgatory.* We are all, symbolically, living along the spectrum between paradise and annihilation. Where we are right now is exactly where we belong. And what we do *next* is part of a grand scheme to explore and test our character, and ultimately to "perfect" it.

The problem is, the tests *we* face can appear so different from others, so *unfair.* We seem to have it so easy compared to other individuals—or whole planetary cultures—who are struggling merely to survive. Still others' lives seem like Heaven already, filled with continual comforts and pleasures and nothing to further "test" them.

But we cannot judge those lives. Nor can we say we're better or worse than those who lead them. Character is fashioned in many crucibles, each for a different purpose. We must accept the crucible given by the Universe *for us*... and then transcend it if and when we're able.

The circumstances in my life are for my own self-improvement. I will start from where I am, and not measure my progress against the lives of others.

4.17

> **What we don't know about death is far, far greater than what we *do* know.**
> CAPTAIN JANEWAY: EMANATIONS: 48623.5

Religion was invented, so the story goes, in order to explain death. Even today, religions which claim to know what happens after death are the most popular. Books about near-death experiences are best-sellers. And holo-suites which simulate scriptural visions of Paradise (or visitations with ancient gods) draw the longest lines—especially on planets where ordinary life is harsh.

The Twenty-Fourth Century offers little more "proof" of life-after-death than do the claims of earlier traditions. And as much as death is embraced by science as part of the natural order, it remains mysterious. Perhaps the most realistic approach is to simply *accept* that Mystery, without needing to know what death holds for us.

Because the more important question is, What do we know about *life?* How do we take advantage of this physical existence of ours to the fullest extent possible?

Even the scriptural accounts of an afterlife teach us less about death than *what's important about life:* That everything we do or think takes us to higher or lower levels of fulfillment; that connecting with The Universe's deepest resources is how we experience heaven; and that if we follow our chosen Path with sincere effort in *this* life, then what we still don't know about death will hardly matter.

What I do know is this: If I take full advantage of my life, what follows will be no less fulfilling.

4.18

The honor is to serve.

LIEUTENANT WORF: PEAK PERFORMANCE: 42923.4

The injunction to *be of service* is so prevalent throughout the spiritual archives that it ranks alongside food, clothing and security as a Primary Need.

The idea of serving others is not some burdensome call to fulfill ones "duty." It's not an obligation to repay others for what you may owe them for years of childhood nurturing, or for the benefits of living in the Federation.

The call to service comes as a voluntary response, at the point in one's life when others' needs are suddenly seen as important as your own. It represents the emergence of a new self, a *higher* self. In spiritual language, it is "the birth of one's own divinity."

A 20th-century Terran playwright, G. B. Shaw, described it these terms: "This is the true joy in life," he said, "the being used for a purpose recognized by yourself as a mighty one; the being thoroughly worn out before you are thrown on the scrap heap; the being a force of Nature instead of a feverish, selfish little clod of ailments and grievances complaining that the world will not devote itself to making you happy…"

Or more simply, "The honor is to serve."

I affirm and celebrate the fact that others are part of what I am. Their needs are part of my needs. My service to them is a gift to my higher and better self.

4.19

There's another way to survive: Mutual trust and help.

CAPTAIN KIRK: DAY OF THE DOVE: Stardate Not Given

It's a common assumption, but mistaken. The instinct for self-preservation does *not* automatically translate into the notion of "Every person for himself." If it *did,* our various planetary races would not have survived to this point.

Galactic archeologists point to no less than fifty planetary civilizations which no longer exist. And the reason, it's now thought, is because narrow selfishness overruled common interest. When survival was at stake, individuals sought their own safety—apart from the group. The wreckage they left behind is witness to that philosophy.

Our own survival testifies to the approach Kirk recommends. Not that we deserve the credit for inventing it. Built into our very chromosomes is a biological predisposition to help one another. And it's almost miraculous. In times of disaster or common threat, people seem to naturally come together, to drop former barriers, to forge the networks necessary to overcome any challenge.

But that "predisposition" can't be taken for granted. It must be nurtured. Our spiritual disciplines keep us connected to one another by reminding us of our connection to the Source which created us all.

And the irony is, it's the most selfish thing we can do.

My personal survival is inextricably bound to the survival of my fellow beings. I help myself most when I freely and gratefully help others.

4.20

Concentrate on getting well... Feel the connection... Our strength is your strength... We're all one circle. No beginning, no end.

THE COOPERATIVE:UNITY:50622.4

First, let's acknowledge that these lines were spoken to Chakotay by ex-drones who once served in the Borg Collective. For Chakotay to put his life into the hands of such a group was clearly a desperate measure.

But let's also recognize that there are times in our own lives when equally desperate measures are required.

Whether we're battling a life-threatening illness, or in the clutches of an addiction, or grieving over a personal tragedy, we too may find that healing eludes us. Our own strength seems inadequate. We lose the will to live.

An ancient spiritual tradition teaches that, when we're suffering or gravely ill, each visit from a member of our community contributes one-sixtieth to our full recovery. In other words, healing is a *cooperative* process. We are meant to draw strength from those around us.

And it's not simply a matter of accepting their "well-wishes." Once we begin to concentrate on recovery, we can consciously *extract* healing energy from them, especially when several are gathered together for our benefit.

We are not weaker for relying on one another in this way. We are stronger. And so are our relationships.

The best medicine for my healing is the help of other people. And I will gladly offer my own presence as a conduit to recovery when others are suffering.

4.21

Honesty is usually wise.

DR. McCOY: FOR THE WORLD IS HOLLOW AND I HAVE TOUCHED THE SKY: 5476.3

As everyone knows, "Bones" was a master at stating the obvious. And yet what seems so obvious in this statement really *isn't*.

Because McCoy wasn't merely applying his dry sense of humor to the old maxim that "honesty is the best policy." The fact is, honesty is only *usually* wise, not always. Sometimes honesty can be too strong a medicine. Most of us can absorb the full truth only in small doses. Which means we ought to think twice before dispensing it to others—especially if there's a chance we're doing so with less than the purest of intentions.

On the other hand, honesty is *still* the best policy overall, despite the rare exception. If we cannot rely on one another's words, lasting relationships are impossible—whether economic, political, or personal. And how true we are to our words is a primary gauge of our character, for our *own* reference if not for others'.

In one of Terra's oldest and most sacred languages, the term *dabar* could mean either "word" or "deed"—as if to point out that speaking is also an action, and our acts are one way we speak to one another. Being "honest" therefore applies as much to our behavior as our words. And striving to make one match the other is wise.

Not usually. *Always.*

I will strive for honesty in both my words and my actions, for each depends on the other.

4.22

We're a part of our environment... We cannot separate ourselves from it without irrevocably altering who and what we are.

AARON CONOR: THE MASTERPIECE SOCIETY: 45470.1

In the words of an old Bajoran proverb, "The land and the people are one." Terra's Native American tradition put it this way: We do not own the land; the land owns *us*.

Just because we are mobile—we walk, we run, we traverse time and space—we are no less outgrowths of our home planet as the root-bound tree. Our very chemistry mirrors our species' planetary origins, as uniquely and accurately as fingerprints identify an individual.

Many people now consider it odd that the ideal single-family domicile on Twentieth Century Terra required its own front and back lawns and private vegetable garden. And yet urban dwellers were only responding to an innate need to remain connected to the earth. Mowing the lawn was an excuse to walk something other than concrete. Tending one's garden was a way to feel the dirt beneath one's fingernails, as had countless generations before.

The call of our chromosomes is *real*. We are poorer if we too cannot dig the soil now and then, if we forget what grass feels like between our toes. To remain connected to our original environment, even if symbolically, is what *grounds* us. Only then can we "boldly go."

Every atom in my body was once part of the environment around me. To live in harmony with it is to create harmony within myself, and with others.

4.23

You reveal yourself best in how you play.

Q: HIDE AND Q: 41590.5

...And the person to whom we reveal ourselves *best*, if we're paying attention, is *us*. Just consider what we say to ourselves in the way we play:

For example, do we spend much of our "rec time" in escapist entertainment or sleep? Then it's likely we're running away from something in our lives, or in our past.

Must we always seek the company of others in order to "have fun"? Then it's possible we feel incomplete or uncomfortable in our own presence.

Do we require competition in all our games, and are we upset if we don't win? Then chances are we feel insecure about who we are at some deep level, and we must continually "prove ourselves" in order to feel worthy.

These are simplistic analyses, of course. But the point is, what we do in our "time off" is a kind of self-portrait. By being more conscious of that portrait, we not only gain greater self-knowledge, we gain more *self-control*.

Because play is a chance to experiment on ourselves without the usual pressure to perform. Through play we can test another way of being, free another side of our personalities, find strengths we never knew we had.

We set the precedent for serious self-transformation —by not being so serious about it!

Play means not having to perform my "usual" role. This week I will put aside at least one day to play, and meet the more relaxed and joyous "me" within.

4.24

This is important—you and I. Things change, but not **this**.

CAPTAIN SISKO: FOR THE CAUSE: Stardate Not Given

In the midst of constant flux, we can find solace and strength in the stability of our relationships.

Not that our personal relationships don't change. We learn, we grow, we find new interests, we set out on new paths—all of which can't help but impact how we relate to one another.

But not *whether* we relate to one another.

Stable relationships aren't based on personalities, but on the *person*. We don't commit ourselves to the surface features someone may exhibit. (Actually, some of us *do* commit ourselves to physical beauty or wealth or having similar likes and dislikes; but we're trying to overcome that kind of superficiality, aren't we?) It's the self *behind* those impermanent features that we are engaged with. It's the core individual whose identity continues through all the changes, who remains the same in spite of all the extra pounds and wrinkles. And social upheavals.

The ability to see through those "exterior things"—even past our personal disagreements—is not only the sign of a mature relationship, but a measure of our spiritual growth. To remain committed to another person is to understand something essential about ourselves.

The opportunity to form a new relationship is a gift from The Universe. Maintaining my connection to another person affirms the higher Self within me.

4.25

I have found myself and my place. I know who I am.

SPOCK: THE FINAL FRONTIER: 8454.1

Here is the affirmation we all long to make someday, the "place" we all want to be in, the sense of identity that's beyond physical location, or time, or circumstance.

One ancient spiritual tradition called it *gnosis,* from the Greek word for "knowing." It means knowing not only Who We Are, but what our purpose is in the Scheme of Things. It means seeing ourselves not merely as others might describe us, but *as The Universe envisions us.*

It is a humbling, yet empowering view. Because knowing our place gives us permission to play our unique role to the fullest, while allowing others to play *theirs.* And like pieces in a jigsaw puzzle, our lives suddenly... *fit.*

The question is, how do we arrive at this place?

The path is different for everyone. And yet the same. It involves what another ancient tradition calls "following your bliss." The fact is, The Universe *wants* us to know Who We Are, and what our unique purpose is. And its surest clue is that feeling of lasting fulfillment we get only when we pursue certain kinds of activities and not others—the inner sense that *this* is The Way and not *that.*

Which is not to say things will be easy, or that we'll always be happy. Only that we know it's worth the effort.

I am a "work-in-progress." I may not fully know Who I Am right now. But I'm in the process of finding out; I'm on the way to my "place." And that is enough.

4.26

I'll accept the judgment of history.
CAPTAIN PICARD: THE WOUNDED: 44429.6

There comes a point in our lives when we recognize, finally, how fallible we are. We're not perfect. We can't know everything. We simply do the best we can under the circumstances… and we go on.

But what's amazing is how often "doing our best" fails miserably—or at least yields nothing tangible. At other times it's our half-hearted efforts, or even those miserable failures, that eventually bring the most positive results.

The fact is, we have no surefire way to pre-determine the long-term effects of our actions. We don't know all the variables. We can't predict with any certainty how our behavior will intertwine with the actions of others, whether the consequences will cancel each other out or develop some cumulative effect. No computer ever built can follow any single action to its ultimate "conclusion," much less chart the complex tapestry we weave together.

To accept the judgment of history is to recognize that the outcome is not in our hands. The Universe is the final arbiter of what we do. And the *best* we can do, it turns out, is less a matter of our actions than our commitment to keep "doing", to keep *learning*, to keep unfolding our own spiritual histories—and simply trust The Universe to take it from there.

I act, and I release the results to be whatever they will be. I accept the consequences as an ever-renewing lesson about my life.

4.27

Is truth not truth for all?

NATIRA: FOR THE WORLD IS HOLLOW AND I HAVE TOUCHED THE SKY: 5476.4

We're good at giving lip-service to the concept of Universal Truth, or "equality under the law," or the idea that we are all essential parts of The One.

If only we could *act* that way.

Because when it comes to *applying* these universals, we start making exceptions and readjusting the scales. In Terran history this was called "the double standard." The law was applied only to the masses, not to princes or politicians or the police. The right to vote was only for people who owned land, or had a certain skin color or belief system or bank account. There was one standard for ourselves, and another standard for "everyone else."

Traces of these policies exist even today, if only as the residue of our continuing struggle with an *inner* double standard: With our tendency to see faults in others that are really projections of our *own* faults; with our suspicion of strangers and aliens that really represents a fear of forces within ourselves we don't yet understand; with our dislike of individuals (or whole races) that results from the fact that we have not yet accepted who *we* are.

When we're courageous enough to notice this double standard in ourselves, we should consider it a call for personal growth. Take heart: It means we're ready.

I will apply the same standards to myself as I apply to others—remembering patience and forgiveness, as well as truth and justice.

4.28

Whatever you need is what I have to offer.
NEELIX: CARETAKER: 48315.6

This is no slogan for bootlickers, no song to subservience, no advice to submerge our own will beneath the changing tide of someone *else's*.

For one thing we can serve other people without losing self-respect, or neglecting our own needs.

More important, we must keep in mind that "need" is not the same as "want." Genuine need is not some passing fancy. It is long-term, primal, rooted in Who We Are. What others *want* from us is only rarely what they *need*. And vice versa. Discerning the difference is a skill. *Applying* that difference is the mark of great wisdom.

The Universe offers us whatever we need. (And sometimes even what we *want!*) But it also calls upon us to supply the needs of others—both out of gratitude, and to keep our own pump primed. The truth is, offering to fill another's need fulfills *our* need. And their need, on occasion, is specifically to fill ours. In fact, what others offer us—freely, willingly, seemingly out of the blue—is often The Universe pointing to a need we didn't know we had.

To live in this interdependent circle of need and fulfillment is to experience a "community" that's both practical and spiritual. In it we discover the one need that must precede all the rest: *Each other.*

I enjoy supplying what others genuinely need.
I affirm the giving and receiving which makes my life purposeful and enriching.

4.29

What I've done, I had to do. If I hadn't tried, the cost would've been my soul.

ADMIRAL KIRK: THE SEARCH FOR SPOCK: 8310.3

Few of our actions are significant enough in themselves to radically alter our lives. Most have a cumulative effect, like small steps, one following the other, down a path we've already chosen.

Then again, there are those occasional crossroads that can literally re-engineer Who We Are. They may be opportunities to show a new side of ourselves, to bring out our dormant divinity, or simply to decide to take responsibility for our lives instead of blaming the world.

Perhaps the toughest decision involves the so-called "lost cause," the no-win situation where it appears that nothing we do will make any lasting difference. Or where doing the right thing may even bring us pain and grief. These are the moments when we ask, *Why even try?*

And the answer is, because *not* trying would cost us far more than trying and losing. Because turning away—ignoring the cries for help, or the seemingly endless tide of desperate, needy people, or the injustices in the world (even if they're somewhere *else*)—would rob us of something so essential that it would feel like "losing our soul."

Sometimes, our highest achievement lies not in the end results, but in *having tried.*

As important as the outward effects of my actions are the inward effects of having acted with integrity, of striving continually to be the best I can be.

4.30

It's human nature to love what we don't have.

ENGINEER LA FORGE: ELEMENTARY DEAR DATA: 42286.3

Actually it's more than *human* nature. It's a function of sentience. "Awareness" not only means being conscious of what *is*, but of what *could be*. Or what we *could have*.

There are dozens of sayings—from "The grass is always greener on the other side of the fence" to "The farther the star, the more it sparkles"—that reflect our drive to possess more. Trouble is, once we *do* possess more, we suddenly find ourselves looking for the *next* fence to jump, the *next* stars to reach for. We're never satisfied.

What's worse, our very success reinforces the notion that what's worth possessing are *things* that can be seen and touched. We become fixated on the material world.

We must learn not to take the objects of our desires so literally. The greener grass and the distant stars—or our neighbor's new shuttlecraft, or our neighbor's *wife*—are almost never what we really want. These are symbols, chosen by our subconscious because they are so visible, so touchable. They remind us that we *aren't* satisfied.

Because what we *really* want is more knowledge and understanding. What we would *truly* love is to keep growing, to keep pushing the boundaries of who we are.

Until what we possess, at last, is our Self.

I realize my desire for "things" represents a deeper longing to explore and develop my personal skills and qualities. The greener grass is within me.

SECTOR 5

CORRESPONDING TO THE TERRAN MONTH OF
May

5.01

To take a risk or play it safe... how precious the right to choose is. Because I've never been one to play it safe, I choose to try.

CAPTAIN PICARD: A MATTER OF TIME: 45349.1

Living, thinking, *doing*—these have always been the greatest teachers. They are the seeds of our growth.

We must trust our own capacity to learn from, and be transformed by, the choices we make. The Universe does not oppose us. Nothing holds us back but our fears, our self-imposed limits, our failure to *try*.

Too often we crush our own dreams. And yet those dreams represent The Universe's invitation to spread our proverbial wings, to leave the safety of the nest, to soar higher. After all, we don't really *control* our dreams, do we? They rise like a wellspring from some deeper source. Ignoring them chokes off our own life-changing energy.

The Inner Voyage affirms those deeper sources, that wellspring of energy. It also trusts that when we risk the first step toward our dreams, the next step will become clear, then the next, and the *next*—as if a light begins to illumine our way. If one route is blocked, another opens up. If we enter unfamiliar territory, a guide appears.

And one of the rewards is that *we* become guides for future voyagers. Our example, our journey, emboldens others. And that, in turn, should make *us* bolder.

I am inspired by each new challenge. I will follow my dreams, not so much for where they may take me, but for what they may teach me.

5.02

The expulsion from Paradise... it is a reminder to me that all things end.

SPOCK: THE UNDISCOVERED COUNTRY: 9521.6

The Terran legend Spock refers to is not unlike creation stories found all across the galaxy. In Spock's own spiritual tradition, *Sha Ka Ree* is the mythical planet from which creation spread throughout the universe—and from which Vulcans were banished just as humans were expelled from Paradise. Stories about the Klingon equivalent, *Qui'Tu,* and the Romulan *Vorta Vor,* are embellished with similar themes.

And all of them are meant to tell us that we were not designed for stasis. It is in our natures that we cannot live in an ideal world, where nothing changes because everyone and everything has already achieved perfection. If anything, our sense of *im*perfection is what drives us—to build, to grow, to improve our world and our selves... and to *keep* growing and improving, or cease to exist.

Of course there are periods in our lives when we enter what seems like Paradise, where we can finally enjoy the fruits of success. And we'd be happy if nothing changed.

The Explusion represents the fact that, even when things seem perfect, we still need to keep moving along our Path. Our salvation depends on it. And what sometimes feels like punishment is really the gift of life.

I celebrate that inner Spirit which calls me onward, even if it means leaving behind what's familiar and comfortable. This day is a new beginning!

5.03

Brute force isn't going to do it!

LIEUTENANT TORRES: FACES: 48784.2

The scene was not uncommon in the "movies" of the mid Twentieth Century. An actor would be tuning an old vacuum-tube radio, adjusting its dials, unable to get it to work until—*whack!*—he'd spank it like some disobedient child. Suddenly the radio would crackle to life, the broadcast now coming in strong and clear.

A good whack may be primitive and irrational; but it also strikes a familiar chord. It symbolizes our own frustrations with making things "work"—not only inanimate objects but our relationships with each other. And if patience and persuasion can't get the job done, there's always, well, *brute force.*

Force, however, can never be the final answer. Even when applied to individuals (or nations) who are clearly wrong. Even when the results seem to justify its use.

Because the negative effects of coercion don't simply fade away. And because the crucial lessons about finding ways to live together as interdependent communities *won't have been learned*—not by those who were coerced, nor by those who did the coercing.

All appearances to the contrary.

And that's the real danger: That appearances will fool us into thinking the underlying problem is solved. Or that slapping the radio won't make the problem even worse.

Resorting to force is our common enemy.
The battlefield is in my heart. The strategy is love.

5.04

I know you're afraid. I just want you to know that, no matter what happens, I'll be here with you.
KES : PHAGE : 48532.4

Sometimes it's not our words people need. It's not even our assistance—whether in the form of financial help, or taking over their responsibilities if they're sick, or "fixing things" that happen to go wrong.

It's our *physical presence.*

How easily we forget that the quality of our lives depends less on external conditions than internal experience. When we listen to our fellow crewmember tell us about a job-related problem, or a broken relationship, or concerns over health, it is rare that he or she wants help in finding some concrete solution. We share our tragedies because it's our *feelings* that need "fixing."

By listening to another's woes, by acting as a sounding board, we bring healing. Simply "being there" works miracles. Sharing the same physical space, without uttering so much as a single word, can express all that another person longs to know: *You are not alone.*

A beloved scripture ends with the words, "I am with you always." It's reassuring enough to remember that we remain linked to The Universe at some deeper level. But nothing speaks louder than our willingness to *stand in* for that Divine Presence... here, now, in the flesh.

My greatest gift to my loved ones is not in doing, but in being; not in my presents, but my presence.

5.05

Don't believe your eyes.

CAPTAIN JANEWAY: CARETAKER: 48315.6

It's not exactly that we should *dis*believe what we see. It's just that we shouldn't define Reality solely according to what our eyes tell us.

The Changeling is perhaps the most graphic example of the fact that visual data isn't enough. Humans possess at least four *additional* senses because no less could insure the species' survival. Some humans—and several other species—possess still *more,* from telepathy to precognition. Different evolutionary histories have encouraged different combinations of these sensory abilities; and each species develops its own characteristic set, usually before consciousness has even emerged.

Some scientists suggest that consciousness itself developed as just one more "sensory ability"—the ability to rise above the physical senses in order to better analyze the data they provide, and in the process to perceive one's *self.* The "spiritual sense" is only a natural extension of this new perception: That information about the physical world is limited and sometimes downright deceiving; that much of what's important to our survival comes from a deeper, non-material source. And if our spiritual sense is a bit underdeveloped at this point, perhaps we should start "believing" our ears and our eyes a little *less.*

I affirm that there are ways of "hearing" and "seeing" that transcend my physical senses. I will develop those abilities through regular meditation.

5.06

One of the most important things in a person's life is to feel useful.

CAPTAIN PICARD:RELICS:46125.3

We're not going to consider our *own* desire to feel useful here. Most of us don't need to be reminded that performing a valuable service fills an important need in us; that helping others makes us feel good. Today's task is to remember that *others* need to feel useful, too.

Look around. Consider the younger members in your community—brothers or sisters, school children; even the youthful "gangs" that seem to populate every planet. Know that all of these growing selves are searching for roles that affirm their worth, their *value* in some wider scheme. That is their birthright as sentient beings. And if we—all of us—can't offer them positive roles for acting out their self-worth, they will invent their own.

And what about those at the *other* end of life's spectrum? Have we found *them* roles, too?—so they might continue to express a lifetime of learning and experience? Or are we content to simply find them a "home"?

One of our most important spiritual qualities is an ability to imagine ourselves in other people's shoes. We know what it feels like to be needed. Now imagine *others* wanting to feel the same way.

Now find a way to *do* something about it.

This week I will ask both a child and an elder to play a valuable role in a family or community project. I willingly accept the possibility of failure.

5.07

I have been told that patience is sometimes more effective than the sword.

LIEUTENANT WORF: REDEMPTION, PART I: 44995.3

To act, or not to act; that is the question.

Then again, *not* taking action is also an act. Which means it's an option that should at least be considered.

Starfleet officers—even trainees—often find this option the most difficult. After all, leaders want to appear "decisive." *Doing something* suggests assertiveness. *Not* doing something seems weak, indecisive. Egos become more important than strategy. And it's not just a matter of appearing strong to *others*. It's our own conceit that no conflict or issue can be solved unless *we* have a hand in it.

And yet strategy depends on precise timing, on waiting for just the right moment. To be drawn into a fight we're unprepared for, or to let someone else set the terms for an engagement, can be a crucial blunder. *Not* striking back—or "turning the other cheek" as one of Terra's Holy Ones once described it—can set in motion forces that are far more powerful than swords or phasers.

Sometimes these forces for reconciliation are already in motion. Things will often "take care of themselves" if only we'd let them. But first we must be still long enough to remove our ego, to listen to the guidance of The Universe… to *be patient*.

I will act, not re-act. With each new day, I will practice the patience that allows The Universe to work in and through my actions.

5.08

The end cannot justify the means.

DATA: REDEMPTION, PART II: 45020.4

Six words. Four basic components. The same ones, in the same order, are embodied in a thousand different languages. So often does it appear throughout the galactic record, in exactly this form, that it can lose its impact.

Fortunately, there are a few effective variations.

Like: Nothing good can be accomplished if the methods are evil. Or: When we set the goal, we thereby determine which options we can employ to achieve it. Or from scriptural sources: One cannot arrive in the Holy City through the Gates of Sin. Or, from Vulcan: To separate the destination from the journey is not logical.

Or this, perhaps the most radical variation: The destination *is* the journey. The end *is* the means.

Which is simply to say that we can't arrive at our goal *except by living out its effects in the present.* We cannot make war to achieve peace. We can't isolate people in prisons in order to free them from their anti-social tendencies. And we certainly can't be saved by letting others make our choices *for us,* by letting someone *else* save us.

"Means" is everything. Getting there is *being* there. Working toward salvation *is* being saved.

Actually, the "end" could never justify the means. It's just what gets us out of our chairs.

I will set goals not so much for the conditions I hope to achieve in the future, but for the conditions I will create now, as I work to achieve them.

5.09

> **You have got to make use of what you have. If you need a hammer and you don't have one... use a pipe!**
>
> **MAJOR KIRA**: RETURN TO GRACE: Stardate Not Given

Kira's advice isn't meant to remind us of our innate creativity, or to inspire us to be inventive—although that would certainly be good advice. Her words are aimed more at our need to accept who we are, and the specific weaknesses and limitations implied by that.

After all, many of us weren't born with hammers in our hands. Or silver spoons in our mouths. On the contrary, a lot more of us were born with (or we've managed to develop!) some pretty serious handicaps.

There was a time when use of the word "handicap" was frowned upon. However, the word need not be taken negatively. In certain sports, for example, a "handicap" is a disadvantage that a player *willingly accepts* in order to make the game more fair, to "level the playing field." A severe handicap might even be *self*-imposed, so that a player might push himself all the harder, and thereby improve his competitive skills more than otherwise.

Perhaps we come into this life having accepted or imposed such handicaps on ourselves—in order to push our own limits, to find and exploit personal qualities and inner resources we might not otherwise realize we had.

The most important "hammer" is not the one in my hands, but the one within me. I accept what I do not have, so I might make better use of what I do.

5.10

What you want is irrelevant. What you have chosen is at hand.

SPOCK: THE UNDISCOVERED COUNTRY: 9521.6

Our choices have a power of their own. And once set in motion, the events which flow from our choices can turn in unexpected and unfortunate directions.

We may offer the usual excuses: There were physical factors we couldn't have foreseen. Other individuals complicated things; they weren't supposed to get involved.

Sometimes nothing we do will improve or reverse a bad situation. And we end up saying things like, "If only I'd known!" or "This isn't how I planned it."

The harsh truth is, what we originally wanted becomes irrelevant. Sometimes *worse* than irrelevant. Because if we continue to dwell on how the situation "should've" turned out, on what we "planned" would happen, we can lose touch with the realities we must deal with *now*.

We can take solace in our good intentions later. In fact, people have a surprising capacity for forgiveness if they learn what we *intended* to do, despite the fact that we damaged them by what we actually *did*.

In the meantime we must take responsibility for what's "at hand," for the consequences of our previous choices. Because accepting responsibility is *also* a choice—one that carries its own power to harm, or help us grow wiser.

I affirm the power I wield—for better or worse, for both myself and others—by making choices. And I will be stronger for accepting their consequences.

5.11

The answer to the puzzle is... too simple for most humans to understand. All life, all consciousness, is indissolubly bound together. Indeed it is all part of the same thing.

LWAXANA TROI : HAVEN : 41294.5

How easily we are fooled by the apparent complexity of nature—*and* the seeming complexity of our own lives!

We're baffled by the hidden agendas in our relationships, appalled at our own ignorance of ourselves, frustrated by unforeseen events that turn our best-laid plans into smoldering ruins. So we invent the notion that life is terribly complicated, that it's a physical struggle between separate, opposing forces we'll never fully understand. And we thereby "explain" our own inability to cope.

In science, however, the best—and most powerful—explanation for any phenomenon is the *simplest* one that accounts for the most data. The idea that our physical lives spring from consciousness, and that our consciousness springs from a much deeper source that underlies *all* life, is just such a simple but powerful explanation.

What seems so complex are only manifestations of The One. By envisioning ourselves bound together with the same Consciousness that created the universe, we are no longer separate entities. Spiritual growth—both communal and individual—begins with this realization.

Beneath the surface, Life is One. No matter what challenges I face today, I will envision myself linked at the deepest levels with everything around me.

5.12

Our species can only survive if we have obstacles to overcome... Without them to strengthen us, we will weaken and die.
CAPTAIN KIRK: METAMORPHOSIS: 3219.4

Most of us, frankly, don't look forward to the obstacles life keeps throwing in our path. We'd prefer things to go smoothly. We'd rather proceed in a straight line than stumble toward our goals on a zig-zag course, or find ourselves pushed backward.

The roadblocks we face, the unexpected turns, the doors that slam after seeming to open in welcome—all of these obstacles can frustrate, depress, or even anger us. It can be reassuring to remember that The Universe is still in control, still guiding us. And sometimes the roadblocks are put there specifically to force us in another direction, onto a path where things *will* go smoother, where the doors along the way will remain open and welcoming.

But sometimes there *is* no other path. Sometimes the obstacles must be dealt with directly, and either we overcome them and succeed, or we don't.

We must be content at such times to realize that these too are for a purpose. Even our failure to overcome them can teach and strengthen us. Pushing against a mountain is doomed only if we think we're actually going to move it. If we do it simply to keep in shape, we succeed!

The obstacles in my life are meant not so much for me to move, but to move me *to become a stronger person. They are opportunies to grow spiritually.*

5.13

Our only influence is by example.

CAPTAIN PICARD: HALF A LIFE: 44805.3

It's fortunate that so many of us put less of a premium on what other people *say*, than on what they *do*.

Because "practicing what we preach" holds us all to a higher standard. And because the best measure of what we believe can be found in our behavior. If we give lip-service to certain principles, but we don't *follow* them in practice, is anyone really fooled for long?

History and personal experience demonstrate that lasting "control" over others cannot be achieved through force, or by threats of hellfire, or even through the Rule of Law. All we can do—all we *must* do—is simply live our lives as we would want others to live theirs; to act as if our Articles of Faith could only be formulated in actions; to *embody* the truth, not merely embrace it.

There is tremendous power in teaching others by embodying one's principles. Witness the fact that the Most Revered Ones throughout the galaxy have rarely been warriors or politicians. Neither are they unapproachable sky gods who rule from a distance, as if direct contact with us would somehow contaminate them. Rather they were individuals who *modeled a lifestyle*, who earned our respect precisely because they lived among us. And what they could do, *so can we*.

I will let my whole life stand for what I believe, trusting that others will see (and perhaps follow) the light which The Universe embodies in me.

5.14

The ability to recognize danger... to fight it or run away from it... that's what fear gives us. But when fear holds you hostage, how do you let it go?

CAPTAIN JANEWAY: THE THAW: Stardate Not Given

The last part of the Captain's statement hides a clue. Because if we can "let it go," fear can't hold us hostage in the first place. At least, not without our permission.

Which means *we* are ultimately in control. The ability to overcome our fears is already in our possession.

Imagination is part of it. Picturing ourselves doing the very things we fear can be a powerful tool for developing confidence and courage. From speaking in front of large groups to climbing great heights; from high-pressure job situations to red-alert battle conditions—whatever your fear is, simply guiding yourself through a mental simulation sets the psychological precedent for overcoming it.

And it's not necessary to *eliminate* our feelings of fear, either. The key is simply not letting them stop you.

The other part, of course, is testing yourself in real life. What's important here is not expecting immediate success, but rewarding yourself for even the smallest move in the right direction. Simulate, test, reward.

Only *we* can hold ourselves hostage. The fact that we *do* means we still have something to learn.

My fears hold me back until I have learned the lessons they are designed to teach me. I will meditate, learn, thank my fears and release them.

5.15

We consider our families one of our strengths.

COMMANDER RIKER : RASCALS : 46235.7

The point here, of course, hinges on what the word "family" means. The social unit known on 20th-Century Terra as the "nuclear family," for example, was among the more artificial definitions that could be found throughout the galaxy. One mother, one father, and 2.5 children living contentedly in the land of security-gated suburbia was not only a fantasy, it was lightyears from the species' own evolutionary roots.

Studies of humankind's origins—and emerging sentient societies elsewhere—show that the natural family extends far beyond the "birth parents." Uncles, aunts and grandparents play almost as great a role. Mothers and fathers of neighbor children, who can augment (or even substitute for) the biological parents are essential.

A family enhanced by the proximity of several generations and a diversity of role models literally moulds our initial concept of Self and the larger world. It's not just that our family is one of our strengths; without it we are less than we might otherwise be. Our hard-wiring *requires* it.

If all of these relationships aren't there for us through biology, we must create them ourselves... For our own sake. For our children's. And our neighbors' children.

My personal development does not happen in a vacuum. I honor and celebrate what The Universe teaches me through intimate family relationships.

5.16

What's important is what **you** think.

CAPTAIN SISKO: THE WAY OF THE WARRIOR: 49011.4

No, *Deep Space Nine*'s resident Emissary is *not* giving us permission to think only of ourselves, nor to disregard the opinions of others. What he *is* saying is that we, individually, are the ones who must live with our decisions. *We* are the ones most affected. Not only our actions, but our innermost *thoughts,* have karma. We will inevitably reap their consequences, both positive and negative—if not immediately, then over time. In fact, it's the *long-term* effects of our thoughts that constitute their real power.

In recognizing that power, Sisko knew, we are also encouraged to accept responsibility for them. Because if our thoughts can affect us *that* much, we'd better learn to control them. Or at least come to terms with them.

Yet some of us still don't want to. We prefer to rely on what other people think since, that way, responsibility for our happiness or success is someone else's problem. And if we seek others' guidance, and make our decisions based on what *they* think, we also avoid blame if things go wrong. "I was only following your advice" becomes our repeated refrain. And, repeatedly, we fail to grow.

The Universe can transform us only through the thoughts *we* have, and the choices *we* make. To value what *we* think is to take our lives into our own hands.

I need the opinions of others to add perspective to my own. But I accept final responsibility for my decisions, my thoughts, and my own happiness.

5.17

> **When a man is convinced he's going to die tomorrow, he'll probably find a way to make it happen.**
>
> GUINAN: THE BEST OF BOTH WORLDS, PART II: 44001.4

The self-fulfilling prophecy is one of the most insidious—and at the same time miraculous—facets of the human mind. "As a man thinketh," the Terran proverb goes, "so he *is*."

And the fact is, human beings *do* view reality through a variety of filters based only in part on direct experience. Perhaps *more* important is what we've been told as children. Because, just as we learn our primary language before we're even aware of it, we also absorb our basic world-view: Whether it's out to destroy us or save us; whether other life forms are competing with us for slices of a finite "pie" or sharing the infinite resources of an infinite universe.

Fortunately, ever since the link between matter and consciousness was proven experimentally, we've known that we can change our "filters"—and therefore reality itself—by changing the way we think. If it's true that a deep-seated belief in our imminent demise makes us succumb more easily when our life *is* threatened, the opposite is equally true. More than most of us realize, our lives are truly in our own hands.

I accept full responsibility for what happens to me... both now and in the past. I will change my circumstances by first changing the way I think.

5.18

May the great bird of the galaxy bless your planet.

LIEUTENANT SULU: THE MAN TRAP: 1531.1

There has been quite a bit of speculation through the years about what Sulu meant by his reference to the "great bird of the galaxy." Was he referring, indirectly, to the *Enterprise* and the positive legacy it left behind on its flight of exploration? Or maybe to some *other* starship?

Was he drawing on religious symbolism, where the bird represents Spirit—or, in some traditions, God?

(Some historians even speculate that a legendary figure, perhaps a specific visionary from Terra's pre-Federation past, was the "great bird" of Sulu's blessing.)

Whatever the case, the bird *is* a meaningful symbol for the inner workings that bless us with spiritual growth. In many cultures, birds represent nurturing and guidance. We can imagine ourselves hatched into a cozy "nest" with others like us, force-fed while we grow in self-confidence and strength—and sometimes "taken under wing" when the world outside seems cold and frightening.

But at some point it becomes necessary to leave the nest and spread our own wings. In some cases we are literally *pushed* out—and it ends up being for our own good, because only then do we find out what we were destined for: To fly even as the great bird flies.

I am grateful for the nurturing of The Universe. As I learn each new lesson, I know I will be sent out to test my spiritual wings. But only when I'm ready.

5.19

> **Once you detach yourselves from your emotional responses you come closer to controlling them. Eventually they will be eliminated altogether.**
>
> LIEUTENANT TUVOK: INNOCENCE: Stardate Not Given

First of all, Tuvok is not talking about eliminating *emotions*. He's talking about eliminating emotional *responses*—those knee-jerk, psycho-physiological reactions that can cloud our judgment and interfere with performance.

The distinction is critical. Because even Vulcans recognize that emotions serve a purpose in most other humanoid species. Emotions draw our attention to events and situations that have potential importance for us. They help us mobilize our physical energies so we can effectively deal with those events and situations. But they are singularly *in*effective by themselves. We must bring our mental and spiritual resources into the response process.

Unfortunately, we can't do so unless we see our Self as separate from our emotions, as a "higher" Being merely *using* the language of emotion. This is the "detachment" Vulcans (as well as Buddhists and Hindus) refer to.

In time, like training wheels on a child's bicycle, our emotional reactions cease to be necessary. We know what's important without having to *feel* it. Our bodies respond without our emotions having to slap us awake.

And we can save our emotions for better things.

I am not my emotions. I will seek to understand the messages they are sending me, then release them.

5.20

May fortune favor the foolish.
ADMIRAL KIRK: THE VOYAGE HOME: 8390

It's always humbling, if not infuriating: What we *think* should happen often turns out to be completely wrong. Our most carefully-conceived plans, our most logically-constructed schemes, end up in the porcelain dumpster.

And then some fool comes along with nothing more than a hunch—or worse, a *vision*—and everything magically falls into place.

Throughout galactic history, the most revered prophets and visionaries were originally regarded as "fools." Maybe because others couldn't see the possibilities, or only the *negative* ones. Maybe because the majority were operating strictly on what was "rational" or "practical"; on what could be deduced from "the facts."

But facts represent only a narrow band on the spectrum of reality. "Foolish" is a term people use to describe whatever lies outside their own visual spectrum. It's also a label for imposing that narrow vision on others.

Not that others' myopia should restrict *us*. We must learn to trust our own insight, our own intuition. Which doesn't mean acting on every idea that pops into our heads. It simply implies a willingness to take seriously what might at first seem foolish. And, like the prophets, to be willing to "act like fools" for what we believe in.

I will act on the vision The Universe instills in me, considering others but not substituting their vision for mine. And I will accept the consequences.

5.21

There's an old horsetrader's adage about putting too much weight on a young back. ...Don't want it to break under pressure.

CAPTAIN PICARD: PEN PALS: 42695.3

There are scores of similar adages throughout the Quadrant. While horses figure in only a few, all make an analogy between the loads borne by a primitive culture's beasts of burden and the "weight" *we* carry through life.

And the analogy is simply this: Just as a young animal must become accustomed to lighter loads before heavier ones, we too need to "build up" to more demanding responsibilities and concerns. Especially *spiritual* ones.

The reason is as obvious as learning the alphabet before the classics. The corollaries are *less* obvious.

The first corollary is that we shouldn't judge others by the spiritual progress *we* may have made. Regrettably, many of us treat other people who are just becoming aware of their spiritual responsibilities as if they should know better. We hold them to standards of ethics and discipline we ourselves have only recently taken on. As one of the ancient Holy Ones advised, we must "...forgive them, for they know not what they do."

Secondly, *we too* are still "young" in many ways. We shouldn't put too much pressure on our*selves* either. The Inner Voyage isn't easy. Let's take it one step at a time.

I must develop basic spiritual skills before mastering the more advanced ones. The "weight" given me by The Universe does not exceed what I can carry.

5.22

We are all part of a greater community. We cannot ignore it.

MIRASTA: FIRST CONTACT: Stardate Not Given

The trouble is, we *can* ignore it. And often *do*.

What we *can't* ignore—at least for very long—are the consequences for refusing to join the greater community. Because if we attempt to maintain our isolation, we lose in the long run. *Every*body loses.

The practical benefits of joining are obvious: New markets and new technologies; new solutions to common problems; exposure to new ideas, new art, new culture.

Not that there aren't potential risks. But centuries of interplanetary experience, under the guidance of the Prime Directive, have shown how distant societies can link together productively without losing their identities and their roots. After all, it is our different perspectives and histories that make community so enriching.

So it is on the spiritual level—individually and collectively. Only as we view the One Truth from different perspectives can we fully absorb its riches. Only as we see the different words and forms Truth takes can we recognize the rich meaning within them.

And only in relationship with others can we discover the richness within our own lives.

I celebrate my inter-relationships with, and interdependence on, others. I affirm who I am, and who I can become, within the greater community.

5.23

You must have faith that the Universe will unfold as it should.

SPOCK: THE UNDISCOVERED COUNTRY: 9521.6

Just as some variation on The Golden Rule is found all across the known universe, so too is this sentiment.

The Universe is lawful. Though we may not always know *why* a specific event happens as it does, we can rest assured that present circumstances are the inevitable, lawful result of prior events. Even wormholes and "future causation" are part of this matrix.

Sentient life is no less lawful. Our consciousness, our "inner lives," are also embraced by causation. This isn't some straightjacket we wear; it is the very foundation of our transformation.

Because if we're not happy with our present circumstances, there are specific steps we can take to change them—however painful or difficult they might be. Our realization of this fact should empower us.

It is also empowering simply to recognize in all these laws a deeper, unseen Reality which underlies the universe. And since every event is an expression of that Reality, there are no accidents. Spiritual Paths acknowledge this as "grace," or "the Divine Plan." Events conspire toward Life, toward growth, toward *wholeness.*

And as it is with the universe, so it is with *you.*

I will live as if everything that happens is purposeful. My life and my growth are as natural and necessary to The Universe as they are to me.

5.24

If there is a Cosmic Plan, are we not part of it? Our presence at this place, at this moment... could be a part of that fate.

COUNSELOR TROI : PEN PALS : 42695.3

Even though we're all busy working on our own personal plans and goals, we must never lose sight of the wider Plan of which we're part. Because as we grow more spiritually aware, it's only natural to begin receiving occasional "casting calls" from The Universe—offers for us to play some important role in a larger cosmic drama.

At such times other people's needs, or even some life-transforming event, must take precedence over what we happen to be doing at the moment. It may be frustrating and sometimes painful to put aside our own "work." We may be so wrapped up in our own lives, or so convinced we're already doing something important, that we'll even pretend not to hear this call. But our response is crucial.

For one thing, if *we* expect help from the Spiritual Network, if we believe that people often come out of the blue to help *us* just when we need it—and they *do*—we too must be willing to perform the same service for others.

But the other thing is, the Cosmic Plan doesn't call on us arbitrarily. More often than not, what we think is a side trip on our Voyage turns out to be exactly the direction we needed to go, and teach us just what we needed to learn.

I am part of the Cosmic Plan. I am grateful for the help The Universe gives me on my spiritual path, and I gladly offer assistance to others when called.

5.25

Our ambition to improve ourselves motivates everything we do.

QUARK: PROPHET MOTIVE: Stardate Not Given

For many of us, "ambition" carries as many negative connotations as positive. In its neutral sense, the word simply refers to the inner drive that impels people toward their goals. But that drive is often seen as self-serving and ruthless. Ambition is the proverbial bull in a china shop, the loose phaser, the win-at-all-costs, take-no-prisoners assault that tramples anything that gets in its way.

This kind of ambition values goals over people, the "end" rather than the "means," the destination more than the voyage—or what we learn *during* the voyage.

In one of his more reflective moments, Quark puts ambition in its place. We should strive not for trophies or achievements, he implies, but for the personal development required to *earn* them. We can easily misinterpret the ambition we feel as directed toward some external objective, toward the "thing" we're doing. But if that's so, we haven't given our subconscious minds enough credit. Because the real objective is always internal, and what we're really "doing" is *improving ourselves*.

The more we become conscious of this fact, the more likely we'll discover what it is we need to learn—and then make our primary goal *learning* it.

Hidden within my external goals are clues to how my inner Self wants me to grow. I will focus less on "achieving," and more on learning my lessons.

5.26

War is never imperative.
DR. McCOY: THE BALANCE OF TERROR: 1709.1

Though McCoy was referring to the clash between nations, war is ultimately a product of our *inner* conflict. If we would practice peace in our personal lives, war not only wouldn't be "imperative," it would be inconceivable.

Unfortunately, there are enough people who *don't* practice peace to ruin prospects for everyone else. And even if we've learned not to respond to these aggressive types out of anger or revenge, shouldn't we at least give them a taste of their own medicine? In fact, don't we have a *responsibility* to forcefully teach them a lesson?

No, because overcoming force with *greater* force only teaches an aggressor that he wasn't powerful enough. Meeting angry words with *more* angry words only justifies feelings of animosity. The cycle escalates.

We can break that cycle only by doing the one thing the aggressor doesn't expect—because it's the last thing *he* would do in the same situation: Reach out in love.

One of Terra's Sacred Ones advised us to "turn the other cheek" after being assaulted. Which doesn't mean simply allowing yourself to be whipped into submission. It means standing your ground, staring into the soul of the other person, believing so strongly in the divinity of that soul that the aggressor can't help but see it himself.

That's the way to teach him a lesson.

I stand for peace in all I do. I believe in the goodness hidden in others, and I believe in my own.

5.27

You should know the dangers of opening old wounds.

ADMIRAL KIRK: THE WRATH OF KHAN: 8130.3

There are reasons why we sometimes don't heal our wounds, why we often bury our painful experiences under a false pretense of "It's okay" or "It didn't really bother me" or "I just don't have the time to deal with this now." There are also reasons for suppressing the memory of pain altogether, as if we weren't wounded to begin with, as if the events that hurt us never really happened.

And the usual reason is, *we weren't ready to learn from them at the time.*

There is nothing demeaning about this. The adult who was abused as a six-year-old child *couldn't* have learned anything at the time, wasn't spiritually equipped to transform the pain. At age twenty, perhaps. Or thirty.

The point is, sooner or later our old wounds must be reopened so that genuine healing can finally take place. And even when we're ready it's still dangerous work.

Because we must be prepared to feel the pain again. We must seek to understand ourselves and the others involved, both as the people we *were* and the people we *are*. We must forgive. Most of all we must be committed to assuming full responsibility for our feelings and our actions, to stop affixing blame and start taking control.

Know the danger. But seize the opportunity.

I am not the person I was. I have grown. I am ready to heal my wounds and grow even more.

5.28

The road from legitimate suspicion to rampant paranoia is very much shorter than we think.

CAPTAIN PICARD: THE DRUMHEAD: 44769.2

It's always tempting to blame our problems on others—on our competition, our enemies, or the latest intergalactic conspiracy. Our fears and insecurities become a function of the external world. We aren't responsible.

But our biggest danger isn't the external world. It's the way we *react* to it. And we *are* responsible for that.

Perception is part of it. Admittedly, we sometimes have a right to be suspicious of others based on previous experience. But if we automatically take that next step, if we begin to *expect* the worst, we put on blinders. Goodness can't be seen, much less experienced. The world turns into an evil place where bad things are just waiting to happen. Our paranoia poisons everything we touch. And what's sad is, we aren't even aware we've made a choice.

We could just as easily choose to perceive the good. But it's more than perception. Positive expectations can literally bring out the kinder, more harmonious elements in other people. Our conscious projection of non-violence and goodwill—a force Hindus call *ahimsa*—sets up an energy field that can physically transform our reality.

And the wonderful thing is, the road to *that* reality is also very much shorter than we think.

The power to transform the world lies within me. I will consciously project goodwill to everyone I meet.

5.29

We all create God in our own image.

COMMANDER DECKER: STAR TREK/TMP: 7412.6

The story is the same on virtually every planet which is home to sentient life. Insofar as a Supreme Being is envisioned at all, that Being is initially seen in the "likeness" of the life forms who envision it.

Naturally, this god "evolves" as their understanding evolves. To begin, it is simply bigger or more powerful than they are. It will have arms, legs, ears and eyes, even though these appendages and organs are not necessary to the god's actions or awareness. It will also have emotions—which usually means it tends to be jealous and vengeful as well as compassionate and forgiving.

As in human history, the Being eventually becomes more than a mere extension of what we *are,* and represents the very best we *can be.* This is often symbolized in miraculous events wherein the Supreme Being enters the planet's history to save us from our baser qualities.

But as progressive as this new "image" is, it still largely depends on the scope of our imagination. And that is why idols and images ultimately cannot save us: We must open ourselves to the Source that can draw out the potential we never realized we had—the capabilities that elude us precisely because we can't yet conceive of them.

Though, fortunately, we can *connect* with them.

I submit to the Mystery which is Ultimate Reality. Though I envision the best I can be, I do not limit my spiritual growth to what I can imagine now.

5.30

Therapists are always the worst patients. Except for doctors, of course.

DR. CRUSHER: THE LOSS: 44356.9

This isn't just about therapists. Or doctors. It's a meditation for people who think they know so much about the process of healing—or about relationships, or religion, or gourmet cooking—that they find it almost impossible to admit that they might ever need anybody else's help.

In short, it's a meditation for, and about, *us.*

Because all of us have some kind of "specialty." We've all become experts on some area of life, either by studying it, or living through it, or because it's our job. And all that expertise gives us the sense that no one else could possibly know the subject like *we* know it.

Which may very well be true. But it's also true that we can never know *everything*. And we can almost always benefit from the fresh insight that only someone *else* can provide—someone not as emotionally involved, not as committed to the way things are "supposed to be done."

Some of our greatest scientific advances have come not from senior professors at The Academy, but from their newly-recruited research asssistants. That doesn't mean the elders are no longer needed. It simply means that our own hard-won knowledge, combined with another's insight, may yield the answer neither of us can find alone.

I am only one of many people on this Voyage. My own knowledge is essential, but not always sufficient. I am grateful for the help of others.

5.31

But then again, all good things must come to an end!

Q: ALL GOOD THINGS...: 47988.1

If so, this would surely seem to be one of the most *depressing* truths imaginable.

Why must all good things end? Why can't goodness, once achieved, be kept forever? Why are the times of rest and peace so short-lived, and the struggle so unceasing? Why shouldn't we be able to enjoy the blessings we've toiled our whole lives for—indefinitely?

We're forgetting one important factor here: Our own responsibility for what happens.

Because in most cases it's not as if someone *else* is taking away the "good things" we've earned. It's in our natures to extract what we need from the present situation, consolidate what we've learned, enjoy our new level of achievement... *and then move on.*

Which simply means that all good things come to an end only if we want them to. And the truth is, even what's "good" has only so much to offer us before we tire of it, before we need a new challenge. We may not be consciously aware of that need. Like a child whose parents tell him it's time to leave the carnival, we may protest and sulk a bit. But we are only following an even *greater* good: The path to our own spiritual destiny.

The good is there to enjoy, and to encourage me to keep moving along my Spiritual Path. The end of one good thing is the beginning of another.

SECTOR

CORRESPONDING TO THE TERRAN MONTH OF
June

6.01

Logic clearly dictates: The needs of the many outweigh the needs of the few.

SPOCK: THE WRATH OF KHAN: 8130.3

What The Universe continually affirms is that every one of us is bound together in an inter-dependent Web of Life. No single individual is so isolated that his existence doesn't matter, or that his actions affect no one else.

Yet every higher life form enters the material world with the same Prime Directive: *Survival of self.* In its biological infancy, each individual is preoccupied with its own needs, usually to the exclusion of others.

Personal growth, however, begins with the realization that others *can't* be exluded. Making others part of Who You Are becomes increasingly essential. Throughout the galaxy, wherever The Inner Voyage (or some other "spiritual path") is practiced, its success depends on a radical redefinition of "self." Slowly, by stages, we incorporate others: Family, friends, mates, community, all life forms, the universe. The boundaries separating us gradually disappear until others' joys and sorrows become *our* joys and sorrows… their needs, *our* needs. And vice versa.

Ironically, those who lose their narrower self—even to the point of sacrificing one's life, as Spock did—insure a legacy which makes the ancient promise of immortality seem pale by comparison.

Today I will practice inter-dependence by putting the needs of others first. I will make at least one new friend, or re-connect with a friend I've neglected.

6.02

You are not alone. Do you understand—? We are in this together now!

CAPTAIN PICARD: LOUD AS A WHISPER: 42477.2

What is the most significant moment in your personal history? In human history? In the history of the galaxy?

It is the point at which we finally realize that our lives, our destinies, cannot be separated from one another. It's the revelation that, from princes to paupers, from Klingons to Cardassians, we are all in this struggle *together*.

One of Terra's pre-modern cultures had a very specific word for this life-long struggle: *Jihad*. Often mistakenly interpreted as an armed conflict against other political or religious groups, *jihad* referred primarily to the struggle *within oneself*—the effort to redeem one's own soul from inner turmoil, from greed, anger, sloth and selfishness.

Even in the case of armed conflict, the real enemy is never the other individual or group. It is our own primitive tendency to divide ourselves, to build walls rather than bridges. It is the world view in which we see one another as material rather than *spiritual* beings, as competitors scrapping over a finite slice of the pie instead of fellow workers in a universe of unlimited possibilities.

We need each other. And those who come to this realization share the responsibility of setting the example for others to follow. Do *you* understand?

*I understand that the real struggle is **within us, not with each other**. I will look there for the things I must change—and there for the strength to change them.*

6.03

Don't be afraid of your darker side. Have fun with it.

COUNSELOR TROI: FRAME OF MIND: 46778.1

"Darker" is one way to describe it. But the darkness has less to do with a certain "side" of us than how little we *understand* it. And what we don't understand, we fear.

When we act in ways we can't explain, or when our emotions surprise us, chances are we're operating under the influence of this "darker side." Our surprise—or, in some cases, our *embarrassment*—should be seen as a cry for help, a call to get back in touch with that deeper, more "primitive" region which comes to us courtesy of the Animal Kingdom. *And* to deal with needs and feelings we've probably repressed for the better part of our lives.

Not that we're being asked to suddenly vent all those repressed feelings on the world. What our darker side requires of us is simply to acknowledge and respect its existence, in the same way an adult admits to the inner legacy of the child he/she once was.

In fact, just as the adult can have fun by recapturing the spirit of that child—the anticipation of each new day, the endless game-playing and exploring, the sense of wonder—we can also have fun with our "primitive" side.

When was the last time you climbed a tree barefoot, or danced around a campfire? Or spent an *entire day* eating, sleeping and snuggling with someone you love?

I will set aside time to honor the physical needs and emotions that are an essential part of who I am.

6.04

Why does everyone say "Relax" when they're about to do something terrible?

ENSIGN KIM: NON SEQUITUR: 49011

Perhaps the most cynical answer to Kim's question is, "To tempt us to lower our shields just before they fire the photon torpedoes."

But the truth is, people more often tell us to relax when they're about to do something on our behalf—something they sincerely believe is for our own good. Perhaps they think they know better. Or they suspect we're about to make a mistake, and since they're more experienced we should stop worrying and let *them* handle it.

What's so "terrible" is not so much the possibility that things may turn out badly. It's the fact that we'd rather do it ourselves. *We need to do it ourselves.*

Our jobs may not give us a choice. But when it comes to our own personal lives, we mustn't allow others to act for us. Even if they know better. Even if we'd prefer to relax while someone else does the work.

Not only must we insist on our right to "learn by doing," we must remember that others have the same right. Not only must we be allowed to take the risks and make the mistakes that lead to our own personal growth, we must guard ourselves against doing the things for others that might prevent *their* growth.

I no longer depend on others to do for me what I should do for myself. I can offer advice to others, but what they do is up to them—and The Universe.

6.05

Notice your mind working... how it plans for the future, visits the past. Notice those thoughts and set them aside. Turn your attention to the white light that is your breath.

LIEUTENANT TUVOK: BASICS, PART I: Stardate Not Given

Our minds are wondrously precise, theoretically flawless instruments. Below the surface of our awareness, they work constantly—managing our bodily functions, tracking events in the world around us, analyzing past actions and consequences in order to plan our future.

The trouble is, we can interfere with the flow of that process by trying to do *consciously* what is best left to our *sub*conscious. Knowing when that's happening is tricky, of course. But if we experience feelings of unfocused fear, or can't seem to concentrate—or perhaps we're uncharacteristically "grumpy"—chances are that our conscious mind is pushing itself into areas where it doesn't belong.

Tuvok's instructions summarize a meditative exercise (known as *v'passana* on Terra) designed to free our subconscious from such interference. The first step is simply to "notice" that our mind is doing its job already, accept that, and then calmly direct our attention elsewhere.

Focusing on our breathing is a galaxy-wide technique for concentrating so strongly on one thing that distractions, even consciousness, temporarily fade away. That's when we do some of our best work!

I breathe in calm, I exhale tension. I breathe in clarity, I release confusion. I am refreshed!

6.06

Over the years I've learned that sometimes you just have to punch your way through.

CAPTAIN JANEWAY: PARALLAX: 48439.7

The word "punch" may derive from a pugilistic sport once popular on Terra, and still practiced on several other pre-technological planets. As the Captain uses it, however, punch is neither violent nor even physical. It's something we *have*, not something we do.

"Punch" is a state of mind. It's the recognition that barriers exist only if we allow them to stop us; that meeting resistance is a sign that we're making progress; that opposition means we're on the verge of a breakthrough.

And when we finally *do* break through, it's not so much because we've beaten the opposition as *outlasted* it.

The most important characteristic of punch is not raw power. It's persistence. Overcoming our addictions, or our grief, or our personal flaws, rarely happens in a single swing. It's a struggle over time—a fight in which we renew our determination every time we're knocked down, celebrate every moment we manage to stay on our feet, and continuously affirm the meaning it gives our lives.

"Punching our way through" is less about right hooks than the right attitude; less about hammering our opponents than forging our own character. Sometimes the sweetest victory is simply making it to the final bell.

Today I will not back away from the fight. I will stay in the ring, go the distance. I will feel my strength and my joy increase as I finish each daily round.

6.07

An answer? I don't even know the question!

CAPTAIN KIRK: STAR TREK/TMP: 7412.6

It's a common problem. Our search for knowledge is rarely thwarted because we can't find answers. More often it's because we haven't asked the right questions.

How we ask is critical. Sometimes, for example, our questions make assumptions that immediately point us in the wrong direction. Like the question, "Which religion is true?" We assume that a religion describes an objective reality, and, like some scientific equation, if it's not accurate it must be "untrue." But the truth is, religious traditions are more or less subjective means for linking us with realities and resources which are beyond these finite packages we call "words." And what successfully links one individual to those resources may not work for another. Asking if it's "true" misses the point.

Other questions contain similar misleading assumptions. "Which planetary race is superior?" "How can I achieve happiness?" "What's the best way to earn love?"

The way we formulate our questions restricts the answers we can generate, or even whether an answer exists at all. Too often we limit the possible responses only to what we expect, or what "fits" with previous knowledge.

Instead we must learn to ask in ways which free The Truth to reveal itself. We must risk being surprised, challenged, even offended. That is the price of growth.

The Universe is ready to answer fully only if I will open myself fully. If I seek, truly, I will find, truly.

6.08

If you could experience the Link, you'd know why nothing else matters.
CONSTABLE ODO: BEHIND THE LINES: 51149.5

We're going to regard what Odo says here less as a positive recommendation than a cautionary statement. Because any activity which becomes so consuming that "nothing else matters" can be downright dangerous.

True, we need some method for looking at our lives from a wider perspective. Whether we're connecting with our "Higher Source" or simply reviewing our long-term goals, we often come to the realization that much of what we do is trivial, or wasteful, or even self-defeating. But we can also trivialize our *whole lives* if this "wider perspective" ends up making our daily activities seem pointless.

The purpose of going on what others have called "The Hero's Journey" was never to enter some higher dimension and *stay there*. It was to discover the Truths we could access only in that realm, then bring them back to *this* life. Likewise, in one of Terra's oldest traditions, the highest achievement is not merely to reach Nirvana, but to return to human existence and help others find their way, too.

Genuine encounters with divinity are marked not by a desire to leave this world. They're marked by a greater respect for it, and by a deeper commitment to living in the present as completely, joyfully and gratefully as we can.

I experience the Link by feeling the presence of resources and loving relationships all around me, above me and within me, each day of this life.

6.09

> **I have found that humans value their uniqueness—that sense that they are different from everyone else.**
>
> DATA: SECOND CHANCES: 46915.2

Data was correct, of course. But there is a dark side to his observation as well as a brighter side.

The fact is, throughout human history, an individual's sense of being "different" from others has usually been connected with the idea of being *better*. More often than not, "I'm not like you" has been a way of saying "I'm superior." Or "My country/culture/religion is superior."

Which is ironic: When most individuals or countries feel compelled to assert their own superiority, it's usually a sign that, deep in their souls, they suspect they're *not*.

But even this sentiment hides a piece of the truth. Because what we *really* suspect, deep in our souls, is that we're all "better" if we maintain and even celebrate our differences. The "brighter side" is that we *shouldn't* be cookie-cutter copies of one another. And even if we are basically the same, making ourselves "unique" in some way is essential to our own—and our society's—happiness and success.

The advantage of uniqueness is written all over the evolutionary record. Species that maintain diversity survive the inevitable natural disasters and epidemics. So do individuals. So do *we*.

> *My differences don't make me better than anyone else. They make us better... together.*

6.10

When one has a difficult job to do, personal reasons can be quite an incentive.

GUL DUKAT : INDISCRETION : Stardate Not Given

There are many things we must do in life, even if we don't feel particularly inspired to do them. Our jobs, for example, or our responsibilities to family. Or perhaps a project we volunteered for out of some perceived "duty."

Some of those tasks are difficult and ongoing. Others would be quick and easy once we started; yet even these we often put off because we "can't work up the energy."

We could quit, of course. We could decide not to finish the task, to *un*-volunteer our services. But that course is usually more damaging—to our own integrity and self-respect if not to our relationships.

So we must somehow *find* the inspiration, despite the challenges. We must invent our own "personal reasons."

And fortunately we *can*. Because in every task there is something to be gained, something meant specifically for *our* benefit, something that fuels our spiritual growth.

We have only to identify the potential lessons. Or we can add our own "selfish" goals, to use the upcoming job as an excuse to learn new skills, expand our knowledge.

Or we can simply reaffirm that The Universe is still guiding us. And our inspiration comes from trying to find out *where*.

It is natural to feel burdened by the difficulties that lie ahead. But I feel even more uplifted knowing how much wiser and more experienced I'll be afterward.

6.11

I can only speculate about my programmer's motives.

THE DOCTOR: THE CLOUD: 48546.2

Fact: We, individually or collectively, did not create the universe. Neither did we create ourselves, or the rules by which we and the universe operate. We can only discover and apply those rules—and then only by going boldly out, as voyagers, on Life's Grand Adventure.

The Reality which "programmed" these rules into the very nature of things transcends our finite lives not merely by some theoretical order of magnitude. That Reality is not simply wiser or more powerful—or any *other* superlative description we might think of. It is utterly beyond our comprehension precisely because we cannot "think" in the terms which apply to it.

The most we can do is to make analogies and inferences. Or, like the holographic doctor, to "speculate."

Not that we *should*. One of Terra's pre-Stardate cultures (sometimes compared to early Klingon) considered such speculation as *dhanna*—idle conjecture that can't be proven, and more often ends up creating division.

Better to accept that there are some things we will never know, to cultivate an appreciation of The Mystery… and then simply *to get on with our lives.*

I will spend my time on those things I can affect or learn from, and not pretend to know what is beyond my capacity to know.

6.12

Stop being so rational. Try using your imagination once in a while.
ENGINEER LA FORGE: THE NEXT PHASE: 45892.4

There's a subtle difference. If someone "stops being rational," that's not the same as "being irrational."

*Ir*rationality is the condition of *seeming* to use reason and logic, but making deductions that are unsupported or downright mistaken. Like the paranoid schizophrenic who argues that we are all Romulan agents: He purports to use logic, yet refuses to acknowledge the unfounded assumptions his argument is based on. That's irrational.

Geordi isn't asking anyone to defy the rules of logic or refuse to consider possible mistakes in their thinking. He is simply reminding us that there are ways of "knowing" which don't involve evidence and deductions and linear thought. Our imagination is one such way.

The visions that flow from our subconscious are not merely fantasies we create. They display vital information about us and our world *in non-verbal form.* Often that information contains answers we've been seeking through rational methods, but haven't had enough data to "compute." Or maybe we *have* all the data without knowing it consciously. And maybe we've been blocking it because it leads to a conclusion we're uncomfortable with.

Our imagination can break through these conscious barriers. If only we would stop *thinking* now and then.

My imagination is one more resource for accessing the truth. I will use it to complement my reason.

6.13

In spite of human evolution, there are still some traits that are endemic to gender.

COUNSELOR TROI: THE ICARUS FACTOR: 42686.4

In several ancient Terran and Klingon texts, we find prayers to various dieties which read something like, "Lord, thank you for not making me a woman."

No doubt there was a time when these prayers were taken literally. After all, being a male in these societies was a distinct advantage. As the traditions evolved, however, such prayers became less and less statements of male "superiority" than affirmations of one's sexual identity, male *or* female. The woman devotee could just as meaningfully pray, "Lord, thank you for not making me a *man*."

Within this affirmation is the realization that each of us *could* have been the opposite sex. Our gender in this life may not be an accident; but neither is it essential to our deeper, spiritual being. We wear our sex as clothing.

Still, it's clothing for life. Our outer wear makes us different from half the population. And those differences, as the Counselor says, are endemic. We can't ignore them.

What we *can* do is realize that they serve a purpose. Not only in terms of our species' survival, but in providing lessons we could not learn otherwise. And one of those lessons is to learn to wear your clothing with pride.

My sexual identity is a gift from The Universe. I will find the joys, and celebrate the unique lessons, available to me only through this *gender.*

6.14

Remembrances and regrets... They, too, are part of friendships.

CAPTAIN PICARD: PEN PALS: 42695.3

Sometimes "the ties that bind" have as much to do with the bad things that happen in relationships as the good.

So often we think of a friend as someone with whom we enjoy only positive, happy, mutually-beneficial experiences. Or at least someone with whom we can "get along." In fact, if we *haven't* been getting along for a while, we figure it's time to start looking for another friend.

What it's *really* time for is to *not give up so easily*.

Because the strongest relationships not only weather the inevitable seasons of sadness and the ordinary disagreements; they survive periods of outright conflict.

In friendships, too, we can lose perspective in the heat of the moment. We may say harsh words, act in anger, or inappropriate passion. Later, we may regret our behavior—or at least recognize that any continuing problems needn't outweigh the mutual benefits.

Remembering—even regretting—what we've done to each other can sometimes forge even closer bonds. In retrospect, we realize that these are the moments that have forced us to grow, to mellow, to redefine ourselves.

Vinegar and oil get along so well not because they dissolve into one another, but because they *don't*.

"Good" memories don't necessarily mean "happy" ones. If I grow through my relationships—even those that have hurt me—I transcend regret.

6.15

I do believe there is more within each of us than science has yet to explain.

LIEUTENANT TUVOK: INNOCENCE: Stardate Not Given

With a few notable exceptions, this affirmation is as close as most Vulcans come to traditional theology. In the language of earlier times, Tuvok would be classified as neither an "atheist" nor "theist," but as an *agnostic*—one who does not assert the existence of a Divinity, but who won't *deny* one either.

As long as science can't explain everything, "supernatural forces" will be invoked to fill in the missing pieces. And since sentient species commonly attach the same attributes to these forces as they see in themselves, (like personality and intention), another divinity is born.

However, believing in a divinity is not a requirement of "spirituality." Tuvok, like Spock, still managed a vibrant inner life. He practiced physical and mental disciplines designed to enhance his capabilities and his sense of personal fulfillment. And he occasionally drew on inner resources, the mechanism of which he might be unable to explain, but which had a verifiable effect on his reality.

Using such techniques is only logical, whether or not we can explain how they work. Sometimes, in fact, allowing the mystery to remain *is* the explanation of "how."

And that is a kind of theology in itself.

Knowing **how** *something works is less important than* **that** *it works. The deeper Science is applying the principles I discover, not analyzing them.*

6.16

We shield it with ritual and customs shrouded with antiquity. It brings a madness which rips away our veneer of civilization... the time of mating.

SPOCK: AMOK TIME: 3372.7

The Terran equivalent is more to the point: "Love makes us do crazy things." And compared to our usual preference for suppressing emotion, to remain rational and logical and "civilized," love *is* a kind of madness.

But it is also entirely natural. The instinct which drives us to form loving relationships and physical unions has played an essential role in our species. It *deserves* to be celebrated in ritual and custom. And enjoyed in real life.

Not that our particular brand of the Vulcan *Pon farr* gives us permission to let our instincts run rampant. We are still fully responsible for our actions, whether they are products of our reason or the effects of our glands.

On the other hand, by acknowledging this "madness" we can be prepared for it. Better yet, we can *transform* it. Because the rush we feel at the sight of physical beauty is really an avenue for connecting with *all* people, and all creation. The passion that rises within us comes from the same pool of energy we can use to fuel our daily work, to inspire our spiritual growth, to *feel* the Life this Universe has granted us... to feel how truly precious it is.

The "madness" of love is The Universe's open invitation to renew my connection to all people and all Life. I accept.

6.17

Without cooperation we will get nowhere.

CAPTAIN PICARD: THE CHASE: 46731.5

Even if we could handle the entire assignment on our own, we shouldn't. Even if no one else could match our ability, perform the task as efficiently, or finish it near as quickly—we should never insist on doing any job by ourselves when we *could* use others.

Because community is our ultimate destiny. We cannot claim to be responsible for "only our own souls." Our lives are too intertwined with, and dependent on, others. Even the rare individual who no longer requires spiritual guidance must still seek out other people on which to demonstrate his/her spiritual skills. Personal transformation doesn't happen in a vacuum.

But neither does it require diluting our individuality in a communal melting pot. Cooperation isn't about suppressing the strong, personal qualities we've developed to this point. It means using them to their fullest.

Sharing one's skills and unique perspectives *in community* is actually the fullest expression of our individuality. As Picard might explain it, "where" is a location that can be defined only in relationship to others. "Nowhere" is the place we end up when we think we can go it alone.

In the sacred language of ancient Bajor, the translation of the word closest in meaning to "hell" is *no place*.

My personal skills become most valuable when I use them cooperatively. My individuality is refined and redeemed through my relationships with others.

6.18

I fell in love with you without knowing how lonely it would be to live without you!
NEELIX: JETREL: 48832.1

Much as we try, we can never make "deals" with our affections. We can't calculate our love, divide it up, send some of it here, some there, or withhold it until certain conditions are met.

We can't, that is, without doing serious damage.

Our emotions have a definite logic of their own. Not that they're always "right" or appropriate. Not that we shouldn't control how we express them. It's just that we can't determine beforehand exactly how we're going to feel about something or someone. Or how strongly.

We hear people say, "I refuse to get involved with anyone because I might get hurt." Or "I'll care for somebody only if I get something out of it." Or "If you won't love *me*, I won't love *you*." This kind of emotional deal-making doesn't lead to control; it leads to *denial.* Our emotional responses and affections don't stop; we only end up suppressing them. *And* losing touch with our selves.

That's serious damage.

Admittedly, affections are risky. We *can* be hurt by love. We *can* give more than we "get"—assuming we're keeping score. But that's the cost.

And holding back our love costs far more.

Genuine love flows through *me, not* from *me.*
My joy is not in keeping it, but keeping it flowing… unconditionally.

6.19

> **...The important thing is to cherish whatever time we have together, whether it's a day or a decade.**
>
> KES: JETREL: 48832.1

Often we can change things. Often we can't. And all-too-often we spend so much time brooding over what we wish we could change that we fail to enjoy what *is*.

This tendency to let our "real lives" slip through our fingers while we brood (or fantasize) is especially evident in our relationships. Either we have such high expectations for our friends or mates that we fail to appreciate who they *are* (or else we never find any friends or mates to begin with). Or we're lucky enough to *have* friends; but we spend so much time wishing we had *more* time with them that we can't enjoy the time we *do* have together!

It's good to "want more," to have high expectations, as a first step toward a new, more enriching reality. But those expectations must not blind us to the riches we already have. Because we gain far more by *learning to cherish what is,* than by constantly striving after what's new.

Better yet, we also develop a skill which pays off in every *other* area of our lives. To "cherish" something is to experience it fully, to extract all the goodness and joy available to us right *now* if only we would open ourselves to it. And once we do, days and decades lose their importance, because living in the present is as good as it gets.

I will learn to cherish my days rather than count them, to enjoy what I have before asking for more.

6.20

I'm still recovering from all those desserts I had last night!

COUNSELOR TROI: LIAISONS: Stardate Not Given

Whatever the currency, we pay for our addictions.

It's a weakness common to most sentient species. And the possibilities cover the spectrum: From drugs to sex, from gambling binges to shopping binges, from over-indulging in desserts to over-indulging our jobs.

Chances are we'll hear warning bells before others begin to notice. Whether it's a psychological signal like guilt, or a physical one like pain, we can thank our own subconscious for trying to get a message through to us.

The worst thing we can do is ignore it. Dismissing our inner warnings can induce a self-inflicted schizophrenia which makes it even harder to regain control of our lives.

The next worst thing we can do is "rationalize" our addictions. Enlisting logic to support our unhealthy habits is like rewriting the Constitution to empower a dictator.

The *best* thing to do, it turns out, is to openly admit when we've lost control over some aspect of our lives. It is also the *hardest* part.

The consolation is, we're in good company. Because virtually everyone has suffered from an addiction at one time or another. And those who choose the road to recovery often come to know themselves—and therefore The Universe—better than most people ever will.

If I lose control I can regain it—with the help of others, and with the awesome strength within me.

6.21

Don't think about it. Just do it.

COMMANDER SISKO: EXPLORERS: Stardate Not Given

Do we think about walking, moving, breathing?

We *can* think about these things. But unless we're just starting to learn (or *re*-learn) these functions, we've probably mastered them well enough to release conscious control. In other words, we just *do* them. And we free our conscious mind for other things.

This process of "mental releasing" isn't meant only for motor control functions. It applies to *life* control functions, too. For example, we don't need to exert conscious control in order for the universe to continue delivering its blessings to us. We should be *grateful*, certainly, for the physical and spiritual riches we enjoy. But concentrating on *receiving* those riches, as if we need to remind The Universe to do its job, is more likely to short-circuit the process than insure speedy delivery.

Similar to our own bodies, the Body of Life has many natural processes we can "release" once we acknowledge that they are flowing, or that they simply exist. Like the process of personal growth. Or the process of receiving just what we need, right when we need it. Or the process of being exactly where we should be at exactly this moment, on our own one-of-a-kind spiritual journey.

Some things we do by just *letting them be done.*

The Universe is taking care of me right now. I am walking The Spiritual Path without having to think about each step. I am doing it. It is being done.

6.22

You can't **make** someone love you.

COMMANDER RIKER: TRUE Q: 46192.3

Oh, but how we *try!*

Flowers, lavish gifts, dinners—we offer these baubles as if they are personal qualities someone can fall in love with! Yet, ironically, the things we do to "win" a potential lover are often the very things we *won't* do after the victory is achieved. The flowers and gifts are merely "start-up costs" for the relationship, rarely indicative of the lifestyle we intend to live afterwards. Are people really fooled?

Constantly. But not for long.

Because drawing attention to ourselves in this way is really pointing at someone we're *not.* And the people who are likely to be attracted by this sham are the people who, in the long run, we wouldn't *want* as friends or lovers.

All we can ever offer anyone else—the only thing that's genuine anyway, that's representative of the relationship someone can expect from us—is *ourselves*... Who We Are. Or perhaps who we're trying to become, assuming we *are* trying.

The bottom line is simply this: Be real. Be yourself. Be patient. Do what's in your heart... but only if it's *you* and not merely the means to an end. The person—soul mate, lover, friend—meant to find you, *will.*

Maybe they have already.

I attract those relationships that represent my own current development. If I present the real "me" to the world, I will attract others who are also genuine.

6.23

We think of ourselves as the most powerful beings in the universe. It's unsettling to discover that we're wrong.

CAPTAIN KIRK: ERRAND OF MERCY: 3198.4

Now and then we get into the groove. We're on a roll. We feel like nothing can stop us, nothing can go wrong.

Maybe it's because, for once, we're doing all the right things. We're meditating regularly; our attitude is optimistic and confident; we interact with people on a positive, respectful, supportive basis, and they respond in kind.

Then we hit the proverbial Brick Wall.

And because it's the last thing we were expecting, we crumble. Having forgotten what adversity was like, we lose our resiliance. We not only don't bounce back, we end up falling lower than ever before.

Call it a Spiritual Reality Check. Occasionally we need an unsettling, or even *humbling*, experience to keep us grounded. For humans, in fact, it's the essence of our identity: Human, humble, *humus*—of the earth. That's what the word means.

Keeping ourselves in perspective—filled with divinity, yet subject to the vagaries of material existence—is actually a source of strength. So, too, is being openly and joyfully appreciative for what we have, what we *are*.

Including the fact that we are *not* the most powerful beings in the universe.

Omnipotence would quickly grow boring. I am grateful for challenges, and the resources to face them.

6.24

I am proud of what I am. I believe in what I do.

ENSIGN CHEKOV: THE WAY TO EDEN: 5832.3

This time we'll *start* with our daily affirmation, by repeating Chekov's words just as he spoke them. Go ahead: Say them to yourself. Again—aloud. And *loud.*

Now once more… and *mean* it this time!

Of course, some of us can't seem to "mean" it, no matter how loud we shout. After all, what if we *aren't* particularly proud of what we are? What if our lives are full of activities we *don't* believe in—at least not passionately? Most of us are still searching; we're far from perfect; we're still on that long, laborious journey to becoming the person we'd like to be. Surely we're not being asked to *lie* to ourselves, to pretend to be something we're not.

Actually, there's no need to pretend. To realize you're on that journey of "becoming" is a proud tradition in itself. To recognize that you're imperfect, that you're still searching, is to believe in the Self within you which *is* perfect, which is the culmination of your search.

Besides, we aren't being asked to be proud of the outward roles we may play in this life—whether teacher or Starfleet crewman or migrant spacedock worker. Our deepest pride comes from what we already *are,* what each of us always will be: *A child of The Universe.* To repeat Checkov's words is to be transformed by that.

So once again, say it. Aloud. Loud. And *mean* it.

I am proud of what I am. I believe in what I do.

6.25

Peace in your hearts. Fortune in your steps.

COMMANDER CHAKOTAY: INNOCENCE: Stardate Not Given

As we grow spiritually, the practice of well-wishing becomes almost second nature. And it's not simply a matter of respecting the laws of karma.

True, wishing good fortune on others brings more positive effects into one's own life, just as hoping others will meet disaster creates negative karma for oneself. But that's not *why* we wish others well.

After all, when we pray that others might be blessed with life's riches, it's not like we're giving away the store. We don't *own* the store, anyway. Wishing someone happiness and peace isn't offering them anything they don't already deserve as children of The Universe.

What it *does* do, however, is draw us into closer alignment with The Universe. *Its* plan for healing and salvation now becomes *our* plan. *Its* mechanism for enlisting consciousness in the ongoing task of creation becomes *our* mechanism.

If we are sincere—if we can wish peace and good fortune even upon our "enemies"—The Universe will trust us with the power to make those wishes come true. Our very thoughts begin to transform the world.

By then, they will have already transformed *us*.

Today I will verbalize to others the blessings that I know The Universe holds in store for us all. I will be patient as my well-wishing slowly takes effect.

6.26

The Prime Directive has many different functions, not the least of which is to protect **us.**

CAPTAIN PICARD : PEN PALS : 42695.3

We often regard the policy of non-interference as a measure to protect other planetary cultures *from us.* The policies of colonial powers, after all, were often responsible for the total destruction of their "less-advanced" neighbors. By not allowing those societies to undergo their own natural evolutions, their speeded-up development was artificial, temporary. Not to mention that unimagined treasures and traditions were lost forever.

But *we* have much to lose, too, by forcing ourselves on other planetary cultures. Jumping into a situation without knowing the full story can be dangerous. It can entangle us in ways we can't foresee. Also, we often react emotionally rather than objectively in such encounters; and by the time we know the facts, the damage is done.

Each of us would do well to learn the *personal* application of The Prime Directive, too: Not to react emotionally, based mostly on *surface evidence,* to conditions or events in other people's lives. Not to assume we are more "advanced" than others, and therefore that we must have all the answers to their problems. And most of all, not to interfere with the natural course of growth and change.

Unless *their asking us* to help is part of that course.

Not only are other people's lives sacred, where they are in their lives is sacred. As part of the universal community, I will lend help... if I am asked.

6.27

I am not concerned with pleasure. I am a warrior!

LIEUTENANT WORF: JUSTICE: 41255.6

In a sense we are *all* warriors.

We strive to defend what's right and true. We struggle for peace and wholeness, both in our communities and in our selves. And we must work daily toward these goals with a sense of discipline and duty—as if achieving them matters more than the personal inconvenience and sacrifices they inevitably require.

It's not that we can't enjoy things along the way. It's not that achieving these goals shouldn't be pleasurable. In fact, what most of us learn is that Right and Truth and Wholeness yield the *greatest* pleasures, the highest bliss, the deepest fulfillment. It's just that aiming specifically *for* the pleasure at the end of our struggle, instead of concentrating on the struggle itself, is the surest way to miss it.

Many ancient spiritual practices made a similar mistake. Spiritual novices were often told that our final goal was "getting to heaven." But the *real* goal should have been—and still *is*—doing the things that, if done mindfully and wholeheartedly, will *result* in what is meant by "heaven." In other words, heaven isn't the goal, but the by-product of *having achieved* our goals.

And therein lies a world of difference.

Today I will focus on being the best person I can be, not because of the pleasure I expect to gain, but because that's the goal I set for myself.

6.28

But will you respect me in the morning?
COMMANDER RIKER: ANGEL ONE: 41636.9

Riker's half-serious question reflects the social insecurity common in cultures where one sex dominates the other. The fact that females held most positions of power on Angel One may be a rarity, but it isn't unheard of. (For those keeping a galactic scorecard, males are the dominant sex in 83 percent of known planetary cultures. Of those cultures, 92 percent would be regarded by Federation standards as "primitive".)

But Riker's question also reflects a larger issue. The truth is, all of us occasionally do things which may seem appropriate or necessary at the time, but which we come to regret later. The dawn of another day, symbolically speaking, often brings a new light to the acts we committed in the preceeding "darkness"—when we allowed ourselves to be guided primarily by emotion or physical need; when we acted out of fear rather than strength; when we didn't know what we *do* know now.

And the question we ask of others—"Will you still respect me?"—really means "Can I still respect my*self?*"

To ask the question ahead of time is to already know the answer. Whatever you're thinking of doing, *don't.*

The problem is, what if we already *did* it?

Hint: Look up "forgiveness" in the Index.

To forgive myself today for what I did yesterday, is to respect the person I can become tomorrow.

6.29

Parted from me and never parted. Never and always touching and touched.

SPOCK: AMOK TIME: 3372.7

Relationships are a mystical thing. Admittedly, there is a physical dimension: A being together, a "touching" and being "touched"—if only in the sense that we respond physically to one anothers' presence. Our brain waves literally change; our senses reset themselves at measureably higher levels of sensitivity.

But there is a spiritual dimension, too. And it's not just that the mere *thought* of another person can generate these same physical responses. Or that, when we're separated from a loved one, we can find emotional comfort in our memories of them. Special relationships go deeper than thoughts and memories. They open up avenues of communication and connection between what The Ancients called our "souls".

In truth, our souls are already connected. A caring, committed relationship simply lowers the veil that gives us the illusion of being "separate." We become increasingly aware of an identity which transcends our bodies—even our location in time—so that, despite our parting, we are never parted. We are always "touching."

Relationships are therefore opportunities to explore our own spiritual roots... in others... in The Universe.

And the ultimate discovery is Love.

I open myself to the mystery—and the treasures —which lie hidden in my relationships to others.

6.30

The needs of the one outweighed the needs of the many.

ADMIRAL KIRK: THE SEARCH FOR SPOCK: 8310.3

It's not that Spock was wrong when he traded his own needs (i.e. *life*) for "the needs of the many." Far from it. As Spock would later say, his sacrifice was the most *logical* thing he ever did, the high point of his Starfleet career.

On the other hand, Kirk reminds us, there are times when saving a single life can justify putting many other lives at risk. Not because that one life is so much more valuable than anyone else's. Rather, it's because the attempt to save that one life affirms what is most valuable about *all* of our lives.

Our own identities grow not by feeding our individual egos, not by becoming increasingly concerned with ourselves and our private, selfish needs. Our personal growth, paradoxically, depends on exactly the opposite—on becoming increasingly *un*selfish, on seeing *others'* needs as inseparable from our own.

The now-legendary Search for Spock was therefore more than a rescue attempt focusing on one individual. It was a symbolic act, a galaxy-wide demonstration that *caring for one another is what gives our lives meaning.*

As another legend put it, "All for one, and one for all." That is the solution. And *both* parts are equally essential.

There are no impenetrable boundaries between myself and others. Their needs affect mine, and mine theirs. We thrive in community, or not at all.

SECTOR

CORRESPONDING TO THE TERRAN MONTH OF
July

7.01

> **It only knows that it needs. But like so many of us, it does not know what.**
>
> SPOCK: STAR TREK/TMP: 7412.6

Like most animal species, we are designed for action. Despite our capacity for pure thought, our nerves, bones and muscles are meant to move, to run, lift, climb—*do*.

Most of the time, however, we "do" without ever knowing why. Sensing an inner call to be *about something,* we give ourselves over to jobs and activities that soon absorb all our waking hours. But all this busy-ness is like a drug. It numbs our sense that we *don't* know what we're about, that our deepest needs are still going unmet.

Most of the time this addiction will eventually worsen to the point that it draws attention to the very message it tries to suppress. And instead of beating ourselves up for *having* the addiction, we should be resolving the question we've ignored for so long: *What do we really need?*

A five-thousand-year-old Terran tradition charts our spiritual evolution through four stages of "need": From fulfillment of bodily pleasures to personal success; from a life of service to final liberation from all need. If we stop long enough to acknowledge our unmet needs, we can feel ourselves being tugged further along this evolutionary journey. And if we honestly *define* those needs, we can take the next step: We can start "doing"... and know *why.*

Today I will make a list of my life's deepest needs. Each month I will review my list to see if those needs have changed, and to chart my progress.

7.02

Change is at the heart of what you are. But change into what—that is the question.
Q: HIDE AND Q: 41590.5

In the face of constant change, it's reassuring to know that some people can always be counted on; that no matter what happens they will remain just as they are.

And yet, ironically, if someone is too predictable, *too* "steady," chances are they've stopped taking the risks necessary to grow and further improve themselves. We must encourage others to surprise us on occasion, to *not* adhere to our own selfish insistence on stability.

What we should seek for others, as we should seek for ourselves, is not some steady-state, but *steady progress.* Which means having a goal for our lives—even if it, too, will change. Then, if we keep our focus on that goal, what seems like a constant state of turmoil becomes a series of stages in our development. Our identities no longer coalesce around specific, unchanging characteristics, but around *movement toward our life's purpose.*

Pre-modern cultures on dozens of planets institutionalized this "movement toward" by re-naming people at successive stages in their spiritual evolution. The same practice today would probably wreak havoc on Starfleet records. But we *could* reward each other with new "nicknames" to reflect our positive changes. And to better reflect the reality of who we are.

The "who" in Who I Am *may change. "I" am the constant, as is my commitment to spiritual progress.*

7.03

You know as well as I do that fear exists for only one purpose... to be conquered.

CAPTAIN JANEWAY: THE THAW: Stardate Not Given

In its own twisted way it's almost miraculous: Our fear can become so palpable, so intense, that it seems like a separate "personality" we carry around inside us. We can hear its voice as clearly as a scolding parent, feel its icy breath on our necks, its grip like a straightjacket.

These imagined sensations are actually a sign of inner strength. For what they tell us is that we can bring a kind of "reality" to something that exists only in our minds, in order to better deal with it. The personality we've invented to embody our fear is proof that we can also create a figure to represent our *courage*—in fact to represent *all* the higher qualities waiting to be born in us.

One of the most important of these qualities is self-confidence. Ironically, without our fears to actively stand in the way—like a real-life adversary—we could never achieve genuine confidence. We would therefore be less likely to take the risks necessary to learn and grow, and to overcome the *other* weaknesses that prevent us from claiming our full heritage as children of The Universe.

Conquering our fear, then, is the first step. By imagining the courageous warrior within us—already imbued with the power and confidence we seek—our fearful personality will slip quietly... finally... into oblivion.

I will acknowledge and name my fears. I bless them for challenging me. And again I release them.

7.04

...Freedom is not a gift. You have to earn it, or you don't get it.

CAPTAIN KIRK: THE RETURN OF THE ARCHONS: 3156.2

In one sense, freedom *is* a gift. The universe bestows sentient beings with an incredible range of choices and actions—any of which can beneficial... or harmful.

Of course, the universe also "knows" which is which. And it tends to reward those choices and actions which balance individual fulfillment with communal wholeness. It also tends to "punish" those individuals who buy personal gain at the expense of others. Like a healthy biological system, the universe roots out selfishness and greed by making their consequences increasingly intolerable. If an individual continues to disregard others, his range of choices is narrowed, his actions more and more restricted until there are no alternatives available. Freedom—even though once given—can be taken away.

But the flip side is that, if one's freedom is exercised wisely, the universe responds by *expanding* the possibilities. *And* the rewards. Like the steward who carefully invests his master's money rather than spending it foolishly—or worse, burying it in the ground where it will be "safe"—we earn the right to exercise still more of it.

We earn the right to become stewards of The Universe, and of the vast potential which lies within us.

I will honor my freedom by using it wisely: Acting with respect for the universe, consideration toward others, and confidence in my own unique gifts.

7.05

If there's nothing to lose—no sacrifice— then there is nothing to gain.

LIEUTENANT WORF: PEAK PERFORMANCE: 42923.4

Not that gambling has much to recommend it. But putting your hard-earned Federation credits on the line at some deep-space casino *does* symbolize one important Law of the Universe: Nothing of real value can ever be gained without risking something valuable of your own.

Often the only risk is your time—the hours spent learning a new skill, or exploring a different path. But time once spent can't be recovered. We tend to forget how truly precious it is until the universe reminds us there's only so much remaining.

Sometimes the risk is more obvious. *And* frightening. Like putting our lives on the line, or our careers, or our integrity (which all amounts to the same thing). And yet the times when we're *most* afraid can be the least risky. In fact, it may not be a "gamble" at all. Because even our losses can teach us something valuable. And when our very future is at stake, what do we have to lose?

Energy is never lost, only transformed. The positive efforts we make *will be rewarded.* Even if the reward isn't exactly what we expected. Even if it may not come according to the timetable we've established.

I will take risks for what I value most... and for the person I hope to become. No sacrifice is too great to attain that which gives my life ultimate meaning.

7.06

This isn't about rules and regulations. It's about right and wrong. I won't let you cross that line again.

COMMANDER CHAKOTAY: EQUINOX, PART II: Stardate Not Given

Rules and regulations, ideally, are forms for preserving and living out our understanding of right and wrong.

Trouble is, we can sometimes lose sight of that connection. We make "the rules" our final authority, when it's *what the rules represent* that is the real Authority.

It's easy to get them confused. We write down our rules, put them into law books, and make them difficult to change (even if for good reason). Then we build institutions around them, create Federations to enforce them, and otherwise focus on the "letter of the law" and not the spirit. Or the Spirit *behind* them.

And it's at this point that we often need someone else to remind us of the difference. For one thing, our laws are only rough approximations of the universal Order they try to emulate. Worse, because they reflect our own flaws, we may end up using them to pursue our own narrow agendas. Or even our personal vendettas.

Chakotay's warning calls us to a higher standard. We can try to justify our behavior by appealing to "regulations," or even by changing the rules to suit us. But we are truly justified only by acting in conformance with the higher Law. And that we *cannot* change.

I seek to embody the "spirit" of the law rather than the "letter." I focus on the Spirit behind the matter.

7.07

As a matter of cosmic history, it has always been easier to destroy than create.

SPOCK: THE WRATH OF KHAN: 8130.3

The endless debate over the Problem of Evil is not merely about the fact that evil exists, or that "Bad things happen to good people." It's about the fact that evil can undo so much good *so easily*.

Technological progress and affluence are achieved only at great cost to a civilization. And yet a single terrorist can destroy a building, or a starship. The kind of "nuclear exchange" once feared by Terrans—and unleashed elsewhere in the galaxy—can decimate entire planets.

The same imbalance holds on the *personal* level as well. Our own hard-earned property and possessions can be lost in a single "act of nature" or one random act of violence. And if that's the case, how can life ever be fair? Or, put another way, *What is the Universe trying to tell us?*

The answer that's so easy—and so hard to accept—is that the material world is not what's most important. That's the sideshow, the magic trick, the "reality" whose existence depends on a still *deeper* reality. And it's our understanding of *that* reality which defines our progress.

We cannot protect our affluence, our "things," with *other things*. We must undergird our monuments and our technology with a *spiritual* foundation. We must improve our minds, our souls, *together*. Only that will protect us.

Material possessions are secondary. My true foundation lies within. I will help others find it there, too.

7.08

How do we know about any of us?

DR. McCOY: STAR TREK/TMP: 7412.6

The short answer to the good doctor's question is: We *don't*. If only because we rarely allow it.

We routinely keep secrets from one another, perhaps hoping to use what we know for our own private gain. We hide behind our own personal cloaking devices, thinking that if others saw us as we really are, they could never love us. Deception is the name of the game.

We even manage to deceive our*selves*: Pretending we're in control when we're not; learning to suppress our emotions until we no longer recognize them; assuming we've conquered certain passions or overcome temptation when we simply haven't been tested yet.

It's no wonder our own behavior sometimes comes as a shock. We hardly know who *we* are, much less others.

Not that we can't know. Ideally, in an atmosphere of openness and acceptance, we could all present an accurate self-portrait of ourselves to the world—both our flaws and our strengths—knowing that no one is perfect.

Just because most people *don't* is no excuse for *us* not to. In fact, our own fearless self-revelation can be a catalyst for communal change, the example that gives others permission to be themselves, too.

Try setting the trend. And let go of the results.

I must know myself before I can begin to know others. I will openly display who I am, thereby encouraging others to do the same.

7.09

No power in the universe can hope to stop the force of evolution.

COMMANDER RIKER: ANGEL ONE: 41636.9

Historians can point to a phase on almost every planet when the concept of evolution was vilified, or even outlawed. Some cultures still regard it as incompatible with the existence of a higher, purposeful Power.

Which only goes to show how easily we can trap ourselves in the finite boxes we build around The Infinite. Because, rightly understood, evolution is one of the primary *manifestations* of that higher, purposeful Power. To use the language of many sacred traditions, evolution is "redemption" acting visibly in nature, and through time. It is what "grace" *looks like* in purely physical terms.

But it also has a spiritual, "invisible" aspect, too. Because it's an activity which goes on inside us, quietly, inconspicuously, as we learn and grow. It is the force that transforms us from the raw material of self-centered *need* into the refined souls whose greatest joy is to *give*.

To assert that nothing can stop this force is to say, first of all, that we *will* be "redeemed." Spiritual transformation is our destiny, both as individuals and as communities.

Secondly, it says that The Universe is in that ultimate Captain's Chair. The voyage may be no less bumpy, but being part of the crew makes it one fabulous ride.

Whether I accept my destiny or fight it will not alter the outcome. But it will *affect my happiness and satisfaction in this life. The choice is mine.*

7.10

There is no correct resolution. It's a test of character.
ADMIRAL KIRK:THE WRATH OF KHAN:8130.3

The most common Terran view—or at least *western* Terran view—used to be that life's major lessons were concerned with learning to do the "right thing," or giving the "right answer." *Getting it right* became an obsession, as if "it" were something outside of ourselves, an object we chisel away at like some marble statue until it finally duplicates someone else's pre-conceived ideal.

Actually we *are* sculptors of a sort. But the statue we're working on at the moment is only an excuse to continue sculpting our*selves,* to refine our techniques or try new ones; to shape the person we wish to become.

The statues we produce—our achievements—are less important than what we learn in the process. In fact, if we try to carry those statues/achievements around with us as we go through life, we end up being weighed down by them, perhaps even stuck in our tracks. Or in the past.

We need to jettison the idea that "right" is something external. Right is not a resolution in the sense of an outcome or an end-product. It's our resolution, our *resolve,* to develop our character. It's where "correct" is not what we try to *be,* but something we *do* to ourselves.

I resolve to bring my character more and more into alignment with the will of The Universe. I look forward to the tests that help me track my progress.

7.11

If you do not learn from your mistakes, you will be doomed to repeat them.

LIEUTENANT TUVOK: LEARNING CURVE: 48846.5

The very same message appears in a thousand forms throughout the galaxy, and dozens on any single planet.

For example: "History repeats itself for those who fail to learn its lessons." Or: "Even the victor must fight again if he learns not the cause of the war." Or, on a more mundane level: "Unless the divorce leads to self-knowledge, the suitor will marry the same spouse again."

Terra is only one of many planets on which entire religions have grown up around the idea that life's purpose is about learning from our mistakes—and that we *will* learn, even if it takes a thousand lifetimes to do it!

On the other hand, being "doomed" to repeat our mistakes is perhaps too harsh a sentence. We could just as easily look at it in a hopeful light: That the Universe is giving us *another chance* to learn a life-changing lesson; and we wouldn't want to "graduate" until we *did*.

What's even more hopeful is that The Universe provides new opportunities for learning our lessons every day. All we must do is *seize* them, to try something new this time, and *keep trying* until we discover what works.

In fact, it's the learning of this "experimental" attitude that is one of life's most important lessons!

Mistakes represent failed experiments. I will take advantage of any new opportunities The Universe gives me to try again, and finally learn its lessons.

7.12

Lies must be challenged.
CAPTAIN PICARD: REDEMPTION, PART I: 44995.3

We're not talking about what our ancestors called "white lies," those (mostly) harmless distortions of truth designed to preserve social harmony and good will by sacrificing a little honesty. Like: "Oh, Uncle Quark, I was *hoping* you'd get me another bolo tie for my birthday!"

It's the distortions of truth that support prejudice and injustice that can't be tolerated. Or the kind of misinformation that justifies one group's abuse of another: The lies about racial or genetic inferiority; the claims of moral pre-eminence, or divine mandates, or "galactic destiny."

Because the damage is not limited only to those who *suffer* injustice. The people who know the truth and allow the lies to stand are damaged as well. For one thing, their silence makes them partly responsible for the injustices which are supported by the lies. Worse, ignoring lies perpetrated by others makes us increasingly immune to the falsehoods in our *own* lives. Like the notion that we can continue to indulge in our same bad habits without any further harm. Or that our spiritual welfare (or lack of it) doesn't really affect anybody else. Or that we can put off those self-improvements we'd like to make (but haven't yet) because, after all, there's still plenty of time left.

If those lies go unchallenged, it is *we* who suffer.

I will challenge falsehood wherever I encounter it, both for the sake of those who may be hurt, and to preserve my own integrity.

7.13

> **I'm an illogical woman who's beginning to feel too much a part of that communications console.**
>
> LIEUTENANT UHURA: MAN TRAP: 1531.1

It's a logical necessity to admit, sometimes, that we are *not logical*. We are emotional beings, with emotional needs that run deeper than the roles we play and the jobs we have. We need to laugh, to cry; to feel sympathy and joy and meaning. We need to love, to *be* loved.

But there are times when we become so wrapped up in our jobs that we forget these needs. We focus so much on the practical functions we perform as members of a community that we lose touch with our own individuality.

Uhura's words remind us that we mustn't lose sight of the physical self—and physical needs—that support all our various roles and functions. Because even as we link with others, even as we redefine and expand our concept of self, even as we identify more and more with the transcendent Oneness beyond all finite selves—we are still linked to a *specific person,* born into a *specific form,* living at a *specific time* in galactic history.

That person will not be ignored for long, since it alone can act as our "center." It is the strong thread which binds together our experiences, our lessons, our learning.

It is the Voyager that will one day carry us home.

I celebrate the unique personhood of "me." I will not ignore the physical, emotional needs which support my ongoing spiritual journeys.

7.14

I'm just trying to keep to the essentials.
CONSTABLE ODO : CROSSFIRE : Stardate Not Given

Let's take a few moments to consider what occupies our time and energy. If we're honest, most of us will admit that we spend the majority of our time on activities that have little to do with our life's goals, or with our efforts toward personal/spiritual transformation.

True, we have a right to occasional "diversions." Play is as important as work. But the best kind of "play" is *more* than a diversion. Whether we're conscious of it or not, our periods of relaxation and "fun" are really designed to give us a better perspective on what we're doing with the *rest* of our lives. Their function is to remind us what's important, what the essentials are.

And yet, with travel brochures in hand and itineraries full of "things to do," that function is defeated. How many of us return from vacation with a new sense of vocation?

Instead we must consciously set aside time for the task of simplifying, of reflecting on what truly *matters*. A weekly "Sabbath" is good for this. Regular meditation can help enormously. We must learn to focus.

And the point is not to logically prioritize our activities, not to make lists, not to "decide." What's essential in our life *becomes clear* as we quiet ourselves, as we listen to our inner longings. As we let the Spirit guide us.

Today I will search my heart for what matters. I will concentrate on those things so that everything I do contributes in some way to their fulfillment.

7.15

The need to resort to violence and force has long since passed.

CAPTAIN KIRK: LET THAT BE YOUR LAST BATTLEFIELD: 5730.2

Sometimes our words are more an expression of hope than fact. And the fact that Federation Starships are still outfitted with shields, phasers and photon torpedoes is a pretty good sign that the need for force *hasn't* passed.

What the Captain is really saying is that people *can* get along if they make the effort. There are alternatives to force, even when those involved seem utterly opposed.

The process to peaceful solutions has been worked out through trial and error on dozens of planets. That process is known and tested. It works. Two or more "sides" who agree to abide by this process *will* come to an accommodation, and often form an alliance that benefits them in ways they could not have dreamed.

But the cost is nothing less than a change in identity. Because we can no longer think of ourselves merely as members of one isolated community, one race, one planetary society. We must learn to identify more fully with our *spiritual* selves, with that Universal Self where we are already connected, already in communication—where an alliance has already been inked.

It's not a matter of compromising with our enemies. It's a matter of making peace with who we already *are*.

My deeper self is connected to everything, even to those with whom I seem in conflict. I will surrender to that Self, and experience genuine peace.

7.16

Creativity is necessary for the health of the body.

SPOCK: THE RETURN OF THE ARCHONS: 3156.2

The Force which fashions our individual lives doesn't simply give birth to us and then leave us to fend for ourselves. It sustains us moment by moment. It is a continuous Presence which underlies all existence.

Science confirms that the universe is more of a process than a physical "entity." And the primary characteristic of that process is *creation*. From atoms to galactic superclusters, the universe re-creates itself continually—maintaining, renewing, transforming. And what The Ancients called our "spark of divinity" is none other than the creative process moving in and *through* us.

Ironically, we can also "create" structures which block that same creative flow. The pipeline can constrict like clogged arteries, and the symptoms are just as physical. When we suppress our natural urges for meaningful expression we can literally lose our vision and our voice. If we're afraid to try new things, to think new thoughts, to renew our*selves,* our very bodies grow stiff and brittle.

Artists are those who have learned not so much to *control* the creative process as to let *it* control *them*. And in the flow of that energy lies healing.

I open myself to the creative process which is my heritage as a creature of this universe. I will find ways to express what is within me, and be healed.

7.17

I've never been afraid of re-evaluating my convictions.

CAPTAIN PICARD: A MATTER OF TIME: 45349.1

We all have convictions. If we can't articulate them in words, we *do* express them in actions. It's not what we *say;* it's our *behavior* that reveals our beliefs.

The difference between the two can be embarrassing, if not deeply distressing. And the point of this difference is not that we are therefore failures or "sinners." It's that *we're still growing.* We are "works in progress."

To be willing to re-evaluate our convictions is to affirm that we are always working on what we believe. What's ironic is that the people who are *un*willing to question their beliefs are usually those whose convictions are weakest. These are the same people who seek to impose their beliefs on others by force or threats because if they can't convince other people *some*how, they are reminded of their own darkest fear: That they might be wrong.

It takes a strong sense of self to admit we might be wrong. It takes a strong commitment to Truth to welcome new opportunities to test our beliefs. It takes great wisdom to know when our failure is the result of a mistaken conviction, or our own inability to carry out what we say we believe. Because in the end, the real test isn't about convictions anyway. It's about our *character*.

Applying my convictions allows me to re-evaluate them. I am open to what these opportunities teach me about my beliefs, and about my character.

7.18

May the Prophets walk with us.

MAJOR KIRA : FASCINATION : Stardate Not Given

One needn't be religious to profit from the Prophets. Stories about scriptural heroes and ancestors who claimed to speak for various divinities can be instructive for us all. Studies of sacred histories throughout the galaxy reveal themes and truths shared by virtually every tradition. In these common elements is a larger, more universal story about the emergence of life, the advent of consciousness and the responsibilities that come with it.

Viewed from this wider perspective, the words and writings of every tradition's Prophets begin to transcend the boundaries of time and place. If we can see past the specifics, we find a rich repository of information about what makes us *all* tick—whether Bajoran or Klingon, Human or Ferengi. We find examples of what causes our problems, what leads to solutions, how to respond in a variety of situations, and how *not* to. In short, we learn more about our*selves*—at our worst, and our best.

To listen to the words of these Prophets, to reflect on their meaning—whether or not we fully agree—is to converse with them, like we might during a long walk. After we go our separate ways, we can recall that conversation. And as often as it illumines our path, they "walk with us." We couldn't ask for better company.

The story The Universe tells is written in every culture and age. I can find and affirm the eternal Truths by searching the words of all the Prophets.

7.19

One of these days I'm going to surprise you... But not today.
CAPTAIN JANEWAY: PHAGE: 48532.4

It's a healthy attitude: To know that we're not straightjacketed by our past; that we're free to do something radically new and unexpected now and then; that we can always break out of our shells, climb out of our ruts, throw off our previous limitations. Putting people "on notice" is a way of preparing our*selves* for these changes as much as others. It helps keep our options open, and options are essential for growth.

On the other hand, it's also essential to take a vacation from unrelenting growth. We need to periodically consolidate what we know, to live out the lessons we've just learned, to practice being Who We Are Now.

The Universe is written everywhere with the message that there's a time and season for everything. Rest and stability are no less a part of the natural order than chaos and uncertainty. To say "Not today" is to accept and enjoy these seasons of rest, while acknowledging the times of instability and change that lie ahead. Taking full advantage of rest, in fact, is what *prepares* us for change.

Chances are we'll know when the next season is arriving. And we'll be all the more ready to embrace it.

I deserve the periods of contentment and peace in my life. I can be comfortable with who I am today, and still be ready for change tomorrow.

7.20

You could learn something from Mr. Spock, and stop thinking with your glands.

CAPTAIN KIRK: MAN TRAP: 1513.1

The idea is not to turn a deaf ear to the call of the wild, to stop enjoying the way our passions can sometimes transport us to a simpler place where life was *felt*, not analyzed. Having "glands"—sexual or otherwise—is a gift. The point is to not let them rule our lives.

In a broader sense, the point is to not let our *bodies* rule our lives. We are sentient beings, "knowing" beings. And by knowing what purpose our glands and our bodies serve, we can give them their due without losing the self-control that makes us *us*.

The most ancient Terran discipline for giving our bodies "their due" is called *yoga*. From a Sanskrit word meaning "union," yoga is the practice of unifying our minds and bodies/glands into a single entity where every individual component works in harmony with the others. Practiced under a variety of other names across the galaxy, the discipline relies heavily on physical movement and balance, while focusing on one's "inner senses."

Ironically, we must become more conscious of our bodies and glands before we can stop "thinking" with them. We must also forgive ourselves for the times we allowed them to dictate our responses—and we ended up paying for it. Now, at least, we know better.

I will learn a discipline which helps me to unify body, mind and spirit—and I will practice it daily.

7.21

I've never let my past lives interfere with my job.

LT. COMMANDER DAX: REJOINED: 49195.5

As a Trill, Dax might be regarded as a living, breathing example of the ancient concept of reincarnation. In Dax's case, as with reincarnation, there is a more fundamental Self which resides in the body, yet transcends it. The *real* Dax isn't the beautiful humanoid we see, but the deeper entity which also "incarnates" in many *other* successive lives—sometimes as a female, sometimes as a male.

But unlike those of us who must be content merely to *believe* (or *not* believe) in reincarnation, Trills have first-hand experience. Dax can recall her previous lifetimes in great detail—a fact which can create serious problems.

Ironically, *non*-Trills face some of the very same problems. Because even if we don't accept the idea that we've lived before, we still, in a sense, have "past lives" to deal with. The people we are *now* are not the people we were ten years ago. Or even five. We've learned much; we've cast off bad habits and limiting beliefs (or we're *trying* to). And the change in us often feels like a whole new life.

As we continue to grow, the challenge is to remember the lessons of our past lives, while not allowing that to interfere with the better person we've become. *Or* distract us from creating an even better life in the future.

My previous life is a priceless repository of first-hand experience. I draw insight and perspective from that life even as I grow well beyond it.

7.22

Sometimes... you just have to bow to the absurd.

CAPTAIN PICARD: UP THE LONG LADDER: 42823.2

Absurdity, like beauty, is in the eye of the beholder. What seems absurd to one person may seem perfectly logical to another. Or at least not that *il*-logical.

Often it takes someone else's explanation or viewpoint to help us make sense of what happens in our lives. That's why our network, our community, is so important. Alone, we may not have the knowledge or experience to integrate new information. Educators have long recognized that optimal learning proceeds in a series of steps that build upon one another. Out of sequence, events and new experiences can seem haphazard, random... *absurd.*

Unless someone fills in the missing steps for us.

But sometimes even *that* isn't enough. Either no one can make us understand—that is, we just don't "get it"; or *no one* understands. Which is another way of saying that there are limits to what we know. Or *can* know.

To "bow to the absurd" is not merely to acknowledge those limits, but to respect them. Because what we don't know *can* hurt us. "Absurd" is therefore not a label for writing something off, but for reminding ourselves to proceed with caution, to find out more if we can, and to learn to live with our own ignorance in the meantime.

Things often don't make sense. But help is always available, both from others and my Inner Source —if only to support me while I seek answers.

7.23

Maybe necessity really **is** the mother of invention. You never look for something until you need it.

ENGINEER LA FORGE: THE MASTERPIECE SOCIETY: 45470.1

Nowhere is this more true than in spiritual matters. Many of us never go looking for a religious community or spiritual discipline because we prefer to think of ourselves as fully independent, fully self-reliant. Some will hang on to this belief in the face of all evidence to the contrary.

For others, the truth finally breaks through in the form of hard, scientific data about the "soft" boundaries which only *seem* to separate us—or in the realization that our solitary, one-point-in-space/time perspective on life is so incredibly limiting.

Some form of this realization, whether conscious or subconscious, is said to be why religion was invented. Ironically, because it *was* invented is why many reject it.

But an invention—any invention—works insofar as it takes advantage of laws and realities that are *not* someone's invention. Spiritual disciplines, and the traditions which uphold them, can work for us to the extent that they understand these pre-existing laws and realities correctly, and provide a mechanism whereby we can use them to live fuller, more satisfying lives.

How many other inventions do that?

More than the right job or mate or possessions, I need the right perspective. Today I will look for new resources to help me reaffirm and re-invent my life.

7.24

If you lie all the time, no one is going to believe you... even when you're telling the truth.

DR. BASHIR : IMPROBABLE CAUSE : Stardate Not Given

The Terran fable of the shepherd who cried "Wolf!" is retold in dozens of similar folktales all across the galaxy. Like the story of the Klingon sentry who raises so many false alarms that his fellow warriors no longer respond when the real attack comes. Or the account of the Ferengi businessman who forgets to tell just enough of the truth to fool off-worlders into believing his sales pitch.

The fact is, we base our acceptance of what's true on the reliability of the source. We tend to trust our own perceptions first—what we can "see with our own eyes." We rely on other people's testimony only insofar as we respect their track record or proven "authority."

But the real crisis is not about believing what *other* people say. It's whether we can believe in who *we* are. And too often it's our own lies that shatter our belief: Our inability to admit when we're wrong; our substitution of a private fantasy world for "real life"; our unwillingness to take an unflinching, objective look at our own flaws and commit ourselves to the hard work of personal growth.

Before we can believe anything, we must reject our own lies. To know the truth, we must first be able to trust what we tell our*selves*.

The real challenge is to be true to myself. I will be honest in evaluating my own thoughts and actions.

7.25

I have noted that the healthy release of emotion is frequently very unhealthy for those closest to you.

SPOCK: PLATO'S STEPCHILDREN: 5784.2

Just as an infant's cries will grow louder until his caregiver responds to his needs, our own emotions can grow "louder" until we pay them the attention they deserve.

Ignoring those messages will result in either of two outcomes: Our emotions finally explode and disrupt our lives so that we *must* deal with them. Or, like the infant who finally gives up and learns *not* to cry—*ever*—our emotions are driven deep inside us where their energy is twisted into negative thoughts and physical ailments.

Our health, then, depends on keeping our emotional energy where we can "see" it, where we can interpret and respond to the message it is sending us. We do this by accepting it and releasing it, thereby letting it speak to us.

But not where others might misunderstand it.

An emotional outburst can mean something entirely different to someone else. Those closest to us, especially, can react to our displays of anger and sorrow and self-reproach as if *they* are somehow responsible. What's healthy for us ends up hurting *them,* and our relationships.

We must consider the message our emotions convey to others as carefully as the message they hold for us.

I respect my own emotions. And I will respect others by releasing my full emotions only in private, or around those I know won't misinterpret them.

7.26

The best defense is a strong offense. And I intend to start offending right now!

CAPTAIN KIRK: THE EMPATH: 5121.5

The Captain isn't implying that we should stop being polite or respectful. Nor is he suggesting we demonstrate how strong we are by picking fights with everyone.

He's talking about *our attitude toward life.* He's pointing out that many of us have an unfortunate tendency to build protective walls around what we've managed to gain—materially *and* spiritually; that we often become more concerned about keeping what we have than risking it on new gains; that our lives thereby become more like a defensive position than an expeditionary force.

The problem is, we can never live victoriously while in this "protective" mode. Nor can we rise to our potential if we simply *react* to whatever life sends our way. Instead, we must go out *looking* for experience, boldly exploring new territory, taking the risks required for growth.

We must also be willing to raise a few eyebrows in pursuit of our dreams and our life's mission. Perhaps other people *will* be offended after all. But not because we've run roughshod over them. It's because our courageous attitude forces them to wonder what they're missing.

By living fully, we can show them. Right now.

It's okay for me to be forthright in the pursuit of my spiritual goals. As I live exuberantly, even "offensively," I give others permission to do the same.

7.27

Humor... I love it!

DATA: GENERATIONS: 48632.4

Most attempts to define humor eventually come down to this: Either you get it... or you *don't*.

Not everyone is blessed with a sense of humor. Some species, Vulcans included, claim to be utterly unaffected.

Which is simply to say that emotions are as essential to humor as intelligence is. And while even Vulcans can "appreciate" irony and satire, most of us also have a visceral response when we "get it." The usual result is that convulsive expulsion of breath known as "laughter."

For emotional beings, how *much* we laugh is a remarkably accurate indicator of our current mental and emotional health. Because the circuits that process our perceptions of reality, that transmit the data required for thought and action, are the same circuits that allow us to feel humor. And if we *don't* laugh—or we laugh at *every*thing—chances are there's trouble in the system.

Fortunately, the same method used to diagnose our "system" can also be used to treat it. Laughing has a certifiable cleansing affect, literally relaxing muscle tension, releasing repressed energy, restoring hormonal balance.

So find something to laugh at. *Daily.* It may take practice. When you find yourself not only laughing regularly, but at your*self,* the system is probably working just fine.

I will make my daily dose of humor as important as meditating. I will create opportunities to laugh, even artificial ones, until my joy flows naturally.

7.28

There is something to be learned when you're not in control of every situation.
COUNSELOR TROI : THE LOSS : 44356.9

Faith is as much about actions as attitude. But attitude is crucial; and one of the most crucial attitudes is *trust*.

We can think of "trust" as the assurance we feel that someone or something will act *as expected*. Trust means "allowing" another person (or object) to carry out his/her (or *its*) function without our having to be involved. Trust is about letting go, about *not being in control*.

In a sense, we're not in control whenever we board a shuttlecraft or step into the transporter bay. Our lives are literally at risk, but we've learned to trust the pilot and the technology to take us where we want to go. Giving up control is the price we pay. It's a choice we make.

Unfortunately we can't always choose. Sometimes control is taken away from us, or maybe we never had it in the first place. And our lives may be no less at risk.

We can look at these situations as opportunities for learning: That we (and the world) will still survive, for example. Or that *following* has its own rewards, as does leading. Or that other people have wonderful talents if only we'll step back and give them a chance to prove it.

We may even learn that there is another Pilot in whom we can trust, and a Technology that will take us where we want to go. Giving up control is a small price to pay.

I am in the care of a higher power. I will release my need to control, and trust in The Universe.

7.29

> **I can give you a long and boring analysis. Suffice it to say... I don't know what's going on!**
>
> CAPTAIN JANEWAY: PARALLAX: 48439.7

Most of us are quite adept at making excuses. We can rationalize our lack of understanding and invent logical justifications for how little we know. We can even devise brilliant explanations that make our continuing ignorance *seem* like knowledge—what past generations referred to as "smokescreens" or "snowjobs."

But a much better approach to not knowing something is simply *to admit it.* Because when we put our energies into making excuses, there's little left for finding answers. When we try to justify why we don't know or haven't learned, we create a psychological predisposition for *not knowing* and *not learning*.

However, by fearlessly acknowledging that "we don't know," we open the door to solutions. Defending our ego is no longer an issue. Others come to our aid because it's not a matter of "me" or "you" finding the answer, but *us*.

Captain Janeway wisely admitted whenever she had no answers. And she was no less a leader for it. In fact, leadership is rarely about *having* answers. It's about *the search for answers*. It's about inspiring others to join us on that search.

It's about being on the search... together.

> *I am always ready to admit when I don't know. Not knowing is the prelude to my growth.*

7.30

> **Running may help for a little while, but sooner or later the pain catches up with you. And the only way to get rid of it is to stand your ground and face it.**
>
> CAPTAIN SISKO: THE WAY OF THE WARRIOR, PART II: 49011.4

The wisdom of Sisko's statement seems compelling enough. Even *more* so because he himself lived it.

And perhaps now is the time to point out that *all* the sayings and comments in this *Manual* have the ring of truth for the same reason. They aren't merely theories, or some office-bound counselor's idea of how things *ought* to be. Nor are they "revelations" from some ancient text. They are the fruits of experience. They have been *lived*.

Which is how Benjamin Sisko learned *this* lesson. He discovered first-hand that we can no more run away from the events that hurt us than a criminal can "run from the scene of the crime." Because the scene that matters most is the one *within us*. Everything we do is recorded in our minds and in our hearts. Everything in our past *remains present*—as emotions and attitudes... as Who We Are.

Fortunately, when we *stop* running, that too is recorded. Taking a stand, facing the pain, finally *dealing* with the events in our lives also becomes Who We Are.

And we are stronger for it. Not in theory. Not just because that's how it ought to be. But because we *lived* it.

No matter how painful the events in my life, I can live through them. The person I will become once I've faced my past is worth my present struggle.

7.31

The trial never ends.

Q: ALL GOOD THINGS…:47988.1

In some cultures, this is the very definition of "hell": To always be on trial; to continually be in the position of having to prove oneself. Or *im*prove oneself.

Can't we ever take a break from the struggle? Can't we just *be* once in a while, without any expectations?

Yes. As a matter of fact, *that's part of the trial.*

Because knowing when to stop is just as important as knowing when to keep going. Taking breaks to "process" our learning, to reward ourselves for our efforts, to simply relax, is as crucial as our day-to-day struggles.

Actually, as we go deeper into our Inner Voyage, the greatest temptation is to *not* take these necessary breaks. Ancient religions, which were often closer to the natural cycles of struggle and rest, instituted frequent feasts and celebrations for exactly that reason. One of Betazed's early spiritual disciplines, going well beyond Terra's "sabbath," insisted its members take four days of rest for every five days of work or study. (Or face four days of confinement!)

The point is, what we are on trial *for* is our current level of spiritual development. That trial is as continuous and automatic as breathing. But without time to *consolidate*, to simply enjoy *who we are now*, we can easily be found guilty of losing what we thought we'd gained.

I will remember to sentence myself to rest and re-creation. My own testimony will help me judge when it's time to continue my spiritual work.

SECTOR

CORRESPONDING TO THE TERRAN MONTH OF
August

8.01

Worlds may change, galaxies disintegrate; but a woman always remains a woman.

CAPTAIN KIRK: THE CONSCIENCE OF THE KING: 2817.6

It's reassuring to know that some things don't change. The speed of light in a vacuum. Acceleration of mass due to gravity. The Trans-Warp Constant.

And our own *personal* constants. Like the soothing effect of a mountain stream. Or the reassuring resonance in the laughter of children at play. Or the fascination of soft backlight on a woman's hair.

Whether these are scientific "laws" or genetically-programmed response mechanisms isn't what matters. Like Captain Kirk's unflagging appreciation for women, they are simply the things we can count on.

We need a core of such constants to keep us grounded. Part of the strategy for transforming our lives, in fact, is to claim the territory we've come to know—what works for us, what doesn't; what generates certain feelings, and what doesn't. And then to venture out from these "strongholds," adding *new* constants, continually claiming new and higher ground, defining the things we can count on.

And if the galaxies around us start to disintegrate, we can always find refuge there. At least until the dust settles and we go boldly out again.

Over the next week, I will make a list of all the things I know well enough to call my "constants." Each month I will review my list, and add to it.

8.02

I don't pretend to tell you how to find happiness and love when every day is just a struggle to survive. But I do insist that you do survive.

EDITH KEELER : THE CITY ON THE EDGE OF FOREVER : 3134.0

This is bliss: To understand that human life is a series of starts and stops, gains and losses, painful struggle and sweet grace; and to pronounce all of it "good."

But sometimes in the depths of struggle and loss we can lose our perspective. We forget The Big Picture. We are no longer able to envision the smooth sailing beyond the present storm. Life seems hopeless.

Our Inner Voyage is of little value if it cannot help us overcome these inevitable periods of hopelessness. And the Voyage teaches us that, at such times, forgetting The Big Picture is actually the beginning of recovery. Because we are forced to remember that we must still live day by day. To get "from here to there" requires living fully in the moment, concentrating on the details, taking one step at a time. *And* rediscovering that the source of genuine fulfillment is not some outward goal but *within ourselves.*

Inner bliss will come. Whatever our problems, "This too shall pass." What lies beyond *is* worth living for.

Even if, in the meantime, the best we can do is survive.

This is my pledge: I will survive, and I will thrive. The days ahead will make all my struggles worthwhile. I hope, therefore I am.

8.03

Every culture has its demons. They embody the darkest emotions of its peoples. Giving them physical form... is a way of exploring those feelings.

COMMANDER CHAKOTAY: HEROES AND DEMONS: 48693.2

Satan, Shaitan and Shiva; demons and devils and Lucifer himself... The question is not whether these beings are "objectively real," but how we can use them to deal with the negative forces they represent.

We think in terms of opposites: Light and dark; good and bad; success and failure; matter and anti-matter. Dualism gives us a "handle" on reality. We can imagine forces working toward one extreme or the other. And it explains a lot to say we are "caught in the middle."

But our minds are not content with mere "forces." We need to put *faces* on them. We ascribe personality even where it doesn't exist—which is our way of acknowledging that we are *affected personally* by these forces. We have a *personal stake*. We must make a *personal choice*.

Our demons are no less real for being artificial embodiments of the forces we finally choose to oppose. And if we visualize our bad habits, attitude problems and character flaws as "evil entities" with a life of their own—which in a sense they *are*—we enable ourselves to become the very real "heroes" who learn to overcome them.

Religions do it. So do our dreams. Take a lesson.

I must "face" my flaws before I can overcome them. I will name my sins, and then I will be forgiven.

8.04

Whatever my personal feelings, I simply cannot interfere.

CAPTAIN PICARD: HALF A LIFE: 44805.3

We are all connected at the deepest levels, consciously and *sub*consciously; that much is now certain. So it's no wonder we find it difficult *not* to become involved in other people's lives. We are *already* involved.

But it's especially tempting to intervene when our experience allows us to see an approaching danger others *don't* see. How can we just stand by and *watch?*

The Prime Directive—this mandate of non-interference—is nothing if not gut-wrenching. It is often far more painful to allow another person to suffer than to undergo the suffering ourselves. But the fact is, there are well-defined stages of growth in the evolution of sentient life. Some of these stages are chaotic, painful, risky. These are potential "breakthrough stages" when a whole people stand at the threshold of self-discovery and redemption.

There is no substitute for living through such experiences. Outside interference can set a species back generations. Individuals can lose years of growth.

And sometimes the individual is *us*. We can ask for help, yes. We can expect guidance. But if we are to have our own breakthroughs, we must earn them. We must *learn* them. And we must give others the same chance.

I will gladly help when asked. But I must not do for others what they must do for themselves. And I pray for the wisdom to know the difference.

8.05

Look at us! We're each fighting with ourselves!

LIEUTENANT TORRES: FACES: 48784.2

Most of us never get the chance to witness, much less experience, what B'Elanna Torres learned when her core personality was ripped into its two competing components. In her case, the two were Klingon and Human. But they could just as easily have been male and female, or animal self and spiritual self. The lessons are the same.

And the key words are, *"Look at us!"*

Because when our primary personality components fall out of harmony with one another, when they *dis*integrate, they are not so much trying to destroy each other as simply *calling attention to themselves*.

The first thing we must do, therefore, is stand back and *look*. Not join the conflict, but seek perspective. The mode of communication may be primitive, yes; but what is all that fighting trying to tell us? What primal needs are going unmet in our "Klingon side"? In our human half?

The fact is, conflicts within us are appeals to remember and honor the positive qualities that each of our personality components brings to the larger unity of our self. They are calls to restore balance, not to "take sides."

And as it is with us personally, so it is with our communities. So it is with our world.

My conflicts—external and internal—are signs that I need to work on myself. I accept the challenge.

8.06

A no-win situation is a possibility every commander could face.

ADMIRAL KIRK: THE WRATH OF KHAN: 8310.3

One of life's saving graces is that we sometimes learn more from our failures and defeats than our successes and victories. Pain and loss are simply the price we all pay for some of life's most important lessons.

What hurts even more than losing—because there seems to be no lesson to draw from it—is the situation in which *nobody* wins. And how often things turn out this way! Unresolved. Unfinished. Check, but no check*mate*.

But maybe there's a lesson in these frequent "stalemates." Maybe some struggles aren't about winning, but *enduring*—despite no permanent victory. After all, we can't give in to selfishness and greed just because the temptations never stop coming.

Or perhaps the lesson is that our idea of struggle is mistaken to begin with. Perhaps what we see as "conflict" is really no conflict at all. Because more often than not, the people we think we're competing with are those with whom we most need to *join forces* in a common quest.

No-win situations call us to transcend the apparent conflict to the point where we redefine what we're really fighting against, where "winning" is no longer the goal. And that's the point, paradoxically, where *everyone* wins.

The stalemates in my life tell me that I have not yet learned something vital to my growth. I will open myself to the messages they contain.

8.07

In critical moments men sometimes see exactly what they wish to see.

SPOCK: THE THOLIAN WEB: 5693.2

Commitment is good. The ability to focus on a task, to pursue one's objective with single-minded intensity, is a prerequisite for personal achievement.

But sometimes we can want something so much, so desperately, that it's not good for us. Because we can lose sight of our other priorities. We can lose our perspective. Our objective ends up ensnaring us just as surely as the Tholian Web.

And it's not just that we no longer see what's happening around us. It's that we start seeing things that *aren't even there*. Our expectations not only filter out evidence contrary to our wishes, they interpret all evidence only to support them. Our leaps of illogic can be mind-boggling.

Schizophrenia, though rare, is the most extreme manifestation of this condition. But none of us is immune, because even "normal" personalities can fragment if we don't *actively pursue balance* in our lives.

We may have concrete goals, but we must still pay attention to feelings and relationships. We may be willing to work around the clock, but we must still take time out for play and spiritual retreat. We may want to change the world, but the real changes must start *within*.

My first wish is to see the world—and to see myself—as they really are. As I tap into the spiritual resources within me, I begin to clarify my vision.

8.08

There comes a time in every man's life when he must stop thinking and start doing.

CAPTAIN SISKO: PARADISE LOST: Stardate Not Given

Elsewhere in the record, Sisko points out the benefits of having a plan, a "blueprint," for our activities. Whether for a single project or our whole trek through life, a plan provides inspiration and guidance. It helps bring us back to our original vision if we get off track.

But some of us *over*-plan things. We try to anticipate everything. We leave no room for mid-course corrections, or for taking advantage of unexpected opportunities.

Worse, some of us have a tendency to keep *planning* as a way to *put off doing*. Which is not unlike the student who continues his "higher education" year after year in order to avoid actually getting a job.

And yet, once the basics are learned, getting a job *is* the best form of higher education. Likewise, once our plans are roughly outlined, actually *carrying them out* is the best way to refine and perfect them.

In reality, "doing" is simply an extension of "thinking." Planning is the intellectual part. *Applying* that plan adds the physical dimension. Both have their own inherent logic. Each is incomplete without the other.

As the saying goes, we change our lives by changing our thinking. But only when thought becomes deed.

My plans are imperfect. My information is incomplete. But I have faith that The Universe will guide me and supply what I lack—if I start now.

8.09

A ship is only as good as the engineer who takes care of her.

"SCOTTY": RELICS: 46125.3

There's a phase in the evolution of all technological societies, (usually when computers are first coming into use), during which expectations leap far ahead of effects. A kind of disaffection sets in… followed by questions.

Like: With all this new number-crunching power, why hasn't the Federation budget been balanced? Or: With graphics programs that can now simulate practically anything, why isn't art thriving? Or: With access to information only the touch of a keypad away, why haven't we solved all of our problems yet?

Simple. Improving our tools does not improve *us*. The person *behind* the keypad remains unchanged. The computer—or the ship—still relies on someone to operate it, to use it purposefully, to keep it functioning at all.

And all the hardware in the Quadrant can't replace the roles only *we* can play. All our upgrading of technology won't change a thing until we upgrade our*selves*.

We are the engineers of our own lives. The vehicles which carry us along—our bodies, our possessions, our present circumstances—are "only as good" as our own inner sense of Who We Are.

Let us make taking care of *that* our top priority.

I can wait for the latest model computer or personal shuttlecraft. I can no longer wait to begin remodeling myself into the person I want to be.

8.10

We can use all the friends we can get.

CAPTAIN JANEWAY: STATE OF FLUX: 48658.2

The fact that Captain Janeway was only repeating an old cliché makes the message no less true.

But what *does* diminish the message is the selfish twist we sometimes give it, as if the only thing friends are good for is our "using" them—usually to help us get out of the sticky situations we've gotten ourselves into.

Friends are good for that, too, no doubt. But friendship is a two-way street. It's as important for us to help our friends get out of *their* sticky situations as it is for them to help *us*. Because our wholeness and happiness depend as much on serving others as *being* served.

More important, as we grow spiritually, we recognize the need to expand our horizons, to transcend our self-centered interpretation of events, to see our own lives in relationship to the larger Web of Life. Friends—fellow voyagers—provide that wider perspective. They enlarge our experience as we help enlarge theirs. They affirm our own wisdom, as we do theirs. They provide encouragement, show us alternatives we might otherwise miss, and sometimes give us holy hell when we need it.

And the wider our network of friends, the more "useful" we become to The Universe for carrying out *its* goals.

Therein lies the ultimate Friendship.

Today I will seek not so much to "get" a new friend as to be one. I will help others along their journeys, and perhaps they will accompany me in mine.

8.11

> **I sometimes ask those kind of questions...
> Who am I? What am I doing here? What's
> my purpose in life? ...Doesn't everybody?**
>
> KES: PROJECTIONS: 48892.1

The surprising answer, for many of us, is... *No.*

Either the thought simply hasn't crossed our minds to question the meaning of life—which, admittedly, is rare. Or we've asked those deeper questions, found them too unsettling (or flatly unanswerable); and we've made the conscious decision *not* to ask them anymore. Period.

There's something to be said for the latter view. Why bother delving into such questions if no final answer is forthcoming? Or if it only makes us cranky and confused? Or worse, if we end up deciding that life is meaningless after all? Better to take things as they come, embracing both the joys and sorrows, living fully in the moment.

In fact, even for those who find a reflective approach more fulfilling, *not* asking the deeper questions can be a good thing. Because we find our answers to Who We Are only by actively *being* Who We Are. We decide what we're doing here by first *doing something*. We discover our purpose by *feeling* that something we've done has meaning.

In other words, if we would spend our time *being, doing* and *feeling* instead of *asking,* the answers would take care of themselves soon enough.

It is good to ask, but better to be. *Before I can reflect on my life, I must give myself experiences to reflect* on. *Today I will stop talking and start doing.*

8.12

What you were, and what you are to become, will always be with you.

Q: ALL GOOD THINGS…: 47988

It's easy enough to accept that what we *were* remains a part of us, if only in our memories. What's harder to swallow is that what we will *become* is also within us.

Look at it this way: Beyond the present, in the "no time" of eternity, our core identities (sometimes called "souls") are already everything they were capable of becoming. Like an old-fashioned laserdisc which contains an entire audio/visual story etched into its surface—or in this case an *infinite number* of possible stories—our souls are inscribed with all the life journeys we will ever take.

Back in the "now," the laserlight of time is pinpointing only a specific instant in the course of one of those journeys. If we could somehow get *outside* of time, however, we could see the culmination of all our journeys, as well as the evolved Self we will have become by then.

As it turns out, we *can* get outside of time—in our daily meditations. This is where we meet our Higher Self, the self who has already made the journey, who already knows what we were, are, and will be.

By drawing on that future perspective, we can help ourselves *in the present*. And it's not cheating. In fact, it's one of the best stories on our laserdisc.

"My highest potential is already present within me." As I concentrate on this thought, affirm it and release it, I turn potentiality into reality.

8.13

You might as well sit back and enjoy the ride.
CAPTAIN KIRK: METAMORPHOSIS: 3219.4

We are strengthened by struggle. We grow through facing life's challenges, hooking up with new resources, and working to change our conditions for the better.

But some conditions *can't* be changed. Some things that happen simply can't be controlled. The only thing we *can* change in these cases is our attitude about them. The only thing we can control is *how we react*.

An Arabic parable is told about a farmer who can't seem to rid his garden of weeds. Finally he travels to the Caliph's palace—several days by camel—to seek the advice of the royal gardener. The wizened gardener listens, then offers several suggestions. The farmer thanks him, goes home and tries each suggestion... without success. He thereupon returns to the palace to complain that he has tried everything, and still he has weeds.

The royal gardener scowls, thinks for some minutes more. "There is one last thing you can try on your weeds," he says at last. "You can learn to love them."

When we can't rid our gardens of the weeds, when the voyage is underway and there's no stopping now, we can still make a choice. We can decide to accept the experience, and then extract whatever goodness and growth The Universe has prepared for us.

I will seek to change what I am able, find goodness in the rest, and trust The Universe to care for me no matter how bumpy the ride.

8.14

There are times when men of good conscience cannot blindly follow orders.

CAPTAIN PICARD: THE OFFSPRING: 43657.0

We can read Picard's words as a statement with mainly political or military significance—the kind of Principle that might have come out of Terra's famous Nuremburg War Trials, perhaps, or Bajor's Lasting Peace Convention. But even for politicians and soldiers, what it comes down to is the primacy of *following one's own sense of Right*.

Because the bottom line is, we never lose responsibility for our actions. Being under orders, or "under the influence"—or under some *other* kind of compulsion—does not free us from the fact that we still have a choice.

This is not merely some judicial edict so that people can be held "legally accountable." It's a spiritual necessity. Deciding the kinds of actions we will and will *not* perform is how we create Who We Are.

Which doesn't mean we should *never* take orders. We have jobs. We make commitments to perform certain functions in return for certain benefits. We may not enjoy everything we're asked to do. But enjoyment isn't the criterion. Measuring our orders against a Higher Order *is*.

If we find ourselves questioning *every* order given to us, we probably can't see that Order clearly. If we find ourselves questioning *nothing*, chances are we're blind.

The "orders" I am given are valuable opportunities to analyze and fine-tune what I believe in. I will trust my own sense of right to guide my response.

8.15

There's nothing wrong with a healthy fantasy life. As long as you don't let it take over.

COUNSELOR TROI : HOLLOW PURSUITS : 43807.4

Soon after its entry into the Third Millenium, Terra suffered through what later became known as The Lost Decade of Virtual Reality. Following dozens of advanced civilizations before them, Terrans became technologically adept at simulating real-life experiences.

People could "travel" to exotic places without leaving home. They could refine their mental skills and physical abilities against computer-programmed competitors. They could *also* experience endless pleasure with sexual playmates whose only purpose was their satisfaction. Or they could feel the darker thrills of slicing imaginary enemies in half—or even killing "virtual copies" of real people.

The social effects of this technology took little time to surface. It wasn't just that virtual reality could never quite capture the realities of genuine social interaction. (If it even *tried*.) The problem was, virtual reality became a very efficient training ground for *anti*-social behavior.

The lure of our fantasy lives has always been strong. Which is a good thing, since fantasy is one of the most powerful mental tools for redesigning our own futures.

We simply need to remember that, with every fantasy we indulge in, *that's* what we're doing.

I will use my fantasy life to lay the groundwork for the person I intend to become.

8.16

We can hardly hate what we once were.
COMMANDER RIKER: THE LAST OUTPOST: 41386.4

We do not overcome our problems by hating them. We can't forgive ourselves and move into the next phase of our lives if we continue to despise the person we were —even if we recognize the evil and the lies in our past.

For one thing, we have a right to despise the *behavior*, but never the *person*. For another, the basis for forgiving and forgetting is *love*, not hate. To love the person we once were, in spite of the weaknesses and "sins" attached to that person, is the most powerful prerequisite for loving ourselves *now*. Our current state, after all, may seem as imperfect and corrupt to the person we will become, as our past state of corruption appears to the person we are at present.

Besides which, that "past self" was our bridge—our *only* bridge—to the wiser, stronger, more experienced person we've become. If anything, we should be grateful, not hateful. If that person didn't have the roots of goodness in him then, beneath all those flaws and imperfections, we couldn't have come as far as we have.

To love ourselves—past, present, and future—is to realize and accept what The Universe is doing to us.

To love others, is to *mirror* what The Universe is doing to us.

I celebrate the divine re-creation of my Self. I lovingly embrace the person who brought me to this point, and turn to meet the person I will become.

8.17

I'm a doctor, not a decorator!

THE DOCTOR: PHAGE: 48532.4

The Voyager's dour-faced doctor must've had a dozen rejoinders similar to this one. Elsewhere in the record we hear him insisting that he's "not a doorstop," nor "a counter-insurgent," nor "a sex surrogate."

And we can sympathize with his obvious impatience as he fires off these retorts. Because, like The Doctor, we too have been asked to do things we consider "beneath us." We too have been treated by someone as if we were cheap labor for any service they might suddenly require.

So we take offense. After all, we know what we're good at—and what we're *not* good at. It's only natural to get a little annoyed when we're assigned to projects that don't make the best use of our time and talent.

We might consider setting our fellow crewmembers straight. Maybe they don't *know* what our true talents are. Or perhaps they're misusing their authority over us.

But we should also consider the possibility that these people are guiding us toward new and useful experiences that will increase our versatility. And our self-confidence.

It's often no mere "coincidence" that a certain job will be assigned to us that seems utterly unrelated to our personal or spiritual growth. Only later do we realize it was precisely what we needed, at just the right time.

I am a novice, not an expert!—at least in most subjects. I know The Universe is providing valuable lessons for me, even if I can't yet see the connection.

8.18

Maybe it's better to look those feelings in the eye than to keep them locked up.

CAPTAIN JANEWAY: PERSISTENCE OF VISION: Stardate Not Given

In purely physiological terms, "feelings" are the conscious sensations of our own energy coursing through our bodies. Each type—fear, anger, grief, or joy—represents a purposeful galvanizing of inner forces designed to support a physical response to external conditions.

Considering our obsession with appearing "in control," however, it's not surprising that we should regard these sensations as unwanted intruders. So we barely acknowledge them. Or even try to suppress them completely.

And often there are perfectly valid reasons for doing so. We have jobs to do, decisions to make, other people's needs to consider. We can't let emotions distract us.

But once the "crisis" is over, we must unlock our temporary holding cells. We must find a safe haven where we can release and fully experience our feelings. And then we must *stop* ... and "look those feelings in the eye."

Which means stepping back to analyze what may have caused them, and especially to consider what we can *do* with all that emotional energy. Because if we can connect our sensations to an eventual response—a *thoughtful* response—we turn our feelings into wellsprings of positive action. We make them whole. We make them our friends.

I will better understand my feelings, and learn to use their energy more wisely, as I regularly share and discuss them with an "emotional partner."

8.19

Ever feel like you're really not wanted?

ENGINEER LA FORGE: ANGEL ONE: 41636.9

What's your threshold for rejection? At what point do you finally get the message that nothing you do will ever be enough? That it's not even what you *do;* it's... *you?*

Social rejection is one thing. It's a common occurence when two people just don't "hit it off." Most of us have learned to accept that. And we move on.

What's worse is when our ideas and our hard work aren't appreciated; when we've put our hearts and souls into some project and our efforts are ignored, or even dismissed. Our self-worth can drop right off the scale.

But *only if we depend on others for our worth.*

One of life's primary lessons is learning to take satisfaction from the task, not from its outcome or what other people may think. Even where a job is assigned to us by someone else, we must find our *own* reasons for doing it. How can this help *me* grow? What can *I* learn from the experience, regardless of the end result?

And ironically, what often happens is that, when other people see the satisfaction we're getting from a task, they take greater interest in it. When others know we're doing something because we believe in it, and not simply to impress somebody, they're impressed.

What's *also* ironic is, by that time it doesn't matter.

Whether I'm "not wanted" by others is not my concern. Doing what I believe in, and leaving the outcome to The Universe, is.

8.20

You must trust yourselves.

DR. CRUSHER: SYMBIOSIS: Stardate Not Given

Sounds too easy, doesn't it? Just *trust* yourselves and everything will magically take care of itself.

And of course it *isn't* that easy. But not because the doctor's advice is mistaken or simplistic. It's because we seem so unwilling to believe there's a resource within us that we *can* trust to guide us and give us answers.

Furthermore, some of us have *tried* "trusting in ourselves" and we know better than to do that again! The results have been disastrous, or at least not encouraging.

The problem is, trusting in that inner guidance is a learned skill. It's natural to get "mixed signals," mentally speaking. How do we separate the messages our hormones send us from the counsel of our rational mind— and finally from the intuitive urgings of our Higher Self?

But remember: A four-year-old can't just hop on a bicycle and ride it the first time, either.

Remember also that, in trusting "ourselves," we don't rely solely on the limited, fallible resources of our own conscious "ego." The Self we must learn to trust is linked in some subconscious, hyperspace-like way to the wisdom and power of The Universe itself. Through that Self we can access a perspective that harmonizes our own needs with others, that guides us through life's obstacle course to our goals... that trusts *us* even when we *don't*.

I respect my own guidance. I am learning to trust myself even as The Universe already trusts me.

8.21

It will be my job to anticipate your needs before you know you have them.

NEELIX: CARETAKER: 48315.6

In cultures across the Quadrant, a statement similar to this one is spoken—and understood—not in any *literal* sense, but merely as a way of emphasizing one's commitment to be of service. Most of us, after all, sincerely want to help others. But we need to go beyond words.

Try this exercise on a friend or loved one, or even a fellow crewmember: Spend a day—the *full* day—making that person the focus of all your attentions. Wait on them. *Spoil* them. Put yourself in their place and imagine what they might want you to do—not what *you'd* like to do, but what *they'd* like if only they weren't afraid to ask. And then *do* it. Expect nothing in return. At the end of the day tell them you'd gladly do it all again.

The point is, *we need to practice serving others*. In our spiritual transitions from ego-centered selfishness to a broader, "inter-connected self," the hard work of service can sometimes feel unnatural and even unfulfilling. The ego will whisper "Why knock yourself out?" and "They don't appreciate it anyway." And the clincher: "What about your *own* needs? Don't *you* deserve a little attention?"

You *do*. And it will come eventually, inevitably. That's how the universe works. The fact that you'll no longer require it, as Neelix might've put it, is "frosting on the cake."

I will do something wonderful for someone today— joyfully, without being asked, without expectations.

8.22

The true test of a warrior is not without. It is within.
LIEUTENANT WORF: HEART OF GLORY: 41503.7

A "fighter" is an individual who fights battles. A "warrior" is one who knows that battles are merely tactical encounters in a much wider conflict.

The warrior also knows that the real conflict isn't over possessions or planetary dominance. It's the struggle to overcome one's inner demons. It's about discovering that the physical conditions of one's life—what's "without"—are only mirrors for showing us what's "within."

There are several important corollaries, the first of which concerns commitment. Because we must commit ourselves to the long-term. The struggle takes a lifetime.

That's why, secondly, we must be willing to lose a battle now and then if it preserves us to fight a more important battle later. Or if the real lesson is about losing. Or letting someone else win if it serves a higher purpose.

Tactical choices like these shape the people we become. They teach us the value of sacrificing short-term gain for higher goals. They are tests of our discipline, our connection to others, our connection to the deeper reservoirs of grace, of genuine peace.

That is why we go to "war" in the first place. And why the supreme victory is over our own minds and hearts.

I am committed to the life-long effort to become my Self. My greatest ally is The Universe.

8.23

Live now! Make "now" the most precious time!

CAPTAIN PICARD (as "Kamin"): THE INNER LIGHT: 45944.1

One way to determine if our lives are in proper balance is to look at the emotional weight we give to the past, present, and future.

We often hear about those who "live in the past." We know how seductive it is to reflect on years gone by as if they were some kind of Golden Age. To be fair, "selective memory" can be a way to acknowledge all the good we've gained from past experience. But it can also be a sign that we've become pessimistic about our future.

On the other hand, being *too* future-oriented is just as unhealthy. In always looking toward the horizon, we can easily miss the present passing beneath our feet. And the irony is, in planning for this glorious future of ours, we'll imagine ourselves living in *that* "present" to the fullest; but by the time we get there we won't know *how*. Because we won't have had any practice doing it!

If only as "practice," then, we need to concentrate on the present. We need to look beneath our feet *now*, consider how blessed we are *now*, feel the warmth of the relationships and the love that surrounds us *now*.

The past no doubt had its golden moments. The future can be even more glorious. But the present is the only time we'll ever really *have*.

Today—all day—I will be present to the present.

8.24

The problem is not in the stars, but in ourselves.

GARAK: THE DIE IS CAST: Stardate Not Given

The Terran playwright, Shakespeare, was among the first to put it in such poetic terms: When things go wrong, when we're not happy with our lives, we tend to look outside of ourselves for someone—or some*thing*—to blame. Other people are usually at the top of that list. But once we realize that others are really no more in control than *we* are, most of us end up shaking our proverbial fists at The Universe. Or at least at "the stars."

It's understandable why we do. The stars are a potent symbol for "the way the universe operates." After all, powerful forces are obviously at work, distant forces that were here long before *we* dropped in, and they seem to shine on our lives in ways we may never fully comprehend. The best we can do is try to "align" ourselves with them, to figure out their signs and cycles and conjunctions. But the bottom line is, *they're* in charge, not us.

Which—again, symbolically—is true. It's also why the primitive craft of astrology still has its fascinations. But even astrology places final responsibility for our lives *on us.* Because it's still *our* job to learn the rules. And we can act in harmony with those rules, to find the hidden opportunities in them. Or we can pretend they don't exist.

In which case we have no one to blame but ourselves.

"The stars" represent What Is. My "problem" is to accept What Is, and organize my life accordingly.

8.25

> **"34th Rule of Aquisition: War is good for business." "35th Rule of Aquisition: Peace is good for business. It's easy to get them confused!"**
>
> QUARK - LT. COMMANDER DAX: DESTINY: 48543.2

Economics isn't the only domain in which paradoxes are common. One of the perennial paradoxes in science, for example, concerns the nature of light. From one point of view, light is definitely a "particle." From another, it's clearly a "wave" phenomenon. Yet both can't be true.

Which is an obvious clue that we still don't fully understand it. Or that our perspective alters our understanding.

The Ferengi perspective on war is such a case. Admittedly, some businesses thrive in wartime, or at least in times of potential conflict. But over an extended duration, warfare ends up sapping the economy, leaving fewer people to pay for the destruction (not to mention fewer people to fight). Ultimately, war profits are unsustainable.

The paradox here is less about reality than our mistaking short-term gain for what's best in the long run. Most of our problems, in fact, are rooted in this mistake. Too often we make choices that are blind to the long-term consequences, or to the effects on our fellow beings.

Spirituality is about widening our perspective, about connecting not only with the larger community but the farthest future. And having acquired that connection, we're less likely to get confused.

I live in the here and now. Yet I am part of the Infinite and the Eternal. That paradox sustains me.

8.26

Bickering is pointless.
SPOCK: MIRI: 2713.5

Fault-finding, negative criticism, verbal sparring—all these forms of petty argument get us nowhere. Worse, they prevent us from getting *some*where: From moving beyond our frustration with the problem to the search for an acceptable solution; from getting past our state of conflict to the process of compromise.

As long as we let bickering hold us back in this way, it *is* pointless. But our irrational arguing also has a positive aspect—one that Vulcan logic can all-too-easily miss: *Our bickering keeps us talking to one another.*

Because what's even worse than bickering is to stop talking for good. We can never end our conflict and find a solution unless we remain in communication.

And the fascinating thing is, people who are bickering with each other usually understand this, even if subconsciously. We know it's in our best interest to avoid breaking off relations and thereby give our darker sides an excuse to demonize the other person. Illogical as it may seem, bickering can keep us in contact until we finally realize what we *should* be talking about: How to begin working together on the problems facing us.

Bickering is a kind of raw energy—pointless energy. That is, until we seize the opportunity to transform it.

The moment I catch myself bickering with someone, I will remember the message my subconscious is sending me: We need each other to find a solution.

8.27

The lasting peace begins here.

GUL MACET: THE WOUNDED: 44429.6

Centuries ago, there was a Terran ballad with the refrain, "Let there be peace on Earth, and let it begin with me." Bajor's last Cardassian governor echoes this sentiment, not in the sense of expressing hope for one particular planet, but in the simple recognition that, for peace to be achieved *any*where, it must start *some*where.

And there is no better place to start than in our own hearts and minds. Right here... right *now*.

There are risks, of course. To lay down our weapons—whether physical, verbal or emotional—leaves us vulnerable and defenseless. On the other hand, peace will never come unless *some*one breaks into the cycle of violence and counter-violence. Often, the riskier that break, the more unexpected and shocking and even "unwise" it is, the better the chances that peace will catch on.

Unfortunately, peace will never fully "catch on" until a transformation occurs which makes violence and vengeance unthinkable to begin with. And "here"—in our hearts and minds—is where that transformation must take root. Because no matter what shape our world is in, despite the groups and governments and galaxies still waging war, we can at least achieve *inner* peace.

And then the world—inevitably—will follow.

*I refuse to let the world's strife derail my efforts to change my*self*. I will seek peace in my own life and relationships, and let my example inspire others.*

8.28

To become a thing is to know a thing.
CONSTABLE ODO: BEHIND THE LINES: 51149.5

One of the indigenous peoples of Terra had a saying that captured Odo's meaning on a more personal level: "Do not judge others," the saying advised, "until you've walked a mile in their moccasins."

But Odo's statement—along with his ability to transform himself into other "things"—takes in objects and beings of every kind. What's it like to be a tree, losing its leaves in an autumn downpour? Or a butterfly caught in a spider's web? Or a window pane that allows things to be seen through it, yet remains itself *un*seen? Odo knows.

But we too can experience these states of being, and more—through our imagination. By closing our eyes, by quieting our normal senses, we too can "become" the tree, the butterfly, the window... Or another person.

And the effects are almost as breathtaking as Odo's description of The Link, "...merging thought and form, idea and sensation." The universe opens; boundaries fall away. We transcend our usual limitations and narrow perspectives. And then we return to our ordinary lives with more understanding, more appreciation, less inclined to judge, less ensnared by self-centeredness.

"Becoming the Other" is a form of meditation found all across the galaxy. Almost always where peace reigns.

I am open to the viewpoints and experiences of other people and creatures. Even inanimate objects can teach me much about life, and about my self.

8.29

It is often helpful to find elements of commonality.

DATA: LIAISONS: Stardate Not Given

It's more than social training. We are programmed by eons of evolution to notice differences. That's how we recognize people, how we identify objects, how we separate what's important to our survival from what's not.

But this handy survival skill can also raise barriers. Because when it comes to people, differences often take on special meaning. Skin color, facial features, distinctive clothing or customs—all these warn us that we're in unfamiliar territory. We don't know what to expect. Yellow alert; be ready to raise shields!

What we're encountering here isn't our prejudice but our *ignorance*. Biology has hard-wired us to feel a "discomfort" in such situations meant not to drive us apart but to make us *want to learn more about each other*.

Master of protocol that he is, Data points to the proper procedure. The most productive relationships begin by naming the things we share. What common interests and goals might outweigh our differences? How can we see ourselves as fellow voyagers, not as competitors?

Biology never has the final word. Our intelligence is designed to complement what our bodies tell us. In the end, that's what makes the real "difference."

Each time I meet someone new today, I will search for—and name—three things we have in common. I will relate to him or her on that basis.

8.30

What can I offer except myself?

COUNSELOR TROI: SKIN OF EVIL: 41601.3

We often think about gifts in terms of "things"—the kinds of things taken off store shelves, or found in the pages of a NetSpace catalog. We might even think such gifts are meaningful. After all, whole industries exist to convince us that we all *need* these things. And if we *are* convinced, surely others should be impressed when we give them as gifts, right?

Except that it's not the *thing given* that makes the gift meaningful. It is, as the old cliché goes, "the thought that counts." What we're giving—assuming we've given it freely—is a message from our hearts. In the guise of a material object, we're sending our feelings of concern or commitment. (Or sometimes, even if we don't realize it, our *lack* of those feelings.) We may be laying the groundwork for a future relationship, or thanking someone for their kindness, or crying out for attention. Which is why we can receive two identical items, right down to the print on the wrapping paper, but the "gift" is different in each case.

That is, if we can see past the object. The fact that we often *don't* only reveals how materialistic we are.

One of Terra's great mystic poets wrote this: "See first that you yourself deserve to be a giver, and an instrument of giving. For in truth, it is Life that gives unto Life."

Becoming a giver is our greatest gift… to ourselves.

As I give of myself, I reflect The Universe giving Itself to me. I will strive daily to keep that cycle going.

8.31

If we're going to be damned, let's be damned for what we really are.

CAPTAIN PICARD: ENCOUNTER AT FARPOINT, PART I: 41153.7

Let's get one thing straight: The Universe does not damn us. The Universe does not seek to condemn us or destroy us, or threaten us with eternal punishment.

It may negatively reinforce certain actions, yes. But karma is designed to refine and improve us, not punish. Karma is a manifestation of Grace.

Damnation, on the other hand, is a concept invented by people. It reflects an inability—or refusal—to recognize the divinity within others because of certain "unacceptable" actions or beliefs. Or because of who they are.

It's almost certain that we will be "damned" by someone, sometime. After all, we can't do what we need to do and end up pleasing everyone. Nor should we try. To continually compromise our beliefs and behavior in an effort to make ourselves more "acceptable" is not only an act of self-repudiation, it is not possible to begin with.

Picard offers a better approach. Since *some*one is going to damn us no matter what we do, why not *earn* that damnation in the course of doing what we think is right? At least we'll maintain our own self-respect.

And if we listen carefully, all that "damning" starts to sound more and more like... *applause.*

I can't please everyone, but I can please myself. If I am doing what I believe in, the condemnation of others cannot touch me.

SECTOR

CORRESPONDING TO THE TERRAN MONTH OF
September

9.01

> **In this galaxy alone there's a mathematical probability of three million Earth-type planets. And in all the universe three million million galaxies like this one. And in all that... only one of each of us.**
>
> DR. McCOY: BALANCE OF TERROR: 1709.1

We are defined not by our specific location in space and time, not merely by the fact that our consciousness is localized *here* and not somewhere else. We are defined by what we've learned, by what talents we have, by the opportunities only *our* lives can provide.

Even the rare "duplicate selves" some voyagers have encountered elsewhere in the universe are not really duplicates. Rather, they are chances to further define our *true* selves, to discover the unique, core identity which makes us *us*—despite all outward appearances.

It is as if The Universe is calling each of us to affirm our own uniqueness, to identify and reclaim Who We Are... and then to *be* that person *no one else can be.*

A story told by one of Terra's "Pious Ones" recalls a teacher named Zusya. His students asked him why he couldn't be more like their model and prophet, Moses. "When I arrive at heaven's gates," Zusya replied, "the Holy One will not ask me why I was not more like Moses. He will ask, why was I not more like *Zusya?*"

I will treasure the lessons uniquely given for me to learn. I affirm and celebrate the person whom The Universe is calling me to become.

9.02

There's no harm in keeping both eyes open.

DR. BASHIR: DISTANT VOICES: Stardate Not Given

As *DS9*'s doctor suggests here, sometimes our own anatomy provides the most valuable clues about Life.

And not just Human or Vulcan or Klingon anatomy. All across the universe, from simple organisms to complex, species with only a single eye are virtually non-existent. The vast majority have exactly two eyes. Why is this?

In a few cases, it's because two eyes provide two entirely different points of view. Some creatures can see not only what's ahead, but what's behind; not only what's on this side, but *that*. In most sentient species, each eye has roughly the same field of vision, but the "offset" is just enough to provide a sense of perspective, to recreate in our minds the dimensionality that exists in the world.

Caught on yet? The lesson is that a single "viewpoint" isn't enough. Looking at things from at least two perspectives increases our ability to survive, if not thrive. It's not just that we see more of the world around us. The world becomes a *qualitatively different place*. We don't just see things, we experience the space *between* things. We experience relationships. We visualize new possibilities.

Bashir was understating the case. Keeping both eyes open is not merely harmless. Without that kind of vision, one of Terra's holy books warns, "the people perish."

I see *only as I open my eyes to different perspectives. I* know *only as I test my ideas against others. I* grow *only as I seek options, and make choices.*

No choice. You say that frequently. Does that... comfort you?

SEVEN OF NINE: EQUINOX, PART II: Stardate Not Given

Such an easy excuse: "But I had no choice!"

Yet almost without exception, whenever we make this claim, what we're *really* saying is that we preferred another alternative. Or that others in our position would've done the same thing. Or that our decision was dictated by habit or culture, or "nature." It was... *automatic*.

The Inner Voyage, however, is designed to make us *conscious* of what was once automatic. After all, we can't take control of what we do thoughtlessly, without even being aware of the process. First awareness, then control.

Not that we always *should* take control. If we had to think about taking every breath, if we had to consciously *tell* our hearts to beat, most of us would be fertilizer by now. Some things are better done *for* us than *by* us.

But making the choices that affect our lives, that help define the kind of people we are, are not among those things. In fact the really *tough* choices—the ones we too often hand over to someone else—are the very opportunities The Universe gives us to take responsibility, to transform Who We Are. The times we *think* we have no choice are when our power to choose can blossom.

Find a moment to be still. Open yourself to The Infinite. You may lose count of the options!

As I connect with my Source, I am open to new alternatives, new choices... a new, truer Self.

9.04

When has justice ever been as simple as a rule book?

COMMANDER RIKER : JUSTICE : 41255.6

An ancient holy book put it this way: "Justice, justice, shall you pursue." Not "happiness," as a certain political document would later suggest, but *justice*.

In other words, do what's right, do what's best for all concerned, and happiness will naturally follow. Put happiness first and justice will occur only by accident, if at all.

Of course, *how* to pursue justice is no simple matter, even if there are rule books (and holy books) that presume to tell us. For one thing, our self-interest frequently clouds our perception of what's "best"—especially when others may be impacted. On the other hand, how can we ever be sure *what* impact our actions will have on others? Not to mention on our*selves*. Starfleet records—like each of our personal histories—are full of good intentions that ended up having precisely the opposite effect.

Which is precisely why the pursuit of justice is a *spiritual* pursuit. Because it encourages us to transcend our narrow, purely physical view of things; to realize there is a wider perspective that "sees" what's best for all; and to strive, somehow, to gain access to that perspective.

Or rather, *to let that perspective gain access to us.*

Pursuing justice means affirming that I am part of a larger Web of Life. I open myself to the rule book which is that Web. I will act as its agent.

9.05

If you don't join me, don't disapprove of me. Not, at least, until you've tried it.

DR. McCOY: THE CONSCIENCE OF THE KING: 2817.6

The problem is not just that we're too judgmental. It's what we're judgmental *about*.

We criticize others (and ourselves) for minor flaws, all the while ignoring what really matters. We find fault with other peoples' private lives, how they look, their personal likes and dislikes—even their religious practices—when our only concern should be *how we get along*.

Withholding judgment (sometimes called "tolerance") is a virtue for precisely that reason. The fact that someone else may chant a mantra, or worship the Mother Goddess, or wear a turban, or go square dancing nightly, is none of our business. What matters is the kind of *people* they prove to be in their dealings with us and with others.

Admittedly, the practices that engender harmonious qualities in these people may not work for us. But that's just the point: We can't really say until we've "tried it."

Not that Dr. McCoy is suggesting we experiment with everyone else's lifestyle and belief system, so we can render our judgment. "Stay on your own path," is what he's really saying, "unless you truly *want* to join me on mine."

Because the bottom line is not the particular voyage we're on, anyway. It's the kind of *voyager* we become.

I am not in this universe to approve or condemn others, but to improve myself… and to demonstrate the person I am through the way I live.

9.06

Thinking about what you can't control only wastes energy and creates its own enemy.

LIEUTENANT WORF: COMING OF AGE: 41416.2

There's a prayer that appears in the sacred writings of nearly every planetary race, the essence of which is this: "Holy One, let me try to change what *can* be changed. Keep me from trying to change what can*not* be changed. And give me the wisdom to know the difference."

It's easy to see why such a prayer is almost universal. None of us wants to waste precious time and energy on projects that are destined to fail. We'd rather invest ourselves and our efforts where they'll have some chance at paying off. If nothing else, it's simply a case of managing our resources, of being practical.

But there are also *spiritual* implications. If we try to move a mountain that can't be moved, (but we think we *should* be able to move it), we begin to see that mountain as "the enemy." Its refusal to move must be deliberate.

Or worse: Maybe it's not just the mountain. Maybe the whole world is against us. Or maybe we're not "worthy." Maybe there's something *wrong* with us.

Persistence is good. Our willingness to take on ever greater challenges strengthens us. But knowing when to quit, or when to not even try, can be just as important.

Sometimes we need The Universe to help us decide.

I accept the fact that I can't change or control everything. I will seek guidance to know what those things are, and what I can do instead.

9.07

We have a duty to investigate.

COUNSELOR TROI : ANGEL ONE : 41636.9

The line is most often spoken by Starship captains or science officers. After all, to explore new worlds, to seek out new life and new knowledge despite the danger—and then to bring the treasures from that cosmic adventure back home—is the primary mission of Starfleet.

But the line could just as easily symbolize the mission of our individual lives, too. Because Troi's statement isn't just about explorations of the cosmic variety. It's about our duty to explore our*selves*. It's a rally cry to boldly go *within;* to seek new opportunities for personal learning and growth; to be curious not only about how the universe works, but about how *we* work.

Why did I do that? What causes these feelings? How can I improve the way I reacted to this event, or that person's remark, or my own inner compulsions? What standards can I use to find out if I *have* improved?

Our curiosity about life is a kind of faith. It's a faith that makes our existence more interesting, certainly. But it also pays dividends in greater self-awareness and greater understanding of others. As we bring back the treasures of this adventure into our daily lives, we discover that we now have more control, more options, more satisfaction.

Investigating is more than a duty. It's our *purpose*.

I am on a Grand Adventure. I will cultivate my curiosity as one of my most valuable tools.

9.08

You never know what conditions you might encounter. You must be prepared for anything.

LIEUTENANT TUVOK : LEARNING CURVE : 48846.5

In one sense, we *can't* be "prepared for *any*thing." At least not with pre-rehearsed counter-measures and programmed responses. The amount of information we'd need to know is simply too great. Besides, it's impossible to prepare for what we can't even imagine, right?

Tuvok admits as much when he warns us not to make assumptions about future "conditions." Yet he still advises us to "be prepared." Isn't this, well... *illogical?*

Not if we remember that proper preparation also includes what Picard called "readiness." And that's a matter of *attitude*. It's the mental framework that expects the unexpected, that's willing to accept new challenges as the cost of learning. It's the faith that we *will* survive, and that if the conditions are too much for us to cope with individually, then there are other resources we can turn to.

And there *are* such resources. Other people, for instance. Not to mention the resource *within* us: The One whereby we are *already* linked with others; the One that already "knows" the conditions we'll encounter even before we encounter them. And the One through which we are, even now, empowered to cope with anything.

I prepare myself for the unexpected as I link with other people, and as I connect with that Source of wisdom and power that lies within.

9.09

He will triumph who knows when to fight, and when **not** to fight.

COMMANDER RIKER: THE LAST OUTPOST: 41386.4

Triumph, fighting, *not* fighting… all of this sounds so belligerent, so militaristic, hardly in keeping with another Starfleet sentiment about war never being "imperative."

But even as we find peaceful ways to deal with conflict, war and warriors still symbolize something crucial about our existence: Our need to struggle against those forces that prevent us from achieving our highest potential.

In the midst of that ongoing struggle, we must take regular breaks (i.e. retreats, sabbaths) to rest, to gather our own forces, to plan new strategies. Of course, the success of any strategy ultimately depends on an honest, steely-eyed evaluation of our strengths and weaknesses.

Because there are times when picking a fight can only harm us. Like when we carelessly assume we've beaten an addiction, or overcome some other wasteful habit; and we stroll into enemy territory only to discover how easily our untested defenses can be stripped away.

There are also times when we've renewed our strength, disciplined our troops; and now the only way to assert control of our lives is to go back and confront the enemy. Our eventual triumph isn't so much "won" as *reaffirmed.* The real victory has been achieved already—within us.

My spiritual growth emerges from struggle. I will carefully choose opportunities in which I can test, refine and confirm the personal qualities I seek.

9.10

There's only one first time for everything, isn't there? And only one last time, too.

JAKE SISKO: THE VISITOR: Stardate Not Given

"Firsts" are more significant than many of us realize. Not only consciously, but *sub*consciously, they become signal beacons on our Inner Voyage. They are the turning points, the personal breakthroughs, the spiritual "revelations." They symbolize the thresholds of transformation beyond which our lives can never be the same again.

Because our subconscious naturally elevates these events, we should strive to make them *positive* experiences. Or at least be aware of them when they happen.

We can also be aware of *last* times, too—as in the last time we smoked, or the last time we did something dishonest, or yielded to some other temptation.

In fact, by consciously *labeling* some event as "the last time," we can increase the likelihood that it will *remain* so. Unlike "firsts," however, last times are easily reversed. We can always repeat actions we thought we'd stopped, and the change we hoped for is effectively cancelled.

A better approach would be to make every hoped-for change into a "first." The last time we lit up a cigarette becomes the *first time* we took control of our habit. And if we yield to temptation again, at least we see ourselves moving in the right direction. Instead of endings, we concentrate on beginnings. Life is about *doing*, not *un*doing.

Every day offers opportunities to do something for the first time. I will use this day to change my life.

9.11

> **Open your mind to the past... art, history, philosophy... Then all this may mean something.**
> CAPTAIN PICARD : SAMARITAN SNARE : 42779.1

The purpose of an education never has been, never will be, to learn the skills necessary to "get a job." Education provides the tools by which we think, act, *live.*

A good one also traces our origins, searches for the elements that make us what we are. It provides a body of shared knowledge which can draw people together even when their present life experiences are different. From the history of one's own race or planet to an overview of life as it developed throughout the universe, we begin to see ourselves as part of something larger, as meaningful components of a Whole. Our lives have *context.*

Which gives us more control. Because what happens *next* is always connected to what's happened before. Without this perceived connection, events seem haphazard; they don't "follow." *With* it we have a better sense of what to expect—from the future, and from ourselves.

It's the reason many adopted children want to know who their birth parents were. It's why all children long to hear stories about their own past. Again and again.

Because it explain us to ourselves. And with this as our starting point, we begin to take responsibility for our lives.

No matter where I am in my life, I affirm the value of everything that has brought me to this point... for learning, for building on, for re-inventing my Self.

9.12

Is that not the nature of man and woman? That the pleasure is in the learning of each other?

NATIRA: FOR THE WORLD IS HOLLOW AND I HAVE TOUCHED THE SKY: 5476.4

There are phases in every culture when the sexual identities developed by social custom no longer reflect biological reality. The fact that females in most species bear its offspring hardly justifies the division of roles—or the outright subjugation—some societies have enforced.

Inevitably a flashpoint is reached. And either the pendulum swings to the other side, or social regulations are redesigned to enforce an "equality" which ignores *all* sexual differences. Between these two conditions, the latter is vastly preferable. In fact, our spiritual progress depends on the realization that our ultimate identity—the soul within each of us—is neither male nor female.

And yet, we are *incarnated* souls. Our bodies are gifts from The Universe. And our full appreciation for that gift lies in recognizing the biological differences we inherit, and accepting the unique pleasures we can enjoy precisely because we are *this* gender and not *that*.

The benefits are not only physical, but deeply spiritual. Because the underlying message is that we are made whole only as we link ourselves to others, as we use our differences to *achieve unity* rather than create division.

Or as some humans have put it, *Vive la différence!*

I am equal to others not by being identical, but by identifying and valuing what makes me different.

9.13

Even logic must give way to physics.

SPOCK: THE UNDISCOVERED COUNTRY: 9521.6

No matter how many intellectual trophies we accumulate, The Universe always finds some way to bring us back down to earth.

And it's a good thing. Because we can become so smug, so puffed up by our own mental prowess, that we begin to think our intellect is what saves us. Feelings are irrelevant. Relationships are beside the point. Solutions to life's problems are simply a matter of collecting data and putting it under the microscope of Pure Logic.

At least this approach uses logic purposefully. Too often our mental calisthenics become an end in themselves. We enjoy playing mind games, solving all kinds of problems "in theory" while ignoring the fact that the ultimate test is whether our solutions work in the real world. Our ancestors called it "living in an ivory tower."

Spock's reference to "physics" is a call to come down from our ivory towers. Our mental and spiritual studies, after all, become useful only as we can *apply* them in our everyday lives. That's the reference point for all our learning, all our growth—individually and collectively.

Whenever our knowledge collides with physics, The Universe is simply telling us to try something else until we get it right. Otherwise all we are is just "theory."

Learning becomes knowledge as I test it in my life, refine it, and grow more confident in it. In the process I feel The Universe testing and refining **me**.

9.14

Part of being human is learning how to risk new experiences... even when they don't fit into your preconceptions.

ENGINEER LA FORGE: INHERITANCE: 47410.2

Think of "being human" as shorthand for "fulfilling your highest potential." Human, Klingon, or otherwise.

That potential is a quality all sentient beings share, a treasure bestowed on each of us by The Universe. Unfortunately, our treasure lies buried beneath the complex programming our species has evolved for its biological survival. As amazing as that program *is,* it can take us only so far. In fact, if we assume that our highest potential is defined strictly in terms of biology, the program will effectively block any further growth. We become like stunted caterpillars, content to crawl when we could be soaring like butterflies... unwilling to emerge from our cozy cocoons when divine transformation is our destiny.

Unlike the caterpillar, our transformation requires our assent. And the best way to *give* that assent is to break free of our preconceptions: To imagine that we can soar even if we've spent most of our lives crawling; to allow a new concept of our world and our*selves* to emerge, even if our present concepts are comfortable, familiar, safe.

The caterpillar can't imagine being a butterfly, yet becomes one. How much higher we soar if we *can* imagine!

I grow not by staying comfortable, but by leaving my cocoon. I earn my spiritual wings not by flying close to the ground, but risking the heights.

9.15

Stop trying to kill each other, **then** worry about being friendly.

CAPTAIN KIRK: ELAAN OF TROYIUS : 4372.5

So often we get things backwards. We speak before thinking, act before considering the consequences. Or we *don't* act, missing an opportunity we should've taken.

Of course there are times when we must speak or act—or *not*—without having time to properly analyze the situation. We may have little more than intuition to guide us. (Not "impulse." *Intuition*.) We accept the fact that mistakes are fairly common in these cases; and most people will forgive us if they think we acted in good faith.

What's *not* easy to forgive is when someone premeditates an action they know is wrong, trusting that they'll be forgiven later. It's shocking how many people routinely do this. It's *more* shocking to catch our*selves* doing it.

Because we corrupt our sensibilities if we cynically use divine grace in this way. To hurt others, intending to make up afterwards, is to *play act* at forgiveness. It leads to the *pretense* of regret, not heartfelt sorrow. It stifles the sincere desire for change that produces genuine transformation. The people we end up hurting most is *us*.

On the other hand, if we premeditate reconciliation and friendship with other people, we also become reconciled with our own feelings. *And* with the divine nature within us.

If I pre-plan my actions at all, it will be to do only those things for which I will not require forgiveness.

9.16

You are going to have to make some hard choices about your future. And you can't make them if you're going to ignore the truth.

DR. CRUSHER: TRUE Q: 46192.3

Spock and Tuvok would readily agree. Because making choices involves logic. Unfortunately, if the data we use is faulty—if we haven't input "the truth"—the most flawless logic will still yield an incorrect conclusion.

Even the most advanced Ship's Computer ultimately depends on the quality of the information fed into it. Perhaps the early computer programmer's motto still sums it up best: "Garbage in, garbage *out*."

So it is as we plan our futures. We make plans based on the rosiest scenario we can imagine. Or sometimes the most *dismal* ones. And it's not that we do this consciously. The truth simply has a hard time getting past our mental and emotional filters. We can just as easily ignore what's in our favor as the harsher realities.

Because of her emotional distance, Dr. Crusher was often able to see what her patients couldn't. We can provide that same service for our friends. And we frequently need that "outside" perspective for ourselves.

Support and guidance are all around us. All we need to do is ask for it. That's what our Spiritual Network is *for*.

I alone am responsible for my choices, but I need not make them alone. With the help of others and my inner guidance, I see more clearly my true path.

9.17

Sometimes things between men and women can get a little complicated.

CAPTAIN SISKO: INDISCRETION: Stardate Not Given

Let's take a quick reading: How are your relationships with members of the opposite sex?

Though you may not know it, what's being asked is nothing less than how comfortable you are with your own sexual identity. *And* whether or not you can transcend it.

Because the complications between men and women depend, first, on how we define our*selves;* and only secondarily on how we regard the other sex. If we don't know what it means to be a "man," we can't expect our relationships with women (or even other men) to be as healthy and fulfilling as they could be. And vice versa.

Equally crucial is our ability to recognize what is *the same* in each of us, despite our sexual identities. Do we know what it means to be a *person* first? Can we see the individual *behind* the physical form, or are we unable to separate the "self" from the body it resides in?

Try this: Imagine what it would be like to take your core identity—what many traditions call the "soul"—and implant it within a body of the opposite sex. *Can* you—?

No wonder things get complicated. We are not only persons, but co-workers, lovers, mothers and fathers. The challenge is finding a balance between our biology and spirituality. The joy is that it takes a lifetime to do it.

My sexuality is one of my greatest gifts. I will use it to discover the inner self that lies beyond it.

9.18

Talk to people... ask questions... learn the truth for yourself.
LIEUTENANT TORRES: REMEMBER: 50211.4

Accepting what others tell us, on faith, can never be a sound basis for Faith.

The "truths" we build our lives around are too important to rest on custom or convention, on what someone says happened two hundred years ago. Or two thousand.

Not because what someone says is necessarily *wrong*. Or because social customs don't play a useful role. It's because we can't fully *know* our truths to be true until we've questioned them, even doubted them... until in some sense we "discover" them for ourselves.

The things that motivate us, that have the power to transform our lives, are the *deeply felt* truths, whose confirmation comes from within. And even if they depend in part on the testimony of others, or words inscribed in a book, their meaning must resonate in our hearts and minds. They must translate into attitudes and actions that make a difference to us personally.

In fact what *doesn't* resonate has no real meaning for us. What can't "translate" ultimately makes no difference.

Our quest for spiritual or religious truth is less about *what's* true than what *conveys* the truth to us—in a way that makes us feel it deeply, then inspires us to act.

The Universe knows what "language" I speak. It is conveying its truths to me right now, if I will listen.

9.19

Wishing for a thing does not make it so.
CAPTAIN PICARD: SAMARITAN SNARE: 42779.1

Actually, the statement isn't as benign as it might seem at first glance. Because our "wishing" for something can often *prevent* that something from ever coming about.

The same holds true for some forms of prayer. As they are practiced on many planets, both wishing and prayer incorrectly place all the power of "fulfillment" *outside* of ourselves. We see ourselves at the mercy of some dictatorial Power which usually doesn't want what *we* want—or at least doesn't care one way or the other. According to this mode of thinking, we are impoverished. We lack. We suffer neglect unless we continually petition this power, or otherwise show how desperate our need is and how granting our wish would make us so happy.

But what we desperately need is to *change this attitude of desperation.* What we need is to stop practicing our own spiritual disempowerment.

At this very moment The Universe is ready to give us our heart's desire. Our desires will often be fulfilled even if we later come to regret it, since taking responsibility for those desires may be an important life's lesson. For most of us, realizing this—*practicing this*—is the key.

Think about it: When you raise your arm you don't wish for it. You *do* it. "Making it so" is not that different.

The ability to make my dreams come true lies in my own attitudes. Prayer is the technology for "making it so" by aligning my Self with The Universe.

9.20

If you're going to judge me, judge me for what I am **now**.

ENSIGN SITO: LOWER DECKS: 47566

Making judgments about others often serves a useful purpose. Judgments help us "package" the experience we've gained, enabling us to form productive relationships based on what we can realistically expect.

But judgments can also be limiting and destructive. If we enter a new relationship with someone based on the negative things *other* people say, we prevent the opportunity for a positive relationship in *our* case. And even if our judgments are drawn from first-hand knowledge, we do damage by casting those judgments in concrete. To judge another too harshly is to deny them the possibility of change. It freezes them at one stage of development when progressive evolution is a law of the universe.

The long-discredited Terran practice of imprisoning criminals was abandoned for exactly that reason: It *confirmed* negative behavior rather than allowing people to unshackle themselves from the past, to be transformed.

What's worse, by denying the possibility of transformation in *others,* we subconsciously tell ourselves that *we're* incapable of change. Instead, we must actively look for—and celebrate—positive changes in others. Not only for their sake, but for our own.

I release others—and myself—to become the highest and best we can be. I will celebrate every change for the better, no matter how small.

Why not try a carrot instead of a stick?

DR. McCOY: METAMORPHOSIS: 3219.4

McCoy's question recalls the medieval tale of the boy who can't get the family donkey to pull their cart. After whipping the stubborn animal with his stick, the boy finally dangles a succulent carrot in front of its nose. The excited donkey lunges forward, pulling the cart with him, and *keeps* moving as long as the carrot is held there.

The debate about what motivates us is largely settled. Negative reinforcement—the stick—has limited value. Pain doesn't tell us where to go; only to stop doing whatever we're doing. *Positive* reinforcement—the carrot—is not only more inspiring, it gives us direction.

What's more, we can apply positive reinforcement *to ourselves*. It works almost as well if *we* dangle the carrot in front of our own noses!

And sometimes we need to. For example, most of us can envision the kind of stronger, more loving person we'd like to become someday. But getting there can be hard work. There may be few rewards, and lots of pain.

Which is why, if we know we're headed in the right direction, we should reward ourselves for every small step we take toward our goals: A night out, perhaps; or a warm bath; or maybe a quiet evening with someone special.

Think what fun we could have rewarding each other!

I will no longer think in terms of "punishing" myself (or others) for failure. I hereby promise only to reward success.

9.22

I suggest you avoid emotionalism.

SPOCK: THAT WHICH SURVIVES: Stardate Not Given

Spock isn't counseling the rest of us to suppress every emotional response we might have. Nor was he suggesting we'd be better off living without our emotions entirely, as many Vulcans (and others) have learned to do.

For most sentient species, in fact, emotions have their own powerful "logic." *And* their own power to flood our systems with raw energy. That energy is designed to be used. To suppress it is not only wasteful, but potentially damaging. Emotions are meant to help us.

Emotional-*ism*, on the other hand, means allowing emotions to *rule* us, not merely "help." Our hormones and nerve-endings are back in the Captain's Chair, just as they were before our species developed consciousness.

It's not that hormones and nerves are bad. They're just not all we can be. Our emotions can't envision the future. They can't imagine consequences. They are blissfully unaware that *we* must go on even after *they've* subsided, leaving us to deal with their effects.

They are also blissfully unaware that they can be easily fooled. A half-baked simulation of reality can create emotions just as intense as the real thing. Emotionalism is therefore a religion of appearances, of the here and gone.

But we are beings of What Is Ultimately Real, and what is Eternal. Let us make *these* our Prime Directives.

I am energized by my emotions, not ruled by them. They can offer guidance, but I chart my course.

9.23

We just have to make the best of the little time we have... we can't waste a second.

CHIEF O'BRIEN : FASCINATION : Stardate Not Given

Even if we *don't* waste a second, we can't do everything. Considering all the star systems we'd like to explore, all the subjects we'd like to master, all the personal qualities we'd like to refine, transform, or just get *rid* of—a single lifetime simply isn't enough.

It's fortunate, therefore, that The Universe does not judge us by our individual Goal Achievement Rates. (Besides, what *we* consider "the goal" may only be an excuse for working on the *real* objective.) What The Universe is concerned with, instead, is whether we've used our limited time *wisely,* whether we've managed that resource with an understanding of *how precious it is.*

The coming day will be unlike any other, if we would only look for its unique treasures. Each new hour offers opportunities for growth, chances to transform our lives, to reach out in service to others. Watching for these hidden, one-time opportunities (even as we stay focused on our long-term goals) gives us a more open and spontaneous attitude toward life. It also fills our time with more spiritual riches than we could ever *plan* to accumulate.

We are, after all, in the care of a Higher Power. Being ready to accept its gifts is the best use of our time.

I will embrace today like a loving friend whom I won't see again. The treasures of The Universe are right here, right now. I will relish every moment.

9.24

Uncontrolled, power will turn even saints into savages... and we can all be counted on to live down to our lowest impulses.

PARMEN: PLATO'S STEPCHILDREN: 5784.2

It was the Terran philosopher, Plato, who first conceived this test of our "nature": Suppose you had a secret ring that allowed you to move among people completely undetected. (Imagine—a cloaking device twenty-six centuries before the Klingons!) If no one could see you, Plato wondered, would you behave any differently? Could you resist the temptation to peek into other people's private lives? Maybe even do harm to your enemies?

Plato took a rather dim view. *No one* could resist doing evil, he claimed, if they could get away with it. Later, St. Augustine would take a similar view. So has Parmen.

And, frankly, many individuals *do* "live down to their lowest impulses" if given the chance. We'd be foolish not to guard ourselves against such people.

But to some extent those impulses are less nature than nurture. Because by being suspiciously on guard against them, we teach one another that they are to be expected. Yet if we expect *high* standards of morality—*and set an example*—people will live "up" to those higher standards.

We have the power to be saints, not savages. It's just a different "power" than Plato was talking about.

I release the Higher Power within me that brings my "impulses" into consciousness, where I can then receive help in transforming them.

9.25

Maybe it's time to stop brooding and start talking.

MAJOR KIRA: THE SEARCH, PART I: 47212.4

By now, most of us have begun to receive the benefits of our private meditations. In fact, whenever we skip our daily "soul-work," even for good reason, we feel like we're missing something. The truth is, we *are*.

But there are times when our meditative practice can turn sour. Like when we use meditation to *escape* our daily life rather than deepen it. For example, we may be going through a crisis in a relationship. Or our jobs may not be going well. We may have done something stupid.

Under such conditions we often find ourselves not so much meditating as brooding. We ponder our sorry state endlessly, rather than seeking inner resources to end it.

The best way to break out of this cycle, ironically, is to *stop* meditating. Instead, we need to find a sympathetic ear—someone who will not offer advice but simply let us "air out" our concerns. And then we need to *start talking*.

Vocalizing our problems is a different process entirely. As we listen to our own words, we begin to separate ourselves from our troubles in a way that breathes objectivity and new insight into our lives. Our very thought patterns refresh themselves, crawl out of their own dungeons.

Through another, we reconnect with our Self.

I do not allow brooding to infect my meditations. I can temporarily substitute spoken words for private thoughts, thereby re-grounding myself in reality.

9.26

Given a choice between slim and none, I'll take slim any day.
COMMANDER RIKER: DEJA Q: 43539.1

This one's about hope. And the fact that even the *thinnest* shred of it can keep us going when nothing else will.

Our uncritical expectations that life will get better *some*day, or that justice will be served *some*day, or that we'll find our true love *some*day—all these "hopes" have enormous power. They are powerful precisely *because* they are so uncritical. Even illogical.

Because if we calculated the odds, if we only knew how slim our chances really were, we might easily give up. By *not* knowing, we allow ourselves to keep trying. And in most real-life situations, it's not our critical faculties or our logical brilliance or our "practicality" that wins out anyway. It is our persistence. It is our dogged, never-say-die, keep-the-faith, thick-headed *persistence*.

In fact, for the really important things in life, the slimmest odds are often the *best* odds. Winning nine times in ten presents no challenge. Fifty-fifty odds may level the playing field, but aren't likely to change us. It's the one-in-a-hundred shot that makes us dig down deep, that forces us to commit fully, that transforms us from opportunists seeking the easiest route into disciplined explorers on The Inner Voyage. That, finally, is where our hope lies.

My success isn't based on "the odds" but on the level of my commitment. I will hope for it; I will expect it; therefore I will achieve it.

9.27

The beginning of wisdom is... I do not know.

DATA: WHERE SILENCE HAS LEASE: 42193.6

Look again. It's not that Data is confused about our concept of wisdom. He knows exactly where wisdom begins: By openly admitting that... *I do not know.*

Get it?

A similar statement can be found in a five-thousand-year-old Bajoran text. And in the ancient record of Terra's most famous gadfly, Socrates. "The truly wise man," as Socrates described him, "is he who knows how ignorant he is."

Which doesn't mean *stupid.* In fact, stupidity is usually an attribute of the individual who thinks he knows everything. This person is open to very little, can be taught very little, and will consequently grow very little.

That's stupid.

In contrast, it is our frank admission that we are ignorant of so much—compared to what there is to know—which starts us down the path of knowledge. It is our willingness to live with partial answers along the way which keeps us open to new information. It is our joyful acceptance that learning never ends which keeps us growing, improving... *alive.*

And that's wise.

I will cheerfully admit when I do not know something. I will ask questions, and I will open myself to the truth, wherever it may lead.

9.28

Your primitive impulses will not alter the circumstances.

SPOCK: REQUIEM FOR METHUSELAH: 5843.7

Most of us wouldn't phrase it quite as delicately as Mr. Spock. Something more like: "You can rant and rave all you want, but it ain't gonna change anything, Charlie." Or maybe: "Once the Terulian wine has been spilled, all the tears on the planet won't put it back in the flask."

And it's true. We can't change what has already happened simply by expressing anger or disappointment or grief. On the other hand, we can't change what's already happened by *not* expressing those emotions, either.

What Vulcans don't readily comprehend is that, for emotional beings, ranting and raving and grieving can be part of our healing process. Or at least helpful in releasing the energy that builds up when life slaps us in the face.

Not that we can't go overboard. We're often blinded by our emotions. We can hurt ourselves, hurt others, and live to regret it. Or, as often happens, we use our "emotional state" to avoid responsibility, to force someone else to pick up the pieces because "We just can't face it."

But all that emotional energy is designed precisely so we *can* face it. That's why it exists: To be transformed into the strength we need to deal with "the circumstances."

Which is what Spock always tried to teach us.

My emotional reactions to situations are what it "feels like" when my body is giving me the energy to face reality. I will use it wisely.

9.29

When every logical course of action is exhausted, the only option that remains is inaction.

LIEUTENANT TUVOK: TWISTED: Stardate Not Given

Sometimes the best thing to do is... nothing.

Which, as we've said before, isn't really "nothing." *Not* taking action is itself an action. Or at least a decision.

And it's not necessarily a decision we reach because we've thrown up our hands and don't know what else to do. It's because a choice we could've made earlier is now easier to accept: We can wait patiently on The Universe.

Though Vulcans might not rush to admit it, logic does have limits. It may be that we just don't have enough raw data to apply our logic *to.* Or perhaps the answers can't be formulated in logical terms to begin with. We aren't able to deduce them so much as "intuit" or *feel* them, or receive them as if by divine revelation.

So when we run into the proverbial dead end, it may be time to turn the usual advice around: Don't just *do* something—*sit* there! In other words, be still... *Wait.*

The Universe, after all, has its own higher logic. Often our problems will resolve themselves if we'd only give them time. Often new options will appear—but only because we've stopped looking so hard. Or maybe we just need to be reminded, once again, who's in control.

Inaction also plays a role in my search for solutions. I must be patient as The Universe integrates my needs with others'—at its own pace, not mine.

9.30

We're all vulnerable in one way or another.
CAPTAIN KIRK: IS THERE IN TRUTH NO BEAUTY?: 5630.7

Ancient Terrans told the story of Achilles, a warrior whose body was magically protected from enemy arrows much as a Starship is shielded from phasers. In Achilles' case, however, one tiny spot on his heel was left unprotected. And that spot eventually led to his downfall.

All of us, it turns out, have some physical or emotional "Achilles heel"—or perhaps several—that can leave us vulnerable, or may even lead to our downfall. And like Achilles, most of us try to keep these "soft spots" secret, so our enemies can't take advantage of them.

The problem is, we also end up keeping them secret from our*selves*. Which is why we're often surprised when certain emotions surface, or we suddenly start behaving in ways that "just aren't like us."

Instead of hiding our vulnerabilities, we need to face them. But not so we can learn how to work around them. These emotional soft spots are our psyche's way of pointing to unfinished emotional business. They are portals into the interior territory we most need to explore, not shy away from. They are the "wormholes" connecting our past hurts to our future healing.

And because others must play a role in that healing, they connect us to *each other*.

I acknowledge the inner work my vulnerability calls me to continue. I accept my psyche's invitation to learn more about myself, and grow even stronger.

SECTOR 10

CORRESPONDING TO THE TERRAN MONTH OF
October

10.01

Perhaps today is a good day to die!

COMMANDER WORF: FIRST CONTACT: 50893.5

For Klingons, as with many of Terra's tribal societies, this pronouncement was often made just before going into battle. But it was less a "battle cry" meant to rally the troops than a warrior's personal declaration of faith. It affirmed that the warrior was prepared to do his or her duty, even if it required paying the ultimate price.

For those of us whose daily battles aren't quite so life-threatening, Worf's statement can still hold meaning. In a symbolic sense, to be ready to die is to affirm what's important in life, to have some concept of what we're living *for*. And when the things we value most are in danger of being lost, we must be willing to "die" for them.

Because if what we have (or *are*) is worth saving, it's worth risking everything to save it. And fortunately we won't face that task alone. On the other hand, if the life we're living *isn't* worth saving—if we've taken a terribly wrong turn without knowing it, if what we've become is a sham, if we've settled for less than we deserve—then we must also be willing to let that life expire.

In this sense, to affirm that we're prepared to die is to release the past, to recognize that it may be necessary to to start over, to reconstruct our lives from the ground up. And either way, we trust the outcome to The Universe.

Each moment holds the promise of a new life. I am ready to give up this life today if it enables me to live a richer, more fulfilling one tomorrow.

10.02

It is a blessing to understand that we are special... each in his own way.

RIVA: LOUD AS A WHISPER : 42477.2

We feel joy and pain. We set goals and strive toward them. We live and love and learn, and eventually die. And hopefully along the way we find a reason for it all.

In so many ways we are alike. And yet we are different. Each of us has unique possibilities. Each develops a set of traits and talents that is ours alone. In the history of the universe, no one else has ever been, or can be, *us*.

To realize that we are "special" is not merely to recognize this uniqueness. It means accepting responsibility for a one-of-a-kind role only *we* can fulfill. And not merely for our own sake, but for others'.

After all, "special" is a relative concept. It assumes a *relationship* in which our uniqueness is the missing piece that helps others complete a larger whole. In fact, all of our pieces are essential. Finding where we "fit" energizes us, gives meaning to our struggles. It is perhaps life's greatest blessing.

But take note: To receive this blessing doesn't require *having already found* where we fit. "Finding" is an action verb. It's an ongoing process. Simply knowing that we *do* fit, somewhere, is enough for now.

I joyfully affirm the role that Universe has created especially for me. Others will help me clarify and recognize my role, as I will help them with theirs.

10.03

Recovery from a great loss involves a great deal of pain. If we try to avoid that pain, we make it harder on ourselves in the long run.

COUNSELOR TROI: THE LOSS: 44356.9

It bears repeating: Our minds may be products of the modern world—inheritors of technology and science and the cultural gifts of an entire galaxy. But our bodies are children of the past, the biological offspring of a localized planetary environment that existed long before our species became sentient. To disregard what our bodies are telling us is to ignore who we are. And what we need.

For example, the pain of loss—what some people call "grief"—is a physical message which demands an equally physical response. We can suppress that message through pain-killing drugs, or by immersing ourselves in our work, or by trying to deal with it on a purely intellectual level since, after all, we *are* rational beings, aren't we?

And yet we can no more dismiss our pain than we can deny the pangs of hunger that remind us to take nourishment. It's true the pangs may eventually go away. But the need that gave rise to them will remain. And if we continue to suppress our hunger—*or our grief*—then what was once merely a call for attention becomes a condition that can threaten our very existence.

Our bodies are *for* us, not against us, if only we will listen and learn its language.

Even in pain, my body is sharing the wisdom of the ages. I will listen for the message beneath its words.

10.04

There is no perfect solution.

CAPTAIN KIRK: PLATO'S STEPCHILDREN: 5784.2

The problem isn't so much that we're unwilling to face challenges. Or that we're unwilling to work. The problem is, we expect too much from our efforts. We want to be *done* with it. We want it solved. We want things perfect.

And yet the testimony of the universe tells us that nothing is ever "perfect." There is no finished state. All is in flux, evolving, ever changing.

If we're mindful—or sometimes just lucky—we can affect the natural course of change in a way that benefits ourselves and others. But we must guard against the notion that we can solve all our problems forever. Or answer our questions with any final certainty. Instead, we should try looking at life like a Science Officer, who builds on previous knowledge, confident that there *are* final answers—at least in theory—but who is satisfied simply to discover one more piece of the puzzle… And then to go on with his work despite incomplete information and imperfect solutions *while the search continues.*

The perfectionist's impossibly high standards can be a convenient excuse to remain uninvolved, to avoid the hard work. And therefore to avoid growing. On the other hand, doing the best we can with the limited knowledge we have—that's as close to "perfection" as we can get.

I'm not perfect, nor do I have all the answers. But I will learn and grow by facing life's challenges with an open, experimental attitude.

10.05

Let's not indulge ourselves in speculation. Can we confine our discussion to the facts?
CAPTAIN PICARD: THE WOUNDED: 44429.6

There's a time for imagination, for unbridled speculation. If nothing else, our flights of fancy can be useful exercises for keeping our minds "limber," for maintaining creative readiness for the *real* challenges that lie ahead.

But sometimes we can't afford the luxury of fantasy-for-the-fun-of-it, or envisioning "the way things ought to be." Reality occasionally dumps a problem on our doorstep that demands a concrete solution *now*. Speculation would only waste precious time and energy.

Worse, speculation is often our (unconscious) way of putting off the decisions and actions that might change our routines—that might change *us*. We can pretend to be dealing with the issues when what we're really doing is avoiding the work. *And* avoiding our responsibility.

Confining ourselves to "the facts" doesn't rule out the use of imagination. It simply reminds us to *stay grounded,* to remember that Truth must be our ultimate foundation. Not what we *wish* were true, but what *is*.

And as much as we can use our power to "go within," to help us *connect* with Truth, the only way to know if we *have* connected with it is by testing our solutions *in the physical world*. By measuring their results... in fact.

I am thankful for my imagination. And I celebrate my ability to develop strategies that will transform and improve my physical reality.

10.06

I'll live. But I won't enjoy it!
ENSIGN CHEKOV: THE DEADLY YEARS: 3478.2

How do we react to disappointment or failure? What do we say to ourselves, what rituals can we use, to help us deal with it and move on with our lives—?

Chekov's response is clearly a common one. What's not so clear is whether he's serious when he says it.

Many of us, however, *are* serious. And unfortunately so. Because we thereby allow disappointment to darken our outlook. We may "live," but in a damaged state that begs for sympathy and closes our eyes to the very opportunities that might allow us to enjoy life again.

The first step to recovery is attitude. "I'll live" is actually a positive affirmation. By saying it, we not only declare our intention to survive the current setback, but to give ourselves the time to heal, to learn, to emerge stronger and wiser than we would if we hadn't had the experience.

Still, ultimate success hinges on what we mean by "I won't enjoy it." If we are determined to let our disappointments ruin our life, that's certainly within our power. But *not enjoying* the feeling of disappointment can also translate into a commitment to move *past* it. Precisely because we *don't* "enjoy it," we'll try again, we'll double our efforts, we'll commit to success or growth or recovery no matter how long it takes. Which is one of life's greatest joys.

I gain from having tried. I discover new resources as I try again. The Universe promises me eventual success. I will learn all I can in the meantime.

10.07

If there is a Cosmic Plan, is it not the height of hubris to think we can—or *should*—interfere?

COMMANDER RIKER : PEN PALS : 42695.3

Hubris: Ancient Greek for giving ourselves more credit than we deserve. Arrogance. Or, as some texts use the term, acting like gods when we are mere mortals.

Riker's question is not simply rhetorical. He's not saying we can't or shouldn't interfere in the lives of others. After all, what if the Cosmic Plan *calls* for us to come to someone else's rescue? *Hubris* might also refer to our arrogance in presuming we know enough *not* to interfere in other peoples' lives when, actually, we *should*.

In other words, nothing is automatic. Taking responsibility for our actions means responding to each new situation with our whole being, not just reacting out of habit or impulse. To know whether we're being called by the Cosmic Plan to play some specific role, we need to ask ourselves—again—what we think that Plan *is*.

The correct response to the question has less to do with *yes* or *no* than "What does The Universe require of me?" We are arrogant only to the extent that we consider our answer permanent. Or that we can arrive at it without receiving guidance from anyone else.

Not the least of whom are those we seek to help.

If I can help, I have the responsibility to consider whether I should. I will listen for the clues that come from within, and an invitation from without.

10.08

What your eyes show you is only the surface of reality.

LIEUTENANT TUVOK: COLD FIRE: Stardate Not Given

In some ways, the primitive mind was more advanced than ours. Before the advent of "scientific law," people were much more inclined to acknowledge other, unseen levels of reality. Invisible spirits who inhabited the rocks and trees were simply a pre-modern method for conceptualizing deeper forces at work—forces with whom people could establish a life-enhancing relationship.

Contemporary science has far surpassed this animistic view, if only in terms of the control it has given us over the physical world. It has also reassured us that there are specific, verifiable actions we can take to affect reality.

But this cause-and-effect view can make us skeptical of anything we can't manipulate in some purely mechanical way. We become accustomed to changing our lives solely through *physical* means, based on the limited view of reality provided by our sense organs.

The unfolding discoveries linking consciousness to matter have once again opened us to the earlier, "primitive" view. Our potential for affecting reality through unseen forces—that is, through meditation and spiritual disciplines—has been validated by quantum physics.

But you'll never know for sure unless you've tried it.

I trust my eyes, but I know there is even more I cannot see. I rededicate myself to that Voyage into the deeper realities.

10.09

**Courage doesn't mean you don't have fear.
It means you've learned to overcome it.**

LIEUTENANT PARIS: FACES: 48784.2

The person who truly feels no fear probably feels little *else*, either. Because the problem with trying to suppress any undesireable emotion is that you usually numb yourself to the *desireable* ones, too. If anything, the fact that your fear can pump you full of adrenaline and put every nerve-ending on red alert is a healthy sign that your emotional channels are open and fully operational.

Courage is often considered an "antidote" to fear, as if it's some drug that's supposed to calm jangling nerves and pump liquid confidence in place of adrenaline. But that analogy is as unfortunate as it is untrue. Because it implies that if we feel fear, we have an excuse not to act. Worse, it implies that courage is also a "feeling."

Courage is *not* a feeling. It is an attribute of our *behavior*. It means taking action even when we *lack* calm and confidence. In fact we are most "courageous" when we are fearful, when we're trembling in our proverbial boots; and yet something needs to be done and *we do it*.

As one of Terra's pre-holographic "movies" envisioned it, our life's mission is not to accumulate knowledge, not to "save our souls," but to *overcome our fears*.

On our Inner Voyage, the three are really one.

*My courage lies in combining these three things:
My knowledge, my connection to divinity, and the
emotional energy which lies even within my fear.*

10.10

It doesn't matter what you're made of. What matters is who you are.

COMMANDER CHAKOTAY: PROJECTIONS: 48892.1

A half-century earlier and seventy thousand light years across the galaxy, Captain Picard had already expressed a similar sentiment this way: "Let us not condemn anyone," he said, "for their bloodlines."

Not that the sentiment was original even then. Three thousand years before, a Romulan general wrote that he had more in common with the Klingons he was fighting than his fellow Romulans who had fled their attack.

In other words, courage and commitment are more important than chromosomes. Standing for something is what counts. Heroism transcends heritage.

Which is as true today as ever. What distinguishes us from others—and what makes us alike—is not a question of race or planetary origin. Or whether we're composed of flesh and bone, bionic parts, or pure energy.

As a great Terran King said, it's "the content of our character." It's the way we relate to the universe and to other living beings. It's whether we tend to think of others as competitors or compatriots; whether we treat the universe as a resource to waste and exploit, or a garden to care for and cultivate.

And thereby cultivate Who We Are.

My body is only a vehicle. In the way I live my life I define my true identity. By the way I treat others I expose—and continue to refine—who I am.

10.11

Sometimes it's the result that counts.

ENGINEER LA FORGE: LONELY AMONG US: 41249.3

Virtually everyone fails more than once before they finally succeed at something. Our failures are never truly failures us if they serve as "practice," if they show us what *doesn't* work, if we learn something new.

But sometimes we've already learned all we need to know in order to achieve our goal. Now we simply need to perform the task successfully, to break that habit once and for all, to act out the ideals we presume to believe in.

Practice is over. It's time for *results*.

Because even though it's healthy to accept failure as a natural part of the learning process, we shouldn't allow ourselves to become *too* comfortable with it. "Failure is okay" can serve as an easy excuse for no longer trying. "Everyone fails" can become a handy slogan for people who've decided that overcoming their faults is too much work, who would rather hide from their responsibility.

During one of Terra's first spaceflights, an accident destroyed much of the oxygen supply. It seemed the "astronauts" would not survive their return trip. The officer in charge of finding a solution put it simply: "Failure is not an option." It would not be enough to *try* to bring them home safely. *Doing* it was all that mattered. They did.

Sometimes we, too, need that kind of pressure.

I accept failure only as a prelude to my success. I already know enough to achieve many of the goals I have set for myself. I am ready. I have the will.

10.12

The riskier the road, the greater the profit.

QUARK: LITTLE GREEN MEN: Stardate Not Given

The same sentiment comes in a dozen shapes and sizes, a few of which we've already seen in this *Manual*. Quark could hardly be expected to keep from putting his own monetary spin on it.

Not that he's wrong. In purely economic terms, we *do* increase our "profit potential" by learning a skill others don't have, or performing a job others won't do. The more unique the skill, or the more uniquely willing we are to take on a certain job, the more economic value we have.

For Quark, "riskier roads" mean opportunities. If the risks were small, if *any*one could do it, the competition would inevitably push prices down. But with higher risk decreasing competition, prices soar. And thus profits.

Of course, this isn't a lesson in economics. What we're *really* talking about is the road which leads to *spiritual* rewards—inner wealth, not latinum. We're talking about valuing ourselves not by what the market would pay us, but by the "content of our character." *And* by our willingness to take the risks required to improve it.

There is another sentiment that also comes in a dozen shapes and sizes, and goes like this: "What does it profit us if we gain the whole galaxy, but lose our souls?"

The greatest risk, it turns out, is *not* taking that Road.

I measure my "profit" by the improvements I make in my character, not in my credit account. Taking risks is the price of transforming myself.

10.13

It's not only a matter of attitude. It's a matter of experience.

CAPTAIN JANEWAY: LEARNING CURVE: 48846.5

Attitude is crucial, of course. A positive attitude can break through the Tholian Webs which keep us bound to our past, or that ensare us in new, unproductive habits and unfulfilling lifestyles. Changing our attitude can not only open doors in the world "outside" us, it can unblock the channels to our own inner resources and energies.

Which is why attitude is called the "warp drive of transformation." But even if it can fuel our journey, attitude can't chart the course. For that we need experience.

There are two types. The first implies increasing ability. If we do something often enough we become "good at it." Eventually we'll have encountered all the variables in the process and fine-tuned our responses. It's all "familiar."

But an equally important kind of experience concerns our explorations into *un*familiar territory. Which means placing ourselves in new situations where we'll be forced to learn as we go; where our direction becomes clear only as we make real choices in the context of real life.

In the sheer act of *living* we learn what books and other people cannot teach us. We give The Universe an opportunity to reveal its truths directly by willingly putting ourselves at risk. And because we *need* to know, we learn.

With that attitude, we can't help but gain experience.

I will look for new opportunities to learn about the world, other people, and myself. I accept the risks.

10.14

No one can deny that the seed of violence remains within each of us. We must recognize that, because that violence is capable of consuming each of us.

CAPTAIN PICARD: VIOLATIONS: 45429.3

It's not just violence. *Every* ancient instinct, every primordial drive, remains buried in our biology, subject to a sudden resurgence under just the right conditions.

Some of us may characterize these latent instincts as "inner demons." Others believe our demons are quite real. Both are ways of acknowledging the legacy of our past while trying to rise above it. In other words, the seeds may still be there, but we don't need to fertilize them. We might even keep some weed killer handy, just in case.

But vigilance against our primitive tendencies is only part of our challenge. The fact is, we may have struggled with *other* inner demons—more modern ones, like an obsession with money or material things, or a case of low self-esteem, or a serious addiction. And having finally overcome them, we assume our struggle is behind us.

Not necessarily. Because the seeds of these problems also remain within us, subject to resurgence. Look at it as The Universe's way of keeping us from becoming too confident. Or for keeping us connected to others who are now having the same struggle... and who need our help.

I will guard against my lowest inclinations by striving to achieve my highest. I grow even stronger by striving to bring out the highest in others.

10.15

We are living beings, not playthings.
CAPTAIN KIRK: THE SQUIRE OF GOTHOS: 2124.5

There are two equally-important themes here: The first is about our relationships with others.

Studies have proven that individuals who commit serious acts of abuse usually have a diminished capacity for imagining the personal lives of other people—that others have hopes and feelings and families, too; that they are conscious and autonomous. That they are *real*.

We all share responsibility for this defect. For we are all guilty at times of relating to others more as "types" than individuals. Instead, we must acknowledge the feelings, the *personhood*, of others in every social interaction.

We must also be wary of "entertainment" that reduces people to objects; that treats life and death so casually. Especially since holosuites and the "popular media" act as substitute teachers for growing minds. It's frightening to think that the rules for social behavior are often learned more by media modeling than by direct experience.

But Kirk's statement is about *us*, too.

It's about the fact that we shouldn't treat our own lives so casually, either. Because the time we're given is irreplaceable. This self is beyond value. We should no more consider our*selves* as playthings than we should others.

In the end, the two can't be separated.

For every person I encounter, I will find some way to acknowledge their presence and affirm their worth. I will thereby reaffirm my own.

10.16

We should not fear the unknown. We should embrace it!

LANEL: FIRST CONTACT: Stardate Not Given

The *Manual* understands "faith" not in terms of dogma or doctrine, or what we merely *say* we believe in. Faith is a characteristic of individuals. It's the set of personal convictions and attitudes each of us demonstrates *by our behavior,* both in public and in private.

And one of the most crucial parts of this personal faith is the way we face The Unknown.

For many of us, "fear" is the operative word. If we can't be absolutely *sure* about the outcome of some new experience, we often won't even try. And yet, ironically, what we *can* be sure of is that if we don't try something new, if we don't seek out new experiences and new perspectives, we can't expect to grow. After all, what we've already done is what brought us to where we are now. And the best way to insure that we *stay* there is simply to go on doing what we've been doing.

To embrace the unknown is to recognize that our fulfillment—our very salvation—lies in what is yet to come. We must learn to see the unknown as a repository of hidden treasures and hidden opportunities, without which learning and transformation are impossible.

And fortunately, each of us has a key.

I face the unknown with joyful expectation. I anticipate new experiences that may change my life—and the lives of those around me—for the better.

10.17

We certainly have the right to exercise control over our own bodies.

COMMANDER RIKER: UP THE LONG LADDER: 42823.2

In recent centuries, the very same words have been used to justify all sorts of social customs. From "reproductive rights" to recreational drug use, the popular justification almost always came down to the claim that "our own bodies" were off-limits, legislatively speaking.

And certainly, allowing outside control over our most primal possession raises grave issues. Where would it stop? If others can control our bodies, why not our minds? And then what happens to personal responsibility?

Actually, it's responsibility, not "rights," that Riker is talking about here. Because unless we have some private domain over which we are the sole judge and jury, we can never *learn* personal responsibility. The risk of harming ourselves—even irreparably—is the price we must pay for being allowed to see and *feel* the consequences of our actions in the most direct way possible. And therefore to become fully responsible for them.

Life would be easier if we weren't forced to confront the personal "demons" and addictions that may already have damaged us. Society might run more smoothly if outside authorities could be allowed to "save us from ourselves." But we would never grow into the responsible, fully-realized selves The Universe wants us to be, either.

I accept not only my "right" but my responsibility to exercise control over my own body.

10.18

Sooner or later you're gonna hafta choose whose side you're on. Everyone has to choose sides.

MAJOR KIRA: NECESSARY EVIL: 47282.5

We can't remain neutral forever. At some point we must come to a decision about what's right and what's wrong—at least for the time being, at least for ourselves. That, in fact, is how we *define* ourselves.

But we don't need to choose immediately. We usually have time to consider both "sides," to objectively learn what we can about each. *Not* doing so would close off options and deny ourselves opportunities for growth.

Yet even when we *do* choose sides, that decision need not separate us from others who take the opposite position. Political parties and religions, for example, share many of the same goals, though the tactics to reach them may differ. Choosing one method needn't suggest that others are evil, or that their members are now "enemies."

Neither is our choice necessarily permanent. The view from the "inside" may reveal facts that were hidden to us before. Making a careful choice can require a long, circuitous journey. Often our strongest commitments are made only after we've actively supported the opposing view.

The point is, sometimes we can't begin to decide until we take sides—*any* side. It's only a start. But it *is* a start.

Choosing sides is part of my decision-making process. I will give my choices adequate time to confirm themselves as I live with their consequences.

10.19

Forever is just another day. Forever is just another journey.

LIEUTENANT UHURA: THE CONSCIENCE OF THE KING: 2817.6

It might help to know that Uhura was *singing* these lines, not speaking them. In the context of a song, therefore, the words were probably less for meaning than for effect. After all, no one would seriously compare the entire scope of time to another humdrum day at the office, or a Sunday cruise around one's star system... *Would* they?

Maybe. Especially if the purpose of the song is to point out that "forever" isn't real; that it's only an illusion.

In fact it's an illusion *we* invented. Forever is simply a way of conceiving time. Like "space," it's a concept whereby we take a bite-sized unit of our experience and push it to its theoretical limits. And for no good reason.

Because the concept can end up squashing us. In the context of "forever," our lives can seem so meaningless, so insignificant. Compared to endless time, how can anything we do make a difference? Why act? Why *care?*

Uhura reminds us to keep our feet firmly planted in *what we can experience.* Since we live day-by-day, our individual acts have measurable significance. We can identify these acts, see their effects on ourselves and others, and connect them into a narrative which transforms our lives into a Voyage from Point A to Point B.

And now, once again, we are in the Captain's chair.

My life is no theoretical concept. I accept the gift—and the responsibility—of living in the now.

10.20

Guidance, insight, loopholes... I'll take anything I can get.

CAPTAIN SISKO: FAVOR THE BOLD: Stardate Not Given

It's easy enough to see how guidance and insight can help us along our daily Voyages. But *loopholes*—?

Like some attorney who gets clients off the hook by exploiting unintended omissions in our laws, are we supposed to weasel out of our problems by searching for cracks in the laws of Karma?

Hardly. Sisko isn't advocating anything dishonest here, because "loopholes" in the law—natural law, anyway—aren't unintentional. In fact, The Universe seems to put them there precisely for us to *find* them.

It's a loophole in the law of gravity that permits a satellite to orbit the planet, or allows a million tons of starship to float above its surface. What we call "loopholes" in the law are *part* of the law. So what looks like something that chains us to the earth gives us the power to escape it.

The same thing applies in our personal life. The events that appear to stop our progress actually hide clues to a new, more fulfilling path. The web of circumstances that seem to ensnare us in bad habits and limited choices may act as our springboard to greater freedom.

Once we realize that the forces opposing us can also be used to our benefit, anything is possible.

Even if it seems otherwise, the laws of the universe are designed to assist my progress. Hidden within everything I can't do are the things I can.

10.21

You need to go on with your life. Don't worry about me.

NEELIX: JETREL: 48832.1

It's an admirable thing to say... if only we *meant* it.

Yet how often we tell others not to worry when we mean exactly the opposite! It's a common ploy for inducing guilt. And what we're really saying (or threatening) is, "Unless you *do* worry, you'll prove that you don't care."

Admittedly, all of us remain connected with one another at some deeper level, even when we've "gone on" with our lives. But there are times when we must publicly sever our bonds, when we must *openly acknowledge* the end of certain relationships. We must do this not only for our own sakes—to make "emotional room" for new relationships and new growth—but to release others from any "baggage" that might prevent *them* from growing.

In fact, to release others from constricting emotional bonds is a gift we can give even to those with whom we remain close. After all, to befriend or love someone is to free them to *be themselves.* It means allowing them to follow the urgings of their own hearts. It means not imposing any obligations on them they wouldn't feel naturally.

And that makes possible one of our greatest joys: To be loved by another despite their freedom; to give permission for them to leave, and know they've chosen to stay.

I can bond with others only when I have fully released them, and only when I myself am fully free. That is the price of genuine love; I will gladly pay it.

10.22

Friendship must dare to risk, or it's not friendship.

CAPTAIN PICARD: CONSPIRACY: 41780.2

In an age defined by micro-genetic technology and distances measured in parsecs, genuine friendship is a rare commodity. Having a "relationship" doesn't require it: We can be Starfleet crewmen, co-workers, fellow members of clubs and races and political alliances—even partners in marriage!—without being "friends."

To be a friend means recognizing another person as a fellow voyager on a journey you have decided to take together. The journey is not so much a common path to a common destination; rather, it's a mode of travel during which you pause regularly to share experiences, reflect on the obstacles and lessons, and encourage one another along the path each is taking. Even if they diverge.

But it's more than tea and sympathy. There are risks. Because when a friend falls down, *we* hurt too. What's more, we may see obstacles our friend can't, or we'll interpret the roadsigns differently. Our friendship comes to a crossroads: Should we intervene to keep our friend from stumbling? Or should we simply "be there" to help after they've fallen? Either choice is risky.

To take that risk is the price of preserving friendship. To make *no* choice is a roadsign that says, "Dead end."

I will take risks to turn "relationships" into friendships, and keep existing friendships from turning into mere relationships. My friends are worth it.

10.23

There's only one kind of woman or man. You either believe in yourself or you don't.

CAPTAIN KIRK: MUDD'S WOMEN: 1329.1

It's like saying a woman is "slightly pregnant." The words don't mesh. Either she *is*, or she *isn't*. There is, by definition, no room for qualifiers.

In the same way, an individual can be said to "believe in herself/himself"—or *not*. There is no middle ground.

The question is, *how* do you believe in yourself? Is it a function of self-confidence? Is it about being "right" or "successful" often enough in the past that you can safely assume you'll be right or successful in the future?

Hardly. People can believe in themselves even while feeling unsure about the "correctness" of their decisions or the outcome of their actions. In fact, it's their belief that drives them to proceed *despite* all those uncertainties.

It's the belief that life is less about being right or successful than being honest and courageous. It's about your willingness to try, to make mistakes, to continually push the boundaries of your experience, to recognize your place in a larger whole and to take responsibility for it.

Finally, it's about saying "Yes!" to your own life.

To believe in yourself is to affirm that life has meaning. Regardless of the outcome. Despite the hardships. And even if you still haven't discovered what that meaning *is*.

I can believe this: That my life is good, even when doubt clouds my vision; that I will endure and grow, in failure as well as success.

10.24

Those that hate and fight must stop themselves. Otherwise it is not stopped.

SPOCK: DAY OF THE DOVE: Stardate Not Given

There are two equally important ways to understand Spock's statement. The first interpretation places the emphasis on the word "stop."

Because the things we're all doing wrong in our lives —acting selfishly, judging others, bickering, sometimes even fighting—must be *stopped*. Once we recognize how we're hurting ourselves, we must put an end to the damage. There's no magic solution, no easy way. We simply decide to stop, realizing that The Universe has empowered us to do so. And then we *stop*.

The second interpretation places the emphasis on "themselves." Or, by implication, on *our*selves.

Or by implication, on *you*.

Because nobody can end your bad habits and harmful thoughts *for* you. Someone else may intervene and *make* you stop, yes. But *being prevented* from acting out your lower impulses isn't the same as "stopping" them.

Only you can do that.

And only then can you—and, by implication, any of us—be transformed.

The Universe gives me the power, and the sole responsibility, to transform myself. I accept that responsibility. I accept that power.

10.25

My logic was not in error. But I was.
LIEUTENANT TUVOK: PRIME FACTORS: 48642.5

The trouble with logic isn't with the *logic*. It's with the people who *use* it.

Analyzing any set of facts to produce a logical decision does not insure that the decision is "right." For one thing, logic can only work with the data available to it. Relevant data may not yet be known. Certain factors may not be reducible to the catagories logic can digest.

Worse, relevant details can be withheld by dishonest "logicians", or specifically selected to produce a desired conclusion. Dictatorships throughout human history—and throughout the Quadrant—are populated by such masters of manipulation. And despite their perfectly "logical" policies, they are no less "wrong."

Tuvoc's words, however, are not about defending ourselves against dictators. They're about guarding against our own tendency to let logic *alone* dictate our actions. Or to pick and choose what we consider "relevant" so our own use of logic produces exactly the conclusion we happen to be looking for at the moment.

It's called "rationalizing". We've all done it. We must be vigilant in preventing it. And we must be big enough to admit, whenever we catch ourselves *doing* it again, that we are "in error."

My logic may be flawless. But I will remember to temper it with compassion... and with the perspective I can achieve only by looking beyond myself.

10.26

I'm really easy to get along with most of the time. But I don't like bullies and I don't like threats.

CAPTAIN JANEWAY: STATE OF FLUX: 48658.2

We've all had experiences with "bullies"—people who use their physical size or power to take whatever they want, or to continually remind us "who's boss."

One of the first signs of our developing empathy is the fact that we can get just as angry seeing *other* people mistreated by bullies as when we ourselves are threatened. The playground bully, pitiful child that he is, at least serves to link others together through shared feelings. *My* experience of fear, anger and injustice at the hands of a bully is what makes me all the more sympathetic to *yours*.

But it's our *next* response that changes things. Instead of reacting to the bullies in our lives by threatening them back, we can express our anger like Captain Janeway.

"I don't like bullies" defines the situation in a way that still allows for reconciliation and growth. We desire harmony; do *they* really want to defy a Law of the Universe? We demonstrate our inner strength by not responding in the usual knee-jerk fashion; their noisy blustering, in contrast, only proves how weak and insecure they must be.

And it is that contrast which inspires growth: In the bully who finally sees his own flaws—and in us, by confirming that if even *bullies* can change, so can we.

I no longer react in anger when I feel threatened. I will pause, look for options, and set the example.

10.27

The more they overtake the plumbing, the more they stop up the drain!

"SCOTTY": THE SEARCH FOR SPOCK: 8210.3

What psychologists call "the need to control" is, in most planetary cultures, a primarily *male* characteristic. The trait can manifest positively in the quest for knowledge, or the ongoing search for new ways of doing things. But it can also manifest in a quest for power, or the search for what *can* be done rather than what *should* be done.

And sometimes what should be done is to simply *let go,* to give up control, to trust nature to do its job.

Which has nothing to do with the plumbing on a Federation Starship... except *this:*

The universe has a kind of built-in plumbing, too. Long before our arrival it developed a finely-tuned system for delivering the necessities of life and carrying off "waste." *We* didn't design or install this system. Nor *could* we have. But what we *can* do, instead, is simply allow it to keep flowing—to nurture the process, not "overtake" it; because if we did, we'd almost certainly clog up the drain.

"Allowing" and "nurturing," in most cultures, are seen as *female* characteristics. These traits are manifest in giving birth to the new rather than constructing it; in following our bliss, not chasing it; in aligning our wills with The Universe instead of demanding that it conform to *ours.*

Let this be a parable of The Inner Voyage.

I release the flow of Spirit within me. I allow my higher Self to be born. I nurture the Life I am given.

10.28

I wasn't programmed for any of this! It's just not acceptable!

THE DOCTOR: PHAGE: 48532.4

The holographic Doctor has once again elegantly expressed our own feelings and frustrations. And the frustration, this time around, has to do with confronting new situations for which we have no prior experience.

These "new situations" can be potentially positive as well as harmful. Ironically, we're often just as frightened of success as we are of failure or injury. The problem is less in the outcome than not knowing how to *handle* it.

So we take refuge in habit. Familiar routines give us a sense of security—even when those routines stunt our growth or keep us mired in destructive relationships.

At least we know what to expect, right?

It's the *un*expected that frightens us. Or rather, that threatens our ego. Ego, after all, is our current "programming." It's a superficial "image" of Who We Are *now*. And like someone facing his own demise, the ego will do everything it can to preserve its "life", the Status Quo.

Submitting to this rigid ego amounts to worshipping an "idol." The Universe calls us to reject this image—first by taking responsibility for our own programming, then by *changing* it. And what was once "just not acceptable" becomes our greatest source of joy and fulfillment.

I'm in charge of my programming now. In spite of my fears, I welcome the new situations that lead to learning, growth, and transformation.

10.29

We've seen development at different rates on different planets.
LIEUTENANT UHURA: A PRIVATE LITTLE WAR: 4211.4

A well-documented pattern of evolution can be seen throughout the galaxy: Given the proper conditions, autonomous, sentient life inevitably develops, along with a natural interdependence within that species. This natural "community" is later overshadowed by individualism and privatism; which are eventually brought into a more productive balance between individual and society.

So the course is virtually locked in. But the rates of progress can vary greatly. Or grind to a halt. In fact, many planetary cultures become so mired in the era of individualism—the "I/Me/Mine" stage—that one final, cathartic orgy of selfishness is the only way to break through it.

Unfortunately, if weapons of mass destruction are part of the mix, the results can be disastrous. A few planetary races have had to virtually start over after such a destructive catharsis. And survivors don't always learn the lesson.

So it is in our personal lives. Our ultimate destinations are given. But our rates vary. Side-trips can seem endless. Or we become stuck in various stages, sometimes breaking out of our patterns only at great cost—to others as well as ourselves. But if we become *conscious* of our own development, our journeys seem to go a bit smoother.

We might even learn our lessons "once and for all."

I celebrate the Voyage I've been on, despite its turns and stops, because I know the ultimate destination.

10.30

Tempering is taken to extremes... We'll need a fine edge that won't dull at the first touch of resistance.
CAPTAIN PICARD : PEN PALS : 42695.3

In developing any skill or discipline, there comes a point when practice no longer helps. In fact, *beyond* that point, not only do we stop seeing any further gains, we may begin to *lose* our skills. Why?

Because what we begin practicing is *practicing*. We end up "working out" for the sake of the workout. Or we meditate because meditation is now an end in itself. The connection of our discipline to our "real world" dissolves. Worse, practice *substitutes* for the real world.

To push the Captain's analogy, we must temper our spiritual "edge" not simply to make it glisten in the light, but to increase its ability to cut through the problems we encounter. If we get carried away by all the polishing, we end up with an edge that has no substance behind it. Or one we're afraid to use for fear it may get nicked.

Our spiritual discipline must integrate seamlessly with the rest of our lives. An effective meditation encourages us to immediately seek out opportunities in our daily experience to *apply* what we've learned.

That's why, when you've finished reading this, you'll know just what to do.

Even as I read these words my mind is searching for ways to test the skills I am developing. I accept problems I encounter as part of my daily practice.

10.31

> **Like the man said, "The only thing we have to fear is fear itself."**
>
> ENSIGN KIM: THE THAW: Stardate Not Given

There is some debate whether "the man" Kim refers to was Franklin Roosevelt, the pre-Federation leader who presided over one of Terra's most serious economic depressions—or whether he meant Ru'agh KoHbar, an even earlier Klingon leader who inspired his fellow warriors to repel a vastly superior Romulan invasion force.

It hardly matters. Thousands of leaders from hundreds of planets have made virtually the same statement, many of them recorded millenia before either Terra or Qo'noS *had* any written records. Because the fact is, fear is an almost universal experience. And although it is as irrational as it is universal, it follows certain identifiable "rules."

One of those rules is that *fear feeds on itself.* Our original fear is rarely the culprit. How easily we let it grow, how often we seek out other people with the same fear so we can "justify" our own; and then how others' fears end up doubling and re-doubling our own until a kind of mass hysteria sets in—*those* are the real culprits.

Another rule is that this hysteria is almost unstoppable until it runs its course. Which simply means that the best counter-measure is not to let it happen in the first place.

That which creates our fear is not the enemy. *Fear* is.

I confront my fears as soon as I sense them. While accepting their role in signaling potential problems, I will make sure that "fear itself" isn't one of them.

SECTOR

CORRESPONDING TO THE TERRAN MONTH OF
November

11.01

It's life. You can miss it if you don't open your eyes.

CAPTAIN SISKO: THE VISITOR: Stardate Not Given

Learning how to stay "focused" can take years. Or a lifetime. Still, it's well worth the effort. To know what you want to do, and then to concentrate your whole being on *doing* it, is one of life's greatest pleasures.

But our lives do not take place in a vacuum. (Not even when we're traveling in space!) We are connected to other people, other life. And we need to *remain* connected.

Because as important as our own experience is, we are incomplete if we cut ourselves off from the experience of others. As trustworthy as our own insight is, we can still use someone else's perspective now and then. Especially when we're so focused on one task—or one purpose, or one phase of our life—that we forget everything else.

Or when something bad happens to us and we retreat into our shells. That's often when we need others most: To bring balance back into our lives; to remind us that goodness still surrounds us, that joy is still possible.

The opposite is also true. Because we can sometimes experience such a run of success and happiness that we forget how much tragedy, how much misery, still exists.

But misery is life, too. To open our eyes to it—*all* of it—keeps us linked. If nothing else, to our own feelings.

I stay in touch with my own feelings—and with my self*—only as I maintain my connection to other people, and to the world around me.*

11.02

Spare me the analysis. It's enough that it works!

DR. McCOY: MIRI: 2713.5

Sometimes asking how or why is the worst thing we can do. Sometimes *not understanding* is what "works."

The rational mind is a wonderful thing. Few people would give back their intellect for the unreflective, half-conscious existence of some primordial Garden of Eden. And yet, in harvesting the fruits of the Tree of Knowledge, our minds *do* occasionally get in our own way.

Most of our body's life-preserving functions evolved long before rational thought—and still work best without it. Healing from illness, for example, is a natural process we can short-circuit if we over-analyze or worry about it. Not that we can't use mental affirmations and medical technologies. It's our egotistical need to "control" the process that becomes a problem. If we would only *accept* our healing, we would improve our recovery.

Our emotional and spiritual lives operate in much the same way. If we learn to *trust* our inner resources, to celebrate and strengthen our connection to our Source, we will receive the guidance and healing we seek.

"Let go and let *God*" is the traditional mantra. It's the difference between praying for what we *think* we need, and attuning oneself to a Universe that *already knows*.

I accept my inner, subconscious resources as well as my intellect. I will seek a balance that works for me, and embrace opportunities to test it.

11.03

I find that maintaining protocol reminds us of where we came from, and hopefully where we're going.

CAPTAIN JANEWAY: EQUINOX: Stardate Not Given

Substitute the word "tradition" for "protocol," and you have an explanation for why many religions and spiritual disciplines seem to cling to the past. And why *we* do.

What we're clinging to is not so much "the past" but our *experience*. And our sense of direction.

There's no question that doing things the way we've always done them can hinder our growth. Not to mention that it doesn't always work—especially when we're confronting new situations we've never faced before.

But it's precisely in new situations that tradition can save us. For one thing, what we see as "new" often turns out to be the same conditions dressed in different clothing. If we're too willing to throw out what's worked for us in the past, we devalue our own hard-won experience.

We also lose the formula for self-transformation. After all, we don't automatically rebuild our principles from scratch every time we meet a challenge that requires us to change. We modify our existing theories. We make adjustments to current behavior patterns. We alter course.

Protocol isn't lifeless, unchanging. It evolves and grows just as we do. But not so fast that we forget Who We Are.

In honoring the past, I remember who I am. In tracing my Voyage from past to present, I draw a line pointing toward my future.

11.04

You can't snatch people and put them into your fantasies and expect them to respond.
COMMANDER RIKER : TRUE Q : 46192.3

Back in Terra's early days of imaging technology, there was a thriving religious subculture whose members refused to allow "photographs" to be taken of them. The Amish (as they are still known) were therefore regarded as a bit "quaint." Maybe they were just being careful.

Not because they thought the images contained some sort of magic, like the voodoo dolls that could reportedly be used to "control" the people they resembled. It's just that photographs were such superficial copies of people. They couldn't capture a person's true identity. Nor could they speak for themselves, or *defend* themselves.

Which tempted whoever possessed the photograph to read any personality into the picture they might wish. That fantasy would then become attached to the visual image. And *that* would inevitably affect their expectations and reactions to the *real* person should they ever meet.

Our fantasies about other people operate in the same way. We become boxed in by our "images" and private thoughts about others, rather than letting their behavior and interactions *with us* define who they are.

People need freedom to be themselves, to grow toward their *own* vision, not ours. Only if we give them that freedom do we have the right to expect it for ourselves.

I am not bound by others' fantasies. I am who my thoughts, intentions and actions reveal me to be.

11.05

Who am I to argue with me?

DR. BASHIR: VISIONARY: Stardate Not Given

Conflicted. It describes the psychological state when one part of us says "yes," another part "no." It's the painful condition of having an idea of where we want to be, while realizing how far we have to go before we get there.

In Bashir's statement, "I" represents the self we *can be,* and "me" is the person we *are.* Too often, *who we are* dominates the argument. Which effectively stops further growth. Our present identity, with all its weaknesses and self-enforced limitations, remains in control.

But the very fact of internal conflict is actually a good sign. Conflict confirms that we stand at the threshold of change, and it's only natural to experience some resistance from an ego which fears being replaced.

The Vulcan approach can help us here—first, by simply reminding us that our egos are not our *selves.* Who We Are is a transitory phenomenon, a work-in-progress. And if we look at that "work" without emotion, without attachment, we can begin to decide what kind of person we'd like to be… and then make the logical choices that bring us more and more into alignment with that vision.

Who am I to argue with me—? "Me" considers it an argument. "I" understands that it's really a healthy discussion about how best to realize our potential.

It is natural to experience inner conflict. I trust the Voyage I have embarked on to guide me through conflict to higher awareness, and to my higher Self.

11.06

It was a mistake... I have made some fine ones in my time.

CAPTAIN PICARD: FIRST CONTACT: Stardate Not Given

Recognizing that we're not perfect isn't meant to excuse bad behavior, or to absolve us from the continuing goal of personal and communal redemption. (Or at least "self-improvement.") Indeed, redemption applies *only* to the ongoing refinement of that which is *im*perfect.

Actually, our imperfections are the required first steps toward improvement. It's not just that getting it wrong *precedes* getting it right. That's what *helps us* get it right.

Like Captain Picard, the most inspiring role models in Starfleet history did not breeze through The Academy—or go on to serve The Federation—with spotless records. The same with *human* history. The most beloved Holy Ones were cherished as much for their raw humanity as their "divinity." Even the paradigm Avatars and Incarnations had their moments of blind rage, their dark nights of doubt, their strategic blunders... their imperfections.

And the reason we continue to draw inspiration from these models is precisely because they *were* so imperfect; because they were as fully "human" as *we* are; because they were subject to the same flaws and temptations of living "in the flesh"—and yet they kept going, kept trying, kept growing. And if *they* could, so can *we*.

I will not condone my mistakes simply because others make them, too. Others learn *from them,* transcend *them. I choose to follow their example.*

11.07

We're going to get through this together!
KES:PHAGE:48532.4

Virtually no sentient species has yet been discovered—from one end of the galaxy to the other—whose evolutionary origins designed it for a totally isolated existence. It's true that certain individuals within a species may become accustomed to being alone; a few may even come to prefer it. But their biological make-up practically *shouts* for companionship.

We are, in other words, hard-wired for community.

This is no more evident than during periods of turmoil or personal distress. Even our apparent instinct to withdraw at such times, to "be by ourselves," is a call to be "missed" by someone, a plea to be rescued from conditions that feel like we alone have been selected to suffer.

Except that we are never truly "alone." And we must not allow anyone *else* to remain alone for long. Because study after study has proven that social isolation destroys individuals—and eventually destroys the societies that allow those individuals' wounds to fester. Whether the wounds are real or imagined.

Our personal and communal destinies are as intertwined as the nerves in our brains. There is nothing we can't "get through" if we go through it together. And few things we can't achieve if we *do* it together.

My consolation, my strength, comes from reaching out to others—to give *help as much as receive it.*

11.08

When we do battle, it is only because we have no choice.

CAPTAIN KIRK: THE SQUIRE OF GOTHOS: 2124.5

Almost without exception, people who go out looking for a fight are really at war with themselves. "Enemies" only reflect the inner demons they are still battling.

But even when we've overcome our aggressive tendencies, open conflict with others can sometimes seem unavoidable. Or even the *right* thing to do.

Kirk's fellow crewmembers knew better. "War is never imperative," Dr. McCoy reminds us. "There are always alternatives," Spock would add, raising an eyebrow.

And there *are*. So is Captain Kirk mistaken?

Not if we read between the lines. When we resort to violence, personally or communally, it's not because we *have* no choice. It's because we *think* we have no choice.

Maybe we think we're alone. Or we think no one else can (or *will*) intervene. Or we're so emotionally close to the situation that we can't think straight to begin with.

But that only goes to show how much we need others to point out what we often can't see ourselves. We need a network of people—the more diverse the better—who may have been down this path before; who can help both sides visualize the consequences. And who, together, can keep the peace long enough to let us work things out.

"I have no choice" is a statement of perspective, not fact. I can always call on others, and on my own inner Light, to help change my perspective.

11.09

There are times when it's best just to let things out.

COUNSELOR TROI: PARALLELS: 47391.2

Much has already been said about our bodies' needs—about the importance of keeping in touch with the physical/emotional legacy we've inherited from our species' evolution. And the fact is, if we don't continually work on integrating body and mind, we risk *dis*-integration. Or, in the medical jargon of past centuries, schizophrenia.

Of course, there are layers of social conventions concerning the "proper" expression of physical and emotional urges, as well as sound reasons for *not* expressing them. We learn to control our anger because it might destroy crucial relationships. We restrain our sexual instincts because unchecked reproduction now works *against* our species' survival. We also choke back tears; we stifle our laughter; and we try to hide how frightened we really are.

And the toll can be devastating. Because the psychic energy of all those repressed emotions doesn't just go away. It builds like water behind a dam. Finding ways to rechannel that energy—art, perhaps, or athletics—is essential. But sometimes the best solution is simply to find a "safe haven" where those emotions can be expressed in their most primitive form: To cry in sorrow, pound our fists in anger, and shout for joy. Because dams break.

It is healthy and natural to release my emotions. I will find a private place, or relationship, or group, where I can do so safely, and in mutual trust.

11.10

Curious how my failure, added to your own, should improve your feelings.

LIEUTENANT TUVOK: STATE OF FLUX: 48568.2

It *is* curious. Most of us are so conscious of our own faults and mistakes that we find great reassurance in the faults and mistakes of others. It's a healthy response if it prevents us from being too harsh on ourselves, if it frees us to make the mistakes that precede genuine growth.

But there's a danger: This kind of "reassurance" can easily develop into "delight." And then we start *looking* for faults and weaknesses in others—especially in our competitors, or even our leaders. We begin to revel in scandal, calling out the media bloodhounds to dig up still more dirt, to spell out everything they find in lurid detail.

Why? Because it serves to further excuse our *own* weakness. Because if we concentrate on others' defects we can ignore our own. *And* we can continue to avoid the self-transformation that, deep down, we already know is needed but our egos hope to delay as long as possible.

We need to counter this mindset. Not so much by turning a deaf ear to the latest gossip, or by deciding not to download the latest edition of *Galactic Enquirer*. The solution is to revel in our achievements for a change, to focus on the *good* things we find in each other.

And what's even *more* "curious" is that we'll not only improve our feelings, we'll improve our *lives*.

I will look upon others' faults as a reminder to work on my own. I will find something good in everyone.

11.11

The more we fight each other, the weaker we'll get and the less chance we'll have.

CAPTAIN SISKO: THE WAY OF THE WARRIOR: 49011.4

One sure indication of progress on our Inner Voyage relates to how fully we've overcome our inbred violence.

The biological roots of violence are strong in most sentient species, and usually stronger in one sex. The urge to inflict harm is literally a primitive one, connected with our emergence from the Animal Kingdom. It was the inevitable outcome of our competition for territory, for reproductive dominance, for self-preservation.

But it almost never meant death. Violence was the painful, pre-sentient, pre-verbal message to go find another valley to live in, or another mate to live with—or at least to submit to someone else's rules about where and with whom to live. Killing was rarely necessary to make the point. And still *is* for most non-sentient species.

Ironic that this same non-lethal violence, combined with our technological "progress," has now turned us into killers. It has also brought mass destruction of property and endless arms races, not to mention the stealing of precious resources from other, peaceful uses.

As citizens of the universe, our progress depends on fighting *this legacy,* not each other. Fortunately, the more we recognize our weakness, the more chance we'll have.

Within me are echoes of the distant past. To go on living in the present, I must transcend the past by affirming the person I wish to become in the future.

11.12

Our job is not to police the galaxy.
COMMANDER RIKER: LOUD AS A WHISPER: 42477.2

The policies of governments begin with individuals. People tend to transfer what they believe privately, what works in their own personal lives, to the public level.

It's possible, therefore, to read Riker's words not so much as a statement about Federation policy as a warning to each of us *personally*.

Because all too often we *do* take the role of policeman. We monitor what others are doing, who their friends are; we make judgments. And sometimes we intervene by offering advice, or helping to solve problems—or even by forcing our lifestyle and standards on others.

Such "help" is rarely appreciated, and may even create an atmosphere of resentment or rebellion. Especially if it's ongoing. Or if it stifles others' freedom to make mistakes, to develop their capacity to think for themselves.

Our "job" is to police our *own* lives. In fact, when we find ourselves meddling in other peoples' lives, it's probably because we haven't been policing our own properly. Often, the only way our subconscious can show us the flaws we still need to fix in ourselves is *through others*.

So let's concentrate on cleaning up our own house first. Then, by our example, we'll have far more influence on others than we'd ever have by flashing a badge.

I am responsible for prescribing, and living up to, my own standards. My success in that effort is what translates into a positive influence on others.

11.13

The logical course is not always the right course.

COMMANDER CHAKOTAY: TATTOO: Stardate Not Given

Once again: Logic has its place. But like a computer, it still needs a good operator. Most of all, it needs good data.

Suppose we ask the Ship's Computer to plot the most direct course to a distant star system. Unfortunately, we fail to tell it that a massive black hole lies somewhere between here and there. Or maybe we don't even *know* about the black hole. Chances are, our Starship will end up a few light years off-course due to gravitational effects we didn't account for—assuming our logically-plotted route hasn't drilled us into the black hole already!

Our lives are much the same. There are so many variables that may affect our course, some we don't even know about. We can certainly use logic to give us direction when enough data is available. But we must also polish the skills that help us fly by the seat of our pants.

One of these, Chakotay knows, is *intuition.* Whether we envision this inner guidance system as Higher Self or Spirit or "animal guides," all of us have a course-correcting ability that is beyond logic, beyond conscious thought.

At this deeper level, the right course for us is already laid in. We have only to listen for its "still small voice." In fact, learning to listen is part of our course!

I can know what the right course is for me. As I learn to "listen" through daily meditation, I can also know when changes in direction are necessary.

11.14

I have a human half you see as well as an alien half... constantly at war with each other. I survive it because my intelligence wins out, makes them live together.

SPOCK: THE ENEMY WITHIN: 1672.1

Inner conflict is hardly a new subject on these pages. *Or* in our personal lives. All of us feel the occasional warring of factions within us—between our intellect and our emotions, for example. Or between desire and duty.

Another subject that's not exactly new is the need for some kind of mediating force to make our warring factions "live together." For Spock, the mediator was his intelligence. For many of us, however, that isn't enough.

...Unless, perhaps, we capitalize the word.

Because "Intelligence" happens to be another name for the greater power that *is* enough—to do anything.

It is not necessary to worship that Intelligence the way our ancestors carried on with their gods. We have only to recognize that the Power sustaining the universe also sustains *us*. The Law which balances a star's exploding interior with its own gravitational collapse—and in the process creates light—can also balance the thoughts and feelings which sometimes explode inside *us*.

Our inner conflict is actually a sign of this Intelligence. We can be sure its ultimate purpose is to create Light.

The Intelligence reflected in the universe is also at work within me. Through my inner conflict I become aware of the lessons it is trying to teach me.

11.15

Sometimes the bad memories can be the most intense of all.

ENGINEER LA FORGE: VIOLATIONS: 45429.3

If we admit that Geordi's observation is true, *why* is it true? Why should unpleasant memories be stronger?

First, let's be clear about what *isn't* the correct explanation: The intensity of bad memories is *not* meant as punishment. It is *not* designed to induce guilt. And its purpose is *not* to make us feel bad about ourselves, or "unworthy" to feel joy and fulfillment.

The fact is, in the language of emotion, intensity is almost always a function of *importance.*

If we feel especially bad about something we did, our subconscious is telling us that there is an important lesson to be gained from the experience; and chances are we haven't learned it yet. If we are unusually disturbed by a past event—sometimes even if we weren't directly involved—our body/mind is sending us a signal that there is special significance in that event for us; and we still need to come to grips with some issue it has raised.

Our memories have a practical function, of course. But our feelings about them are meant to teach us, to make us wiser, and ultimately to bring us into a more productive relationship with other people and the universe.

Even my bad memories are for my own good. I will reflect on those that hurt most, and with the help of others learn the lessons hiding within them.

11.16

I'm sure I could be more productive if I didn't have to regenerate every day.

CONSTABLE ODO: FOR THE CAUSE: Stardate Not Given

If only we didn't need sleep! If only we could *use* that extra seven or eight hours a day (Humans/Bajorans), or three hours (Vulcans/Klingons); then we would get so much more accomplished!

Or would we—? Because even though Odo is restating a complaint we *all* have (in his own terms, of course), his characteristic sarcasm betrays a recognition that regenerating (i.e. sleeping) isn't just an annoying necessity. It's actually the best use of those precious hours.

After all, it's not as if *nothing* is going on. Like the Ship's Computer shutting down to optimize its data-banks and run systems checks, our own "down time" enables us to process our experiences and consolidate learning. No artifical version of this procedure is half as effective.

And not only do we need *daily* "regeneration," our productivity is enhanced still more by weekly breaks and regularly-scheduled shore leave.

It's so easy to get caught up in our duties. And it helps our ego to think no one else could do what we do, so we'd better stay on the job. But if "observing the Sabbath" weren't already carved in sacred stone, we'd be forced to invent the practice for our own good. It's *that* important.

Today I will begin meditating on my next scheduled holiday. I will open myself to entirely new places and possibilities my inner wisdom will suggest to me.

11.17

Adopting a siege mentality is ultimately self-defeating.

LT. COMMANDER WORF: TO THE DEATH: 49904.2

Fortify the ramparts. Shut the gates. Batten down the hatches. Here they come again!

According to the siege mentality, it's us against everybody else. Life is a defensive action. KEEP OUT!

Even if it's understandable, it's a bad strategy.

For one thing, building a fence is practically an invitation to have it torn down. Not that destroying someone else's fence is our "right." It's just that people are naturally curious; what do you have that you're hiding? Besides, people are *social* animals; we expect others to interact with us, not build walls of separation and isolation.

What's more, the walls people build to keep others out ultimately *change them*—usually for the worse. Either they become hardened to the rest of the world ("I've got mine, now go get your own"); or they grow increasingly paranoid ("Everyone's trying to take away what I have"). Fortresses breed fear, not a sense of safety.

Our best "defense," it turns out, is to get out *in* the world—to show others who we are, what we believe in, and how we've earned what we have; to show that we are in the world *for* something, not to stand against it.

And the best thing is, The Universe stands behind us when we do that. Which *changes us*—for the better.

My best protection is to simply be Who I Am, without fear, and with respect for Who Others Are.

11.18

This is one puppet who doesn't like her strings pulled.

MAJOR KIRA : VISIONARY: Stardate Not Given

In a sense we *are* puppets. All of us have so-called "heartstrings" that others can tug on to arouse our sympathies. We also have "hot buttons"—sensitive places in our psyches that can trigger anger or jealousy or lust, or cause us to react in other predictable ways.

But most of us don't *like* having our strings pulled or our buttons pushed. We don't appreciate the feeling that we're being "manipulated" by someone else. Worse, we don't like the idea that we *can* be manipulated, that someone could actually bypass our rational minds and play our emotions like a keyboard.

Which is why some of us flatly deny it. Trouble is, that only makes us *more* vulnerable to manipulation. By assuming that no one else can control us, we close our eyes to defenses that might prevent us from *being* controlled. We also fail to accept an important part of who we are.

Ironically, not liking our strings pulled is a crucial step toward transcending our "puppethood." At least we're *aware* of it. Only then can we learn how to prevent it, or how to pull our *own* strings in pursuit of our goals.

We might also learn when The Universe is pulling, and when to just relax and enjoy the dance.

The fact that I can sometimes be manipulated is no dishonor. I am learning what my "strings" are, and how to use that knowledge to my own advantage.

11.19

> **For humans, touch can connect you to an object in a very personal way... Makes it seem more real.**
>
> CAPTAIN PICARD: FIRST CONTACT: 50893.5

And it's not just "objects" that become more real. It's other living beings, other *people*.

Just before the turn of the Millennium, many Terrans began to rediscover the language of touch. Psychologists showed that babies who weren't cuddled and stroked became withdrawn—and sometimes died. People affixed small signs to their personal transports which promoted the frequent hugging of one's children. Or even trees.

The purpose was not only to communicate affection, but to absorb the "reality" of others at the most primitive level. The fact that we can't always translate those messages into words makes them no less meaningful.

Not that just *any*body can send such a message, any time they wish. Touch, without permission, can be a violation of one's personal boundaries. And many of us still have trouble recognizing what constitutes "permission."

But what's worse is when we fail to see when touch is not only permitted, but desperately *needed*. For example, in young people who feel so unloved or unnoticed that violence is the only way they can attract attention.

Touch is our first language. It's time we learned it.

I will learn the vocabulary of touch the same way I learned the language I speak: By using it. But I must also honor the "silence" others may prefer.

11.20

You choose your enemies, you choose your friends. But family... that's in the stars.

CHIEF O'BRIEN: THE ICARUS FACTOR: 42686.4

In one sense, O'Brien's claim seems to contradict other advice you'll find in this *Manual*. Haven't we implied that each of us defines "family" for ourselves? Isn't our support network, and the spiritual tradition we align ourselves with—which we *choose*—our family too?

Of course. But biology is still at our core. Every species has its "blood relations." Even with genetic engineering, we cannot change our heritage.

Nor should we try. The Universe does not toss us into biological units haphazardly. There is meaning and reason for *this* mother and father, *that* brother or sister, *this* uncle and *that* grandmother. Or the lack of them. For O'Brien, "in the stars" is shorthand for acknowledging just how important these relationships are—not merely in terms of our physical existence, but our spiritual growth.

At some point in our lives, it's not uncommon to wish we could replace this biological unit with a different one. But these most intimate relationships, as difficult, as confrontational—and yes, even abusive—as they may be, are those we are destined to learn the most from.

By facing both their pain and their joy, we take on a heritage beyond biology, as deep as boundless Spirit.

I accept the family locked into my chromosomes. I unlock my spiritual self by learning the lessons only these relationships can teach me.

11.21

Are you doing the best thing... or are you doing what's best for **you**—?

DR. CRUSHER: BLOODLINES: 47829.1

It's always a fair question. At face value it asks us whether our actions are mostly selfish, or if we're taking others into account. If we *are*, are we considering the effects of our actions only on those in our own social circle? Or could there be consequences for the wider community? Or on people we may not even know?

The irony here is that "the best thing" and what's "best for you" are ultimately the same. We only *think* there's a difference because our view is so narrow, or only concerned with the short term. If we would consider all the people we touch, if we could account for the long-term ramifications, we'd see how our own particular interests are virtually inseparable from the best interests of *all*.

The problem is, we can't do that. We're not omnipotent. Nor do we always have the time to analyze these things beforehand. Besides, taking care of our own small patch of the universe really *is* our primary responsibility.

But we *can* draw on other people's advice whenever it's practical. We can also "check in" with The Universe through regular meditation and other spiritual exercises.

Because it's along this Path where selfish and self*less* merge... where what's best for you is simply *what's best*.

I work toward the goal of making what's "best for me" what's best for those around me. Starting with family and friends, I will continually widen my circle.

11.22

We don't have to like each other to work well together.

COMMANDER RIKER: THE BEST OF BOTH WORLDS, PART II: 44001.4

Most of us do not work—or live—in isolation. In the course of our daily routines we will interact with dozens of other people. And chances are, at least a few of these people will reflect personal qualities we won't like.

Like... Such a misnomer. Because to "like" someone usually means to *be like* them, to see something we have in common. And yet much of what we see in others are the very qualities we *don't* like in ourselves. So we often end up *dis*liking those who are most like us, and liking those whom we are *not* like (but would *like* to be like).

All of which is simply to point out how fickle our "likes" are, how unreliable they are as guides to interpersonal relationships. Some of our planet's greatest advances, after all, have come from partnerships between people who haven't particularly liked one another. Or worse.

But Riker's advice isn't ultimately about learning to work with people even if we don't like them. It's about learning not to make that superficial assessment in the first place. It's about giving them a chance. It's about giving our*selves* a chance to seek out the goodness in others that makes us "like" them, and allowing others to discover the goodness to "like" in us.

I will think of at least one trait I have in common with each person I encounter today. I will look for the things in my co-workers that make us alike.

11.23

Why is any object we don't understand always called a "thing"?

DR. McCOY: STAR TREK/TMP: 7412.6

Here's the harsh truth right up front: The words we use to "name" an object often convey as much about *us* as the object itself.

Other people, for instance. Whole races have been reduced to their skin colors or prominent features. Members of a particular sex are labeled by a single "function" or physical characteristic rather than by their individual qualities or proper names. This is done (supposedly) because we don't yet *know* their qualities or names. Unfortunately, by sticking people into these simplistic boxes, we can prevent ourselves from *ever* knowing them as unique individuals. They remain mere objects to us; and we thereby remain simplistic and insensitive.

And if we can turn *people* into objects, how much less consideration we give the natural world! Animals, plants, land—whole planets—become "things" to possess and exploit. Which defines *us* as tyrants and exploiters.

"Thing" is a perfectly good word, a useful word. It points. It acknowledges existence. It "stands for" objects until we get to know them better. But in doing so it points to our ignorance. It reminds us that we don't understand.

Ideally, it reminds us to *keep learning*.

My words describe me as much as the objects they represent. I will listen for what they teach me about myself, and about what I have yet to learn.

11.24

I never fully appreciated how difficult and how rewarding it is to be human.
COUNSELOR TROI: THE LOSS: 44356.9

Just to be in the game is an honor. To be born into this world, to be alive and conscious, is a reward in itself.

Not that life doesn't send us difficulties that can make us wonder if being alive is all that great. What's worse, while we're having all those difficulties we end up fantasizing about how things might have been. And far from comforting us, our dreams of a better life only increase our pain. Our ability to imagine heaven makes our current problems seem all the more like hell.

But let's try imagining *this:* Let's say we were given a choice before entering this world. We could have been incarnated as a happy, contented pig—or the calloused, get-up-at-dawn farmer who feeds it. One has a secure, mud-filled pen and all the corn cobs he can eat. The other has twelve-hour workdays... and the stars at night.

In a sense, we've already made the choice. And we make it again at each day's dawning. We trade an unconscious, unknowing, unmerited contentment for the conscious fulfillment we must *earn* by overcoming countless obstacles and character defects.

To "be human" is to finally appreciate that having to earn it *is* the highest reward.

I am grateful for the challenges in my life. I will reward myself for overcoming them. The Universe will reward me for the stronger person I become.

11.25

I suggest that good spirits might make an effective weapon.

SPOCK: DAY OF THE DOVE: Stardate Not Given

When nothing else works, when one of life's sticky problems can't seem to get unstuck, when nothing else can stop the coming storm, we still have one weapon: Our attitude. Our ability to face the storm... *and laugh.*

It would be valuable enough if keeping a positive attitude were simply a technique for avoiding depression—a mental gimmick for minimizing the doom and gloom, for looking ahead to a time when fortune might smile on us again. After all, in the normal cycle of things, bad times *do* eventually give way to good. A positive attitude at least preserves us for that brighter future.

But Spock is being even bolder. He's reminding us that good spirits can effectively *change reality now*.

For one thing, the very cells of our bodies become infused with increased vitality. And because our bodies are connected to the world, external changes are possible.

What's more, in the network of consciousness, a display of positive attitude can evoke a sympathetic reaction in other people. The resulting *communal* positivity not only creates an atmosphere for finding solutions where before none existed, but cancels out negative karma like the effect of two opposing wave forms.

If I can't control external events, I can control my attitude about them. I give up nothing by trying. I take back my life if I succeed.

11.26

What is the point of doing battle if you cannot enjoy the fruits of your victory?

LT. COMMANDER WORF: FOR THE CAUSE: Stardate Not Given

According to many traditions, "spiritual maturity" is demonstrated by an increasing ability to postpone the rewards for one's efforts over longer and longer periods of time. Like the promise of "heaven," it should be enough to know that we are working steadily toward some goal, and that we'll receive the benefits *some* day.

And there's some truth to this. But the fruits of victory can't be delayed indefinitely. We are not only spiritual beings; our material dimension deserves respect. And like the Captain who knows the limitations of his crew, we must give our bodies their due—if only to reinforce positive effort and inspire ourselves to re-enter the battle.

The eventual goal may be to transcend our bodies. But in the meantime we must not pass up opportunities to "stand down" from the struggle, to consolidate recent gains and live in their afterglow; and thereby send our psyche the life-affirming message that The Path may be rocky and dangerous but the views are worth every step.

And something happens: As we become seasoned soldiers of the spirit, we find ourselves growing less and less dependent on the fruits of victory, and enjoying the struggle more and more for its own sake.

My body/mind is a gift from The Universe. I will honor its needs. I welcome new opportunities to earn the rewards which encourage my progress.

11.27

Enjoy these times... it's the time of your life that'll never come again. When it's gone... it's gone.

"SCOTTY": RELICS: 46125.3

If only we could learn the lesson before it's too late: How precious are our lives... and how fleeting is time!

The fact that we have *physical* lives makes the lesson all the more urgent. We are born, we die; and between those two events is a finite period during which we gain experience and try to live out whatever purpose we discover for ourselves. We may not know how *long* that period is. We only know it's finite. Our eventual death is simply the universe's reminder to *pay attention*.

Which is exactly what Scotty is trying to point out. The times we live in, the people we interact with, the very bodies through which we experience our lives—all of these are changing constantly. The precise combination of factors which are present *in this moment* will never come together again anywhere in the universe.

We are therefore advised to "enjoy" these times. Not so much in the sense of "having fun," but in an attitude of *being joyful*; of seeing each moment as the unique treasure it is, and being glad for it; of being open to each new once-in-a-lifetime opportunity for learning... and in giving thanks no matter what its lesson.

Time, like energy, can be transformed into matter. By using and appreciating the time I am given, time no longer "passes." It becomes part of me.

11.28

We all work for our supper. You'll be surprised how much sweeter it tastes when you do.

ALIXUS : PARADISE : 47573.1

We take so much for granted. We accept the ease and comfort our technology gives us with hardly a thought.

And for the most part this is good. By not having to deal with the physical challenges our ancestors faced, we are free to concentrate on more "spiritual" matters—like self-improvement, creative expression, the Quest for Truth.

But there is a price. We can become too lazy, too dependent. We can forget how to "fend for ourselves" if our technology were ever taken away. We can lose touch with the most basic requirements of our own survival.

We can also lose touch with the "simple pleasures" of living. Like the satisfaction of growing the very food we put on our table. Or the pride that comes from helping to build the machines we use, or the homes we inhabit. Or the delight in creating something—out of words, or clay, or sound—for our own personal enjoyment.

Often, our recurring feelings of being "unfulfilled" are simply the result of having too few opportunities to practice self-reliance, to do things for ourselves. To "work for our supper."

Fortunately, it's a situation that's easily remedied.

I will endeavor to link what I do with the benefits I enjoy. I will find projects or hobbies that allow me to "taste" the fruits of my own labor.

11.29

Try to maintain your emotional equanimity. You should not be concerned with success or failure.

LIEUTENANT TUVOK: COLD FIRE: Stardate Not Given

"Equanimity" is simply Tuvok's ten-credit word for "emotional balance." It's the opposite of all those wild mood swings many of us give ourselves—from agony to ecstacy, depression to exhilaration, fear to fearlessness. And make no mistake: We *do* give them to ourselves. Because heightened emotions can sometimes become the drug we use to mask our own lack of direction. We may not feel a sense of purpose, but at least we feel *alive,* right?

The problem is, sooner or later our emotional rollercoaster rides take a toll on our bodies. Chances are even better that they'll damage our relationships.

One of the best ways to regain emotional balance is to detach ourselves from the outcome of our efforts. Not that we shouldn't have goals, or strive to achieve them. It's just that while we're "striving," worrying about whether we'll succeed or fail can distract us. By *not* being concerned with success, we free ourselves to concentrate on *the job itself,* and on doing the best we can.

And that frees The Universe to do the job *It* does best: Balancing our wants with what we actually need.

Which is the *spiritual* version of equanimity.

I can feel alive without using my emotions as a thrill ride. I will control my temperment and my effort, and let The Universe control the rest.

11.30

Rudeness will get you nowhere.

QUARK: FOR THE CAUSE: Stardate Not Given

A lesson in social graces... from *Quark*—?

Even Quark has standards for "appropriate behavior," though they're often at odds with other cultures. One area of agreement, however, is that social interactions are *not* the proper context for venting one's frustrations.

Yet that is frequently just what we do. We bring our unresolved personal issues from one situation into the next. Angry over our jobs or relationships or unmet personal goals, we end up "taking it out" on others—including people we don't even know.

Make that *"Especially* people we don't even know."

Those who work in the public sector, like Quark, encounter this phenomenon daily. From bartenders to sales clerks, the "anonymous" people we meet in stores and public facilities make easy targets for our unhappiness. Since we have no relationship to lose, we somehow feel under no obligation to treat them with courtesy. But *they* are required to treat *us* with courtesy or else we report them to their superiors (which gives us back the sense of "power" we may have lost in some previous situation).

It's not just that these people deserve better from us. It's that practicing courtesy—*especially on people we don't even know*—is a good indicator of spiritual growth.

The person most affected by my rudeness—or my kindness—is me. My first reaction to frustration is to be even more respectful and courteous to others.

SECTOR 12

CORRESPONDING TO THE TERRAN MONTH OF
December

12.01

Make it so.

CAPTAIN PICARD: ENCOUNTER AT FARPOINT: 41153.7

In Terra's venerable story of Genesis, the Creator says, "Let there be light." And lo, there *was* light. The rest of the universe was similarly created by divine command, from plants to planets, from humus to human beings. Words never had such power.

But words themselves aren't what actually *does* the work of creation. Even God needed a mechanism to carry out his order. "Let there be..." is only a symbol for that Universal Order which must precede the *verbal* order.

Likewise, Picard's famous command could have no effect without a proper mechanism—in this case his highly-skilled crew, committed to their interdependent roles and to their mission; and the *Enterprise*, with its arsenal of technology. All of these elements were necessary before "Make it so" could become anything more than wishful rhetoric. But once everything was in place, this "rhetoric" wielded the power of the universe.

That same power lies *within us*. We too can make our wishes "so"—*if* we have the proper mechanism in place. By acknowledging and aligning ourselves with the Universal Order, by affirming our roles in the Interdependent Web of Life, by becoming conscious of the mission that infuses each of us with a unique purpose, our words—our very *thoughts*—become instruments of creation.

As I increasingly align my will with that of The Universe, I strengthen my power to "make it so."

12.02

That is the exploration that awaits you: Not mapping stars and studying nebulae, but charting the unknown possibilities of existence.

Q: ALL GOOD THINGS...: 47988.1

No matter how far we may go on our travels among the galaxies, we are never more than a heartbeat from the primary object of our explorations: *Us.*

Q knew what we only suspected. Stars, nebulae, and alien lifeforms were never really the point. Bringing back new information about the cosmos, or new technology and artifacts from other civilizations—even forming new alliances—are only by-products of The Real Adventure.

Because in pushing the boundaries of the known universe, we are actually expanding the limits of our own minds. In journeying through space and time, we are really charting the hidden dimensions within *us.* By mapping stars and the routes between them, we are not only connecting with one another but to Existence itself.

Many of us remain blissfully unaware that our explorations "out there" are only symbols for this Inner Voyage. And maybe that's as it should be, because the adventure can also be enjoyed for its own sake. But someday, when we look back, we'll see that we haven't so much been on a journey through the universe, as a quest into our *selves.*

Today offers a new opportunity to explore my self. With each new task I redefine Who I Am. With every new challenge I transform my life for the better.

12.03

The lure of perfection is powerful.
SEVEN OF NINE: DRONE: Stardate Not Given

Working to get things "just right" can be a healthy goal. Whether it's a new project or a new relationship, or perhaps a personal skill we'd like to develop—striving for perfection can be a useful mantra to focus our attention.

But if we expect to actually *achieve* it, perfection begins to enslave us. The temptation to keep tinkering until we reach some point where further improvement is impossible can distract us from other needs. We end up losing perspective—*and* the time to pursue other projects and relationships that provide balance. Perfection becomes a merciless taskmaster that can never call the task complete, if only because we can never know when something is perfect.

And there's the rub. "Perfection" has no objective definition. It can therefore never be achieved.

The word is useful when it describes a direction, not a destination. Its "lure" is productive when it encourages us to keep growing, damaging when it refuses to be satisfied.

Ultimately, it is *we* who must decide when we're satisfied. Part of growing, in fact, is learning how to recognize when enough is enough... when it's time to switch gears, work on something else, or simply take a break and enjoy the unique, transitory set of imperfections that is us, now.

I seek not perfection, but the wisdom to know when I've done enough. I accept the flaws that remain, as long as I am making progress.

12.04

Patience is a lost virtue to most. To me, an ally.

CONSTABLE ODO : NECESSARY EVIL: 47282.5

In a world of warp-drives and personal transporters, time is perceived differently. The rhythms of biology are no longer our primary reference. Our "natural" sense of time is redefined by the increasing speed of our artifical devices. Patience is a lost virtue if only because our interactions with technology rarely require it!

But our *personal* interactions are another matter. Here, biology is still the defining factor. "Real time" must be readjusted for the slower pace of thinking and feeling; for the deliberate nurturing of relationships; and for the subtle, cumulative effects which combine to change our lives. One spiritual tradition symbolizes this "living" process in the sacred image of the lotus flower, unfolding itself petal by petal until it is finally revealed in all its glory.

Patience is the quiet acceptance of the fact that some things must be allowed, like the lotus, to unfold at their own pace. Love is the classic example. Likewise developing a spiritual discipline, overcoming our fears, or finding our life's purpose. These things must "unfold." Rushing them can only disrupt or prevent their flowering.

In the process, it's not really patience that becomes our ally. It's *The Universe*.

I won't be rushed by the timetable of technology. I will take time to fully absorb the lessons I must learn. My life is unfolding at just the right pace.

12.05

A good joke just seems to make fear dissolve.

NEELIX: THE THAW: Stardate Not Given

Often true. In fact, even a *bad* joke (which Neelix was known for) can do the job. The question is, *why?*

In the midst of a crisis, most of us have a tendency to focus so intently on our problem that we lose sight of everything else. And fortunately so, since this ability enables us to devote all our energies to finding a solution.

But sometimes our fears have no identifiable source; there is no specific problem to solve. We simply harbor a vague, seemingly-permanent sense of foreboding.

It is *not* permanent. And that's precisely what a joke—or some other distraction—can show us.

By giving us something else to focus on, we step back from our fears for the moment. By the release of tension a good laugh (or even a *forced* laugh) can give us, we extract ourselves from our emotional straightjacket. In that moment, we recognize that *we can control our attitude,* even if we can't control the circumstances.

Better yet, we prove once again that, by controlling our attitude, we *do* control the circumstances. Detached from our fears, we regain perspective, clarity of mind. We reconnect with our inner, healing resources. We remember that, with The Universe, all things are possible.

I can use humor to break through fear. By giving myself opportunities to laugh as I would give myself medicine, I restore balance and perspective.

12.06

Our feelings are what make us all human.
COMMANDER RIKER: THE ICARUS FACTOR: 42686.4

Naturally, the Commander doesn't mean "human" in the sense of a particular species from Terra. He's talking about the one personal quality shared by living, sentient beings everywhere: The ability to *feel*.

But it's more than a mere sensitivity to physical stimuli. All life forms can sense and respond to the external environment. "Feelings" refers to an *interior* sensitivity. And what's being felt is one's own state of mind.

The trouble is, many of us are *so* sensitive to this inner feedback that we've come to fear it—often to the point of more or less disconnecting ourselves from it. Ironically, the very people who show *no* feelings are sometimes the ones who feel *most deeply*. Or at least they could in the past—before some emotional trauma hurt them so badly that their subconscious mind created a shield to prevent any further assaults.

Yet that reaction, too, is "human." So we must not only be aware of our own tendency to "raise shields," we must accept that *others* may be cut off from their own feelings. In that realization, we begin to "humanize" them, which eventually leads to forgiving them. Which in turn re-humanizes *us*, and reminds us to forgive ourselves.

If my own feelings make me defensive, so it must be with others. Today I will lower my "shields," so that someone else will feel safe in lowering theirs.

12.07

Just give up—? I don't think so!

DR. BASHIR : DISTANT VOICES : Stardate Not Given

There's no better formula for success: In striving to achieve our goals, we should never give up. In following our dreams, we mustn't give up. In seeking to transform ourselves, we simply *cannot* give up.

The age-old wisdom about success consisting of one part inspiration and 99 parts *per*spiration is true. It's not intellectual brilliance that ultimately wins out. It's not our good looks. It's not our talent, or money, or even who we know that is most likely to bring success.

It's our willingness to *keep trying,* to stay in the game, to embrace the ongoing struggle. Even more, it's the realization that achieving our goals and dreams isn't the top priority anyway. These are just excuses to continue refining our *character*—to make us more committed, more courageous individuals; to force us to look within ourselves, to connect with the deeper resources each of us has, but we pretend we can get along without.

Few of us will make these life-enriching connections unless we are confronted by some extraordinary threat or challenge. Ironically, it is when we feel defeated by these events, when we are tempted to "just give up," that we are most able to discover and release our true power.

Be still. Try to feel it, *live* it. Don't give up until you *do*.

I may not achieve all my goals and dreams. But I will achieve something even greater by continuing to make the effort, by not giving up.

12.08

I admire gall!
LIEUTENANT WORF: THE SURVIVORS: 43152.4

The omnipedia on the Ship's Computer defines "gall" as "Rudeness; impudence; asserting oneself in a way that ignores authority, custom or convention."

Which is why gall is usually considered a negative personal trait in "polite society." But it can be decidedly *positive* in situations where taking risks is necessary to the achievement of one's goals. Including spiritual ones.

Because among the traits that usually accompany gall is a healthy dose of confidence (bordering on *over*-confidence), as well as a readiness to take a stand for what one believes—even when doing so would invite danger. Klingons call this kind of brazen self-assertion *nuQ'nuH*, while Terrans know it as "chutzpah."

We should all be so brazen. And the fact is, we *can* be. When it comes to asserting ourselves for what we believe, we never face the danger alone anyway. Inspired by our example, others will join us. And since the energies of the universe are drawn to efforts that complement its own redemptive purposes, we have all the support we need.

Try this exercise for developing your own capacity for "gall": Without putting anyone else at risk, do something that flies in the face of convention, or goes against "the odds." Savor what it feels like. Notice how you survive... win or lose. Then do it again. Someday it will matter.

I am confident. The Universe is with me. I take risks for what I believe in, and for my spiritual growth.

12.09

No one can guarantee the actions of another.

SPOCK: DAY OF THE DOVE: Stardate Not Given

There's a saying common to dozens of planetary cultures: "Speak for yourself." Because as much as we may *think* we know someone else, we can never presume to express exactly what they feel or think.

The same goes for "guaranteeing" another person's actions. After all, we can't live inside anyone else's mind. We can't feel what they feel, remember their memories, know every little detail that might affect their behavior.

We have a hard enough time knowing what makes *us* tick. How many times have we surprised ourselves—positively *and* negatively—by doing something we never thought we could (or *would*) do?

When we pretend to know someone else better than we have a right, it's often an expression of our desire to know our*selves* better. After all, we'd like to be able to count on *some*body. We desperately want *some*one to be reliable, consistent... *knowable*. And when we fail our own test, we may transfer those hopes to someone else.

There's another saying that's almost universal: "Know thyself." The good news is, *we can.* By being objective about our own behavior. And by continuing to run the daily diagnostic on ourselves called "meditation".

My first priority is guaranteeing my own actions. As I become aware of my behavior, I can begin to change it for the better.

12.10

Life is full of surprises.

GARAK: THE SEARCH, PART II: Stardate Not Given

We shouldn't be surprised at being surprised.

Life is never 100% predictable. Nor would we *want* it to be. Our lives melt into bland nothingness when things no longer surprise us. An unvarying routine can literally sap our strength and strangle our minds. We begin to shrivel up spiritually; we start sleepwalking through life.

In contrast, we often feel most awake when we don't know what's going to happen next. The only thing we *do* know is that challenges lie ahead, events we can't even foresee are bound to change our lives; and if we don't pay attention, we may learn our next lesson the hard way.

And that's precisely the point: The Universe is still in control, still teaching us its lessons. In fact, surprise can sometimes be the best way to focus our attention on the *most important* ones. If we weren't caught by surprise now and then, we might go on ignoring some essential piece of information, some new experience necessary for our continued growth. Surprise is the "wake-up call," the knock at the door, the bell ringing for our next class.

If we don't think we're ready yet, we're not giving ourselves enough credit.

I am thankful for the surprises in my life, pleasant or otherwise. I know The Universe is using them to point to the areas in my life that need attention.

12.11

For your information, I don't appreciate being deactivated in the middle of a sentence.

THE DOCTOR: LIVING WITNESS: Stardate Not Given

Neither does any of us. The trouble is, it happens all the time. Especially to the people we're talking to. Or *at*.

Because we often forget that the art of conversation is not so much about talking; it's about listening. We're so intent on showing off our brilliance that we can hardly wait for the next opportunity. (And sometimes we *don't!*) We're so starved for attention that when someone tells a tale of sorrow or success, we can't help but go one better.

Taking care not to "deactivate" our conversation partners, however, is a sign that we respect and value their experience—and we don't *over*-value our own. When we listen attentively to what they have to say, we affirm their worth, while acknowledging the divinity within them.

We also give that divinity a chance to reveal what may be important for us at that moment. Because every conversation holds the possibility for discovering something new, something The Universe wants us to know. And the answers to our questions—or prayers—are more likely to come through another person than "divine revelation."

If we only *let* them come. By being open to the Spirit that moves in and through the sentences we exchange.

Today I will practice the art of listening. I will say little, prompting others to say more. By treating their words as gifts, I discover the treasures within.

12.12

It's the differences that have made us strong.

CAPTAIN PICARD: UP THE LONG LADDER: 42823.2

At its best, the Federation has been a grand experiment in learning to live and work together productively—despite a stunning variety of races and cultures. In stark contrast are the nations, past and present, where "ethnic purity" is the ideal. Or where diverse cultures have tolerated one another only because of an enforced "peace."

Not that the Federation's experiment has been altogether peaceful either. Living with differences requires work. Communities must always guard against the kinds of acts which incite division. Individuals must remind themselves (and each other) how much richer the social fabric is when the whole spectrum of colors is woven in.

A community's strength depends on differences, not sameness. What one person can't do, another *can*. As in the concept of teamwork, the experience and talents of each individual is multiplied by every other.

This principle is valid at every level, right down to our own personal lives. Because within each of us is a similar diversity of roles and responsibilities, needs and wants, strengths and weaknesses—some of which may seem to conflict. Our happiness depends not on repressing these inner differences, but accepting and integrating them.

I accept the diversity within me, and the diversity around me. I celebrate the many relationships and inner resources that make me strong.

12.13

> **All the knowledge of the universe, and all the power that it bestows, is of intrinsic value to everyone.**
>
> JETREL: JETREL: 48832.1

As Captain Picard said more than once, "The search for knowledge is always our primary mission." Here, Jetrel is simply trying to explain why.

Why should knowledge be so all-important? After all, isn't there something to be said for the bliss of ignorance? Who wouldn't trade a few I.Q. points—or a few gigabytes of cerebral storage space—for a greater ability to enjoy life? Or for a renewed sense of purpose? Or to feel more *loved?* Aren't these qualities far more valuable to us than the mere accumulation of facts?

Jetrel's point is that "knowing" is *the key* to increasing our enjoyment of life. Knowledge is what gives us the ability to discover and act out our life's purpose. To know the universe, to know someone else, to know our*selves*— as fully as we can—*is* to feel more loved. And to love.

Knowledge doesn't only bestow power. It bestows the power for *good.* It also bestows the recognition that we must use that power to increase everyone's good.

Everyone's. Because if we hoard our knowledge, if we try to use it only for our own benefit, it quickly loses value. Knowledge, like love, increases its worth *as we share it.*

As I make new discoveries about myself and the universe, I will look for opportunities to share my knowledge with others, and for them to share theirs.

12.14

Even the eagle knows when to sleep.
COMMANDER CHAKOTAY: RESOLUTIONS : 49690.1

It's a common reaction: When at last we demonstrate some measure of mastery over our own lives, we may suddenly feel an even greater need to prove ourselves. When we finally assume command over our personal circumstances—which is what the eagle represents—we also assume the role of "spiritual example" for others.

And it's as if we've taken on a new job. *We* are now "the strong one." *We* must be the role model. Others begin looking to us for advice, reassurance, inspiration. Having shown a glimmer of our divine spark, it has now become *our* responsibility to lead the way. If not save the world.

Part of this messianic attitude comes from the understandable desire to confirm that we really *have* seen The Light, that our newly-acquired spiritual gifts are for real and not some fluke. The problem is, we are still fallible, vulnerable, imperfect creatures. We can't be round-the-clock role models. That's far too much pressure.

Besides which we still have our *own* personal needs. For advice and reassurance. For room to experiment, to make mistakes without feeling like we're causing others to stumble. For simply being alone now and then.

Part of spiritual mastery is knowing when to put our lofty self-image to bed and just *be ourselves*.

No matter how spiritually "adept" I become, I am still the same person. Though I soar like the eagle, I share the same basic needs as everyone else.

12.15

I don't think we can start second-guessing ourselves. I think we have to proceed normally and deal with each situation as it occurs.

COUNSELOR TROI: ALL GOOD THINGS...: 47988

There's something to be said for "hunches."

Despite the Vulcan preference for logic, the rest of us rarely make decisions by conscious thought alone. Our *sub*conscious plays a major role—or perhaps *the* major role—processing far more data than our "aware mind" could ever gather, much less keep track of.

Unfortunately, the subconscious decisions (hunches) presented to our awareness often seem too easy. We become suspicious of the fact that we didn't have to think very hard, or do a lot of preliminary analysis. So our logical mind begins reviewing the process and, naturally, can't always determine the basis for our decision. A second decision is made, which is more like a "guess" because now we doubt ourselves. And that's usually a big mistake.

The exception is when we realize that our first hunch is based not on our intuitive decision-making powers, but on some knee-jerk reaction or habit. Or our hormones.

Ultimately it's a matter of looking at the *source* of our decision, not the decision itself. It's a matter of learning to trust a part of ourselves we don't consciously control.

I can feel my decisions are "right" without always knowing how I arrived at them. I will trust my inner guidance, and let my experience confirm the results.

12.16

Kind of exciting, isn't it? We just don't know!

ENSIGN RO LAREN: CONUNDRUM: 45494.2

Most of us prefer to have things "settled." We like our problems solved, our investigations completed, our mysteries explained. It's nice to have a challenging puzzle to work on now and then. But we seem *driven* to put the pieces together so we can get on with our lives.

And yet there's a sense in which *not* settling everything is good for us. To think we know it all, or that we can answer all the Big Questions, is to presume we're larger than Life, to rank ourselves equal to The Universe. To recognize mystery—in fact to *celebrate* that Mystery— is to accept our place in the grand scheme of things.

Which isn't so bad. Just imagine how life would be if there were no riddles left to solve, no facets of ourselves left to explore. The "Hell" described by many primitive religions, in which sinners are subjected to eternal torment, is child's play compared to the condition in which the universe holds no more secrets, in which we know everything about everything.

To realize there will always be something we don't yet know—or perhaps can't *ever* know—keeps us energized, excited... *alive!*

...And humble.

I celebrate the Mystery of existence. I give thanks for the challenges The Universe holds in store for me, no matter how much I've already accomplished.

12.17

I will not destroy life. Not even to save my own.

DR. McCOY: THE EMPATH: 5121.5

The good doctor wasn't talking about viruses or cancer cells, or the hordes of disease-carrying insects that plagued pre-scientific cultures throughout the Quadrant. McCoy would hardly lose sleep over irradiating an invasion of deadly microbes, or destroying a tumor.

What he was pointing to was the larger Web of Life that calls each of us to maintain the natural balance we've inherited from an Intelligence far beyond our own. It is a balance crucial not only to our physical, but our *spiritual,* survival. Because preserving or destroying life has effects that can't be measured in flesh and bone. And because we are linked at levels that transcend even consciousness.

Those who acknowledge this deeper "interconnectedness" share a tremendous responsibility. That responsibility is not merely to respect the natural balance in the way we live, but to openly demonstrate its vital importance to others who have yet to learn.

McCoy was following the path of those who have been willing to demonstrate the primacy of Life in the most radical way. And the most eloquent. Even if we're not as courageous, we can still make the same statement.

I will strive to develop a lifestyle that preserves and celebrates the sanctity of all Life, even as it preserves and celebrates my own.

12.18

You'll learn to build for yourselves, think for yourselves. And what you create is yours. It's what we call freedom.

CAPTAIN KIRK: THE APPLE: 3715.0

The dictionary definition is fine for political debate and historical analysis. But freedom, in a personal sense, gets down to this: *Taking responsibility for your life.*

It begins with the commitment not to blame anyone else for the condition you're in. Others may have contributed, yes; but what you do about it now is *your* decision. Whether you continue to wallow in misery, or face your challenges with a positive attitude, is up to you. To repeat Kirk's words, what you create from your life *is yours.*

Of course, the struggle for freedom is not entirely an inner one. There are always external forces of the kind politicians and historians discuss. From a spiritual point of view, however, outward conditions exist precisely to help us bring our *inner* conditions into better focus. Our material situation represents our own spiritual harmony, or lack of it—or perhaps the spiritual obstacles we need to overcome before we can achieve it.

We may not *like* the thought that the obstacles in our lives reflect something inside us. It's easier to place the blame elsewhere. But *that's* the slave mentality that keeps us where we are. The alternative is freedom.

I accept the hard work that freedom requires.
I declare my independence from old habits and restrictive beliefs. I am the architect of my own life.

12.19

We must fall back on the old axiom that when other contingencies fail, whatever remains, however improbable, must be true.

DATA: LONELY AMONG US: 41249.3

We might also say, "...whatever remains, *however much we may dislike it*, must be true."

The point is, we often make our quest for Truth far more difficult than it needs to be:

First, by having preconceived expectations about what can be considered "true" (i.e., that truth must be logical, or at least conform to the laws of probability; that truth must be complicated; and that if discovering it is too easy, it can't be true).

Secondly, by closing our eyes to answers we may not *like*, or whose implications make us uncomfortable.

Many of us, for example, prefer to think we're self-sufficient enough to overcome our problems, achieve our personal goals, and find happiness—*without* having to resort to any "higher power" for help. We'll exhaust all the other possibilities—or "contingencies," as Data would say; we'll seek fulfillment in material things, or pleasure, or power until, finally, the real answer is all that remains.

What the ancient traditions have taught seems more improbable than ever in this Age of Technology. But the quest for Truth, ultimately, is still a spiritual one.

I clear my mind of all expectations. I will look for answers in the improbable and unpalatable as well as the logical and comfortable.

12.20

I've always believed that what you get when you love someone is greater than what you risk.

COMMANDER CHAKOTAY: TWISTED: Stardate Not Given

Chakotay tells us exactly what's "at risk" in the statement that leads up to this one. "Nothing makes us more vulnerable," he says, "than when we love someone."

Being vulnerable: That's the risk. It's also what scares us. Because to love someone is, in a sense, to give away control. Since we've allowed someone else's welfare to become as important as our own, we can now be affected by what happens to *them,* not only to us.

And it's not just what *happens;* it's what they *do.* Their every word, every act, has double the effect. An affectionate touch can send us into warp. An angry glance can jolt us like a phaser set to stun. Is the ride really worth it?

Yes. For one thing, to explore the depths of feeling we are capable of is to know ourselves better. For another, we learn greater compassion for others, because *every*one struggles with these same issues. Even Vulcans.

Vulnerability is also one of the few portals through which we can link with the larger Web of Life. In order to open ourselves to its riches we must lower our shields, let go of our insistence on "control." In order to feel *its* transforming Love, we must first feel love for another.

How I love others reflects the extent to which I allow The Universe to love me. To love is to release my Higher Power and access the infinite reservoir within.

12.21

Perhaps someday we'll find that space and time are simpler than the human equation.

CAPTAIN PICARD: HIDE AND Q: 41590.5

We may be curious about it, but we can survive without knowing precisely how the universe was created. The mysteries of space/time have their fascinations, but the ultimate questions are still about *us:* How the mind works; how to transform anger into love; what makes us gape in wonder at the stars, or cry at a baby's first steps.

Not that quantum mechanics is a snap. The laws governing the world of matter are more intricate than most of us can imagine. But they are "simple" in the sense that they can be known; and once science settles a question about the material world, it's pretty much settled.

Understanding our *selves,* on the other hand, is a project that never ends. Spiritual knowledge is always open to revision. In fact, the operative word here isn't really "knowledge" at all. To fall back on the cliché, it's *faith*.

The controversy between knowledge and faith—what some see as the conflict between science and religion—was rarely about two competing ways of "knowing." What past religious traditions deplored wasn't so much that science was "incompatible," but that it distracts us from the issues we *ought* to be working on. Like what makes our lives meaningful. Like learning that no fact of science will ever fill the hole in our hearts... *for each other.*

I know what the most important "equation" is: The science of living with others—and with myself.

12.22

After a time, you may find that "having" is not so pleasing as "wanting." It is not logical, but it is often true.

SPOCK: AMOK TIME: 3372.7

The Vulcan saying is much like the ancient Terran one: "Restrain your dreams, lest they transmute into reality."

Yet ironically, many of us would rather hold on to our dreams than the realities they are designed to mold themselves into. After all, we can still *control* our dreams. We can eliminate whatever we don't like with a wave of our imagination. The fantasies we have about the perfect relationship or the ideal job are "perfect" and "ideal" only because we tend to gloss over the hard work they will inevitably require. "Wanting" demands little energy. "Having" comes with lots of strings attached.

Then again, "wanting" does *project* energy. And the universe responds by coalescing its forces around our wants, and finally bringing us the realities they represent.

When we find those realities to be unfulfilling (or even self-destructive), The Universe is probably trying to teach us a lesson. It may be asking us to take responsibility for our thoughts as well as our actions. Or it may be encouraging us to look at our motivations for "wanting." Do we really *need* the things we want? Do we desire some things only because someone *tells* us we should?

Our dreams are mirrors of ourselves. Look hard.

I will dream not so much to have whatever I want, but to want what I already have.

12.23

A structure cannot stand without a foundation.

LIEUTENANT TUVOK: FLASHBACK: 50126.4

This is the bottom line. This is what we've been searching for—or trying to hang on to, patch up, or improve on: A foundation on which we can structure our lives.

There are parables in almost every tradition about the dangers of building on shifting sands, about the need for something solid to support us. Rock, the ideal foundation, symbolizes the things we can depend on, that don't change, that withstand the test of time. It's not surprising that the disciple of a certain Terran Master was renamed *Petros* (meaning "rock") when he founded what became one of the galaxy's leading spiritual institutions.

Not that an *institution* can serve as a foundation. Our foundation must be made up of the same truths that the universe itself is built on. These are the truths that institutions and traditions can only conceptualize for us, then demonstrate how they apply in our daily lives.

Our task is to get down to the original bedrock, with help from those institutions and traditions—or through any *other* resource we may find during our search, not the least of which is that Piece-of-the-Rock within each of us.

And the miracle is, once we have that foundation, the structure on top practically builds itself.

I am restructuring my life, day by day, on the principles I am now learning. As I go boldly on my Inner Voyage, I anchor myself on Universal Truth.

12.24

The king who would be man!

Q : DEJA Q : 43539.1

The sting of Q's remark depends on our awareness of a centuries-old story entitled, *The Man Who Would Be King*. The tale cautions us against our tendency to presume we know what's best for everyone, and if only the world would do as we decreed, life would be perfect.

Except that we often don't have a clue what's best for our*selves*, much less anyone else. And if everyone were to do exactly what we told them to, the world would probably be in much worse shape than it is already.

In other words, let's not appoint ourselves king, when we're really cut out to be humble peasants.

Of course, it's one thing to be humble, and another to ignore (or even deny) the regal qualities we *do* possess. Too often we accept the role of peasant—"man," in Q's hierarchy—when *we are capable of so much more*.

After the liberation of his country, a great Terran leader phrased it this way: "Your playing small doesn't serve the world. There's nothing enlightened about shrinking so that other people won't feel insecure around you. We were born to manifest the glory within us... And as we let our own light shine, we unconsciously give other people permission to do the same."

The true king shows others the royalty within them.

I accept the awesome power within me to create and transform my own life's circumstances, and thereby demonstrate how others can do the same.

12.25

The channels are open and you are tied in.
LIEUTENANT UHURA: THE ENTERPRISE INCIDENT: 5027.3

A more profound statement of spiritual Truth was never spoken. Because the same Source that created the physical universe, that created all life—that created each of *us*—remains connected to us in ways we've only begun to imagine. One ancient Terran tradition described that Source as being "closer to us than our jugular vein." Another explains that we are sons and daughters of The Creator, embraced like a beloved child in a parent's arms.

Some traditions go even further: We are literally gods-in-the-making, sentient beings whose present form is like the caterpillar to the butterfly, the hatchling to the eagle. We are destined to soar. We may need help in learning *how*, but we certainly don't need to ask whether we *may*.

In fact, according to every one of these traditions, we have not only received divine "permission," but all the help we need. Channels to the deepest resources of The Universe are already open, or at least built into the fabric of Reality and awaiting our discovery. Better yet, discovering and *using* those channels requires no "outside" agency, no additional equipment. We are "tied in" by virtue of our consciousness, empowered by an inner Spirit that is the very incarnation of universal, creative energy.

With that energy we can transform ourselves and our world. And we begin simply by saying *Yes* to it.

I say "Yes!" to the power within me; "Yes!" to my connection with The Universe and everything in it!

12.26

**What the future holds no one knows.
But forward we look, and forward we go.**

COMMANDER RIKER: SECOND CHANCES: 46915.2

There is no going back. We can't undo what was done, nor can we live in the past. Why would we *want* to?

Past glories and golden eras seem even more glorious in retrospect. We lose touch with the daily struggles and concerns that made life as much of a challenge *then* as it is *now*. The mistakes we made, the wrong decisions, were not without purpose, not without their lessons. Our present is the diploma we receive for all we've been through in the past. Do we really want to go back to kindergarten and re-learn what we already know?

Armed with all that hard-won knowledge, we can now affect and transform our future for the better. But only if we can see it coming. Only if we're looking forward.

It is still full of unknowns, yes. But that is what's so exciting. The future is not predestined. Every decision, every action, shapes it. The quality of our future lives, the character of the person we will become, is in our hands.

We cannot change the past, but we can redeem it by what we create now. This is what spiritual traditions envision (by various names) as The Messianic Age. But it is not some far distant future; it is *our* future. And the Messiah isn't coming. He is here *now*, in *us*.

I am part of the Cosmic Plan to shape the future. My first responsibility is to my own *future, my own life. If I succeed there, the rest will fall into place.*

12.27

So... five card stud, nothing wild... and the sky's the limit.

CAPTAIN PICARD: ALL GOOD THINGS...: 47988.1

In the Starfleet chronicles which have since become known as "The Next Generation," Captain Picard's closing words represent more than the rules for a friendly game of poker. They are, in a sense, the groundrules governing The Game of Life.

For example, we agree to play the cards we're dealt. We can occasionally improve our hand, yes. But there's no switching cards with other players, or getting more cards than anybody else.

And the cards are exactly what they appear to be. A low card is a low card, not a face card. We cannot *wish* our twos into kings, our eights into aces. Nothing is "wild."

Which also means, thankfully, that the game is not arbitrary, chaotic. As much as the game may seem a matter of "luck," it is not. Astute players can develop and use *skill*—mental, spiritual, and emotional. And even though the advantage is only a few percentage points, it makes all the difference. So *much* so that, for all practical purposes, there are no limits on what we can win.

As the Captain said as he finally sat down to play, "I should've done this long ago." The good news is, there's still time for *all* of us to join in the game.

I will play the "cards" I am dealt. I am holding a good hand. I'm not playing to beat the Dealer, or my fellow players, but to improve my own skills.

12.28

You have no idea what the consequences might be once you involve yourself.

CAPTAIN JANEWAY: TIME AND AGAIN: Stardate Not Given

It's a worthy goal, as Tuvoc says, to "be prepared for anything." But as Janeway reminds us, we never *can* be. The smallest detail, overlooked, can ruin our best-laid plans. And even if everything *does* go "according to plan," the full effects of our actions may not be felt for weeks or years. Or generations.

Which doesn't mean we shouldn't act at all. Nor is it simply an appeal for extra caution, or still more pre-planning. For one thing, we may not have that luxury.

What it means is getting used to *not knowing*—of being able to move forward despite limited information, despite our fear and doubt. And for that we *can* prepare.

We can prepare by actively seeking "experience," by looking for new challenges where the unexpected can be expected. Naturally, we'll want to start with assignments that can't hurt us too badly if things go wrong. But just by putting ourselves in these situations, we automatically learn crucial lessons: That we *will* survive; that there is a "knowing" below the level of consciousness that can guide us; that if we take the leap, if we *do* "involve ourselves" in good faith, The Universe will respond in kind.

And then we'll not only survive... the consequences may just turn out better than we could have dreamed!

I am never, ever alone. I receive divine guidance as I open myself to the full resources of The Universe.

12.29

I can only hope that the future holds even greater challenges.
CAPTAIN SISKO: THE ADVERSARY: 48959.5

If we pause to consider the past year, or the past *five* years, chances are we'll be astounded at how far we've come. We've learned, we've grown. We are changed people. Most of our changes have been for the better.

What's better about us is no accident. Because it's not from having won the Tarkassian lottery. Or because some genie granted our wish. Most of our progress was *earned*.

And most of *that* came from being challenged.

Despite the fact that it was hard, grueling work at the time, having to overcome obstacles and climb mountains was good for us. Even the times we slipped, even when we hurt ourselves, the lessons were worth the pain.

And even if it's a cliché, hardship *does* build character. Because the stronger our opposition, the more we must learn to be creative; the more we must learn teamwork; the more we must search our souls for inner strength. It is our Adversary that brings out the Hero in us.

Which is why Sisko could plead, in all sincerity, for a future filled with even greater challenges. For only then could he—or can *we*—continue to improve.

Our challenges are gifts to grow on. We are not given more than we, with help from The Universe, can bear.

I will list three things I've learned from challenges over the past year. I will think about my biggest challenge today, and what I might learn from it.

12.30

Those little points of light out there... the great Unknown beckoning to us.

DR. BASHIR: THE QUICKENING: Stardate Not Given

Today's space voyagers weren't the first to gaze at the stars and see them as worlds like our own, complete unto themselves, teeming with other lives, other possibilities.

The writings of ancient Hindus hint at infinite worlds beyond our own, just as that tradition embraces the idea of countless lives beyond this present one—all of which are part of some grand Cosmic Plan designed to refine our souls to the point of perfection.

Points of light or points in our lives—these concepts symbolize what lies ahead for each of us. They represent a future we can only dimly imagine, yet which holds such vast possibilities that any direction opens up whole new worlds to explore, and even the faintest glimmer can illumine our spiritual path.

To feel the beckoning of those lights and lives is to accept the responsibility of existence. It is to acknowledge that we are ready to continue our Inner Voyage, to experience new things; to learn, grow... *become.*

We have done well to come this far, through times of happiness and sadness, joy and pain, ignorance and self-discovery. All we know for sure is that there will be more of each. And that we will be better for it.

I accept the challenge of the rest of my life. The strength to move bravely and boldly into my own future is all around me, and within me.

12.31

I envy you... taking these first steps into a new frontier.

CAPTAIN PICARD: FIRST CONTACT: 50893.5

It's tempting to become nostalgic over the journeys we've already completed. We look back and recall the joy of discovery... our feelings of awe and excitement as we encountered new and unexpected possibilities... the thrill of finally breaking through barriers that would end up changing our lives forever.

It's tempting because we forget the agony of learning painful lessons. All we remember is the ecstacy of arrival. Or at least our relief from having to pay any more dues.

And that's as it should be. By envying others who are about to embark on their own explorations, we are sending them a message that their struggles will strengthen them, their pain will pay off. If we tend to gloss over the rough spots, at least we've affirmed that the ride is worth the price of the ticket. Others need to hear that.

But we're missing the boat if we assume the message is only for *their* benefit. Our envy is also meant to inspire *us,* to re-invigorate *our* continuing explorations. Because we haven't exactly reached the end of the ride, either.

What we interpret as "envy" is really our own longing to keep moving. What we feel are the vibrations of our inner voice reminding us that another frontier awaits us.

I will encourage others who are just starting down the paths I have completed. I am strengthened for the Voyages that still lie ahead.

Abbreviations of Characters

AL — *Alixus*
AN — *Anij*

BR — *Dr. Bashir*

CH — *Commander Chakotay*
CK — *Ensign Checkov*
CN — *Aaron Connor*
CP — *The Cooperative*
CR — *Dr. Crusher*

DK — *Captain Decker*
DR — *The Doctor*
DS — *Ensign D'Sora*
DT — *Data*
DU — *Gul Dukat*
DX — *Lieutenant Jadzia Dax*

EZ — *Counselor Ezri Dax*

GK — *Garak*
GN — *Guinan*

JK — *Jake Sisko*
JT — *Jetrel*
JW — *Captain Janeway*

KK — *Captain/Admiral Kirk*
KL — *Edith Keeler*
KM — *Ensign Kim*
KR — *Lieutenant Kira*
KS — *Kes*

LF — *Engineer La Forge*
LN — *Lanel*
LX — *Luaxana Troi*

MA — *Gul Macet*
MC — *Dr. McCoy*
MR — *Mirasta*
MT — *General Murtok*

NT — *Natira*
NX — *Neelix*

OB — *Chief O'Brien*
OD — *Odo*

PC — *Captain Picard*
PM — *Parmen*
PR — *Lieutenant Paris*

Q — *Q*
QK — *Quark*

RK — *Commander Riker*
RL — *Ensign Ro Laren*
RV — *Riva*

SC — *Scotty*
SK — *Cmmdr./Capt. Sisko*
SL — *Lt./Cmmdr. Sulu*
SN — *Seven of Nine*
SP — *Spock*
ST — *Ensign Sito*

TR — *Counselor Troi*
TS — *Lieutenant Torres*
TV — *Lieutenant Tuvok*

UH — *Lieutenant Uhura*

WF — *Lt./Cmmdr. Worf*

Topic/Character Index

A

Acceptance — 4.16/SP - 7.22/PC
8.13/KK - 9.06/WF - 11.02/MC

Accepting Reality — 2.13/KK
2.27/KK - 6.23/KK - 8.24/GK
9.13/SP - 9.28/SP - 11.18/KR

Addictions — 6.20/TR

Admitting Ignorance — 7.29/JW

Ambition — 2.21/KK - 5.25/QK

Apathy — 2.29/JW

Appearance vs. Substance —
2.26/NX - 3.30/TV - 8.09/SC
10.08/TV

Attitude — 1.03/SN - 1.10/RV
3.24/TS - 5.09/KR - 6.06/JW
7.26/KK - 9.08/TV - 10.06/CK
10.13/JW - 11.25/SP - 12.05/NX

B

Balance — 7.20/KK - 8.05/TS
8.07/SP - 11.01/SK - 11.29/TV
12.14/CH

Beginnings — 1.06/SP - 12.27/PC
12.31/PC

Believing in Yourself — 3.23/DX
5.20/KK - 6.24/CK - 8.19/LF
8.31/PC - 10.23/KK - 12.08/WF

Blessing — 3.14/SP - 5.18/SL
6.25/CH

Brooding — 8.18/JW - 9.25/KR

C

Changing Ourselves — 1.31/AL
2.27/KK - 10.28/DR

Challenges — 1.05/RK - 1.10/RV
5.03/TS - 9.26/RK - 10.20/SK
11.24/TR - 12.29/SK

Character — 4.02/CH - 7.10/KK
7.17/PC - 10.10/CH - 10.26/JW

Choices — 1.01/PC - 2.25/DT
5.10/SP - 9.03/SN - 9.16/CR

Choosing Sides — 10.18/KR

Coercion — 5.03/TS

Commitment — 2.18/JW
8.22/WF - 12.07/BR

Communication — 2.15/PC
4.04/RV - 8.26/SP - 12.11/DR

Community — 2.08/BR - 5.11/LX
5.22/MR - 6.02/PC - 6.30/KK
10.02/RV - 11.07/KS

Competition — 4.03/PC

Confidence — 1.09/TR - 1.20/TS

Consciousness — 5.11/LX

Consequences — 8.25/QK-DX
11.21/CR

Constants — 8.01/KK

Controlling — 7.28/TR
10.27/SC

Cooperation — 6.17/PC

Cosmic Plan — 5.24/TR
10.07/RK - 12.26/RK

Courage — 7.26/KK - 10.09/PR

Courtesy — 11.30/QK - 12.11/DR

Creativity — 7.16/SP

Criticism — 1.20/TR - 2.06/SP
2.19/SC - 4.08/SP - 11.10/TV

Curiosity — 9.07/TR

D

Death — 1.11/BR - 4.17/JW
Defeat — 1.24/TR
Deeper Meanings — 2.29/JW
  3.28/RK - 4.04/RV - 10.20/SK
Direction — 2.20/SL - 11.13/CH
Diversity — 2.01/SN - 3.21/SP
  12.12/PC
Doing — 4.13/DT - 8.11/KS
  10.11/LF
Double Standard — 4.27/NT

E

Effort — 1.03/SN - 3.16/PC
  3.22/PC - 4.29/KK - 12.07/BR
Ego vs. Self — 2.06/SP - 11.05/BR
Emotional Energy — 6.16/SP
  7.25/SP - 8.18/JW - 9.28/SP
  11.09/TR
Emotions — 5.19/TV
Emotionalism — 9.22/SP
Empowerment — 1.23/SK
  5.16/SK - 5.17/GN - 9.19/PC
  12.01/PC
Enemies — 4.05/TV
Exercise — 3.07/SL
Expectations — 1.25/LF
  2.26/NX - 5.28/PC - 6.07/KK
  9.24/PM - 10.04/KK - 11.22/RK
  12.19/DT

F

Failure — 3.16/PC - 10.06/CK
Faith — 3.26/KR - 5.23/SP
  7.28/TR - 9.18/TS - 10.16/LN
  12.28/JW

Family — 5.15/RK - 11.20/OB
Fantasies — 1.30/UH - 3.17/GK
  8.15/TR - 10.05/PC
Fear — 1.02/KK - 1.15/WF
  3.13/RK - 5.14/JW - 7.03/JW
  10.16/LN - 10.31/KM - 12.05/NX
Feelings — 2.22/TR - 3.05/TV
  4.06/MC - 8.18/JW - 12.06/RK
Feeling Useful — 5.06/PC
  11.28/AL
Firsts — 2.17/SP - 9.10/JK
Forgiveness — 2.03/EZ - 8.16/RK
  9.15/KK
Freedom — 7.04/KK - 12.18/KK
Freeing Others — 10.21/NX
  11.04/RK
Friendship — 3.06/LF - 6.14/PC
  8.10/JW - 10.22/PC
Fulfillment — 1.27/JW - 2.27/KK
  11.28/AL

G

Gender Issues — 6.13/TR - 9.12/NT
  9.17/SK
Giving — 3.01/DT - 8.30/TR
Goals — 1.04/CH - 1.11/BR
  4.13/DT - 5.08/DT - 6.27/WF
Grounding Ourselves —
  3.18/JW - 4.22/CN - 6.23/KK
  9.11/PC - 11.03/JW
Growth — 2.21/KK - 3.13/RK
  5.25/QK - 5.27/KK - 7.29/JW
  8.04/PC - 8.06/KK

H

Habit — 4.10/DR
Hate — 8.16/RK - 10.24/SP
Healing — 4.20/CP - 7.16/SP
10.03/TR - 11.02/MC
*Higher Power/Intelligence
The Universe/God/Source* —
3.09/OB - 5.29/DK - 6.11/DR
11.14/SP - 12.25/UH
Honesty — 4.21/MC - 7.24/BR
Honor — 4.12/WF - 4.18/WF
Hope — 8.02/KL - 9.26/RK
Humility — 5.30/CR - 9.13/SP

I

Illusion — 3.30/TV
Imagination — 5.14/JW - 6.12/LF
8.28/OD
Individuality — 3.25/DR
6.17/PC
Inner Conflict — 8.05/TS
11.05/BR - 11.14/SP
Inner Guidance — 1.07/JW
2.12/GN - 8.20/CR - 11.13/CH
12.15/TR
Inner Resources — 4.05/TV
9.08/TV
Integrity — 4.29/KK - 8.14/PC
Interdependence — 1.16/DT
2.08/BR - 4.12/WF - 4.19/KK
6.01/SP - 9.04/RK - 11.07/KS

J

Joy — 3.11/Q - 3.12/KK - 7.27/DT
11.27/SC

Judging Others — 1.26/DR
2.26/NX - 4.27/NT - 5.21/PC
9.05/MC - 9.20/ST - 11.12/RK
11.22/RK
Justice — 7.06/CH - 9.04/RK

K

Karma — 5.16/SK - 8.31/PC
Knowledge — 9.11/PC - 12.13/PC

L

Laughter — 7.27/DT - 12.05/NX
Learning by Doing — 1.12/KK
6.04/KM - 8.08/SK - 10.13/JW
Lessons — 2.16/DS - 6.10/DU
7.11/TV - 10.29/UH - 11.15/LF
Letting Go — 1.07/JW - 3.16/PC
4.26/PC - 6.05/TV - 6.11/DR
6.21/SK - 9.06/WF - 10.01/WF
10.27/SC - 11.09/TR
Lies — 7.12/PC - 7.24/BR
Life as Business — 4.15/QK
Life's Mission — 3.27/KK
3.29/JW - 9.07/TR - 10.09/PR
Linking to Source — 1.14/CR
1.23/SK - 12.24/Q - 12.25/UH
Listening — 5.04/KS - 12.11/DR
Living in the Present —
1.04/CH - 1.17/DR - 3.03/AN
6.08/OD - 6.19/KS - 8.02/KL
8.23/PC - 9.23/OB - 10.19/UH
11.27/SC
Logic — 3.02/SP
Losing Touch — 7.13/UH
Loss — 10.03/TR

Love — 2.14/NT - 5.26/MC
6.16/SP - 6.18/NX - 6.19/KS
6.29/SP - 10.21/NX - 12.20/CH

M

Making a Difference — 1.06/SP
Manipulation — 11.18/KR
Material vs. Spiritual — 4.30/LF
7.07/SP
Meditation — 1.17/DR - 3.08/CR
6.05/TV - 8.12/Q - 9.25/KR
Memories — 11.15/LF
Mirroring — 4.08/SP - 11.12/RK
Mindfulness — 6.19/KS - 6.27/WF
Mistakes — 2.03/EZ - 2.16/DS
7.11/TV - 11.06/PC
Motivation — 6.10/DU - 9.21/MC
11.26/WF
Moving Forward — 1.24/TR
5.02/SP - 5.31/Q - 12.26/RK
12.30/BR
Mutual Support — 1.27/JW
3.09/OB - 4.19/KK - 11.07/KS
Mystery — 6.15/TV - 12.16/RL
12.21/PC

N

Needs — 7.01/SP - 7.13/UH
Negative Thoughts — 1.28/TV
New Experiences — 3.11/Q
8.17/DR - 9.14/LF - 12.10/GK
12.30/BR
Non-Attachment — 3.10/WF
11.29/TV

O

Objectivity — 1.19/OD
Opportunities for Growth —
8.17/DR - 9.23/OB
Opposites — 3.30/TV
Others' Opinions — 1.09/TR

P

Pain — 2.24/PC - 5.27/KK
7.30/SK - 10.03/TR
Past Lives — 7.21/DX
Patience — 5.07/WF - 5.21/PC
9.29/TV - 12.04/OD
Peace — 5.26/MC - 7.15/KK
8.27/MA
Perfectionism — 10.04/KK
12.03/SN
Personal Demons — 8.03/CH
10.14/PC - 11.08/KK
Personhood — 10.15/KK
11.04/RK
Perspective — 1.19/OD - 6.08/OD
7.22/PC - 7.23/LF - 8.12/Q
9.02/BR - 9.16/CR - 11.01/SK
11.08/KK
Planning — 1.14/CR - 2.04/SK
8.08/SK - 9.16/CR
Play — 2.09/Q - 3.11/Q - 4.23/Q
Practice — 10.30/PC
Presence — 3.06/LF - 5.04/KS
Prime Directive — 6.26/PC
8.04/PC

Q

Questions — 6.07/KK - 8.11/KS

R

Rationalizing — 10.25/TV
Readiness — 5.18/SL - 9.08/TV
  10.01/WF - 10.11/LF - 12.30/BR
Recovery — 4.20/CP - 8.02/KL
Re-Creation — 1.01/PC
  1.21/PC - 1.26/DR - 3.03/AN
  5.17/GN - 8.16/RK
Rejection — 4.11/SK - 8.19/LF
Relationships — 1.16/DT
  2.18/JW - 4.07/MT - 4.24/SK
  5.22/MR - 6.22/RK - 6.29/SP
  10.15/KK - 10.22/PC
Remembering — 3.18/JW
  7.21/DX - 11.03/JW
Responsibility — 2.10/PC
  5.10/SP - 5.16/SK - 8.24/GK
  10.07/RK - 10.17/RK - 10.25/TV
  10.28/DR - 12.18/KK
Rest — 7.19/JW - 7.31/Q
  11.16/OD - 12.14/CH
Results — 10.11/LF - 10.30/PC
Rewards — 1.05/RK - 1.18/KS
  9.21/MC - 10.12/QK - 11.24/TR
  11.26/WF
Risking — 2.05/RK - 5.01/PC
  7.05/WF - 10.12/QK
Role Models — 5.13/PC - 8.27/MA
  11.06/PC - 11.12/RK - 12.24/Q
Rules — 7.06/CH - 12.27/PC
Running Away — 1.21/PC
  7.30/SK

S

Sanctity of Life — 2.28/LX
  2.29/JW - 4.14/PC

Security — 7.07/SP - 7.26/KK
  11.17/WF
Self-Acceptance — 2.03/EZ
  3.15/TR - 3.20/CK - 4.25/SP
  5.09/KR - 6.03/TR - 9.01/MC
  11.20/OB
Self-Deception — 7.12/PC
  8.07/SP
Self-Discipline — 5.19/TV
  6.20/TR - 7.20/KK - 10.24/SP
Self-Discovery — 12.02/Q
Self-Inventory — 3.04/PR
  7.17/PC
Self-Knowledge — 7.08/MC
  12.09/SP - 12.21/PC
Self-Limitation — 5.01/PC
  9.14/LF - 12.24/Q
Self-Respect — 9.03/SN
Self-Transformation — 9.03/SN
  9.20/ST - 10.16/LN
Self-Worth — 4.11/SK
Selfishness/Selflessness —
  3.01/DT - 11.21/CR
Serving Others — 2.10/PC
  3.01/DT - 4.18/WF - 4.28/NX
  8.21/NX
Sexuality — 9.17/SK
Simplifying — 4.09/PC - 7.14/OD
Slave Mentality — 2.23/SK
  12.18/KK
Spiritual Evolution — 5.04/KS
  5.23/SP - 7.09/RK - 8.12/Q
  10.29/UH - 12.02/Q
Spiritual Knowledge — 5.05/JW

Spiritual Struggle — 5.12/KK
6.02/PC - 9.09/RK - 11.24/TR
Spirituality — 3.09/OB - 3.29/JW
6.15/TV
Stability vs. Change — 7.01/Q
Standards — 7.06/CH - 9.24/PM
Starting Over — 10.01/WF
Stereotypes — 11.04/RK
11.23/MC
Stress — 3.08/CR
Suffering — 2.07/CR
Surrender — 3.31/SC - 9.29/TV

T

Tactics — 8.03/CH - 8.22/WF
Taking Action — 2.02/MC
8.08/SK
Teamwork — 1.25/LF - 6.09/DT
Technology — 3.25/DR - 8.09/SC
Threats — 10.26/JW
Touching — 11.19/PC
Transcending Differences —
2.01/SN - 8.28/OD - 8.29/DT
Transformation — 1.31/AL
3.22/PC
Trust — 1.29/WF - 8.20/CR
Truth — 9.18/TS - 10.05/PC
12.19/DT - 12.23/TV

U

Uniqueness — 6.09/DT
9.01/MC - 10.02/RV
The Unknown — 1.02/KK
10.16/LN - 12.30/BR

V

Values — 1.08/QK - 5.06/PC
Violence — 10.14/PC - 11.11/SK
Vocation — 1.08/QK - 3.19/DT
Vulnerability — 9.30/KK -
12.20/CH

W

Wanting — 1.13/SP - 4.30/LF
12.22/SP
Wealth — 4.09/PC
Web of Life — 6.01/SP - 9.04/RK
12.17/MC
Who We Are — 4.01/QK - 7.15/KK
10.10/CH
Winning — 4.07/MT - 8.06/KK
Wisdom — 1.22/KK - 3.02/SP
7.18/KR - 9.27/DT
Wishing — 1.30/UH - 9.19/PC
Words — 4.04/RV - 11.23/MC
12.01/PC